AGAINST THE
GRAIN

AGAINST THE GRAIN

NORMAN BAKER

Biteback Publishing

First published in Great Britain in 2015 by
Biteback Publishing Ltd
Westminster Tower
3 Albert Embankment
London SE1 7SP
Copyright © Norman Baker 2015

ISBN 978-1-84954-941-7

10 9 8 7 6 5 4 3 2 1

A CIP catalogue record for this book is available from the British Library.

Set in Charter by Adrian McLaughlin

Printed and bound in Great Britain by
CPI Group (UK) Ltd, Croydon CR0 4YY

Contents

Chapter 1

My time in politics was over before it had begun.

So I thought as I surveyed the front page with some dismay. The headline in the *Sussex Express* screamed out: 'Buttering Up Voters Claim'.

It was April 1987 and I was living in an old railway cottage close to the level crossing on the A27 at Beddingham, just outside Lewes. A couple of months earlier, there had been a knock at the door. A man I had never met before, nor heard of, asked me if I would stand for the Liberals for the local council election in May.

'Don't worry, you won't get in,' he told me reassuringly.

I had joined the party some six years earlier in Islington, and promptly forgot I had done so. Eventually someone from the local party contacted me and asked me to go canvassing. I had no idea what this entailed or why we wanted to do it but I gamely made myself available one evening to traipse round the houses that bordered the old Arsenal stadium. The experience was bewildering and one I found rather embarrassing and I resolved not to do that again.

So I became a sleeping member of the Liberal Party, and in fact joined the Green Party as well shortly after we moved to Sussex in 1985, as I liked bits of both parties. I suppose in retrospect I could have been expelled from one or the other had this become known, but at the time, it seemed to me quite a natural thing to do.

Then came that knock on the door, from Gordon Hook, a Liberal councillor in the nearby village of Ringmer. At the time I was scraping by, teaching English as a foreign language, and without any clear idea what I wanted to do, so I decided that standing for election might be an interesting diversion, and agreed on the basis that I would not win.

Although I confess I have used a similar reassurance myself a number of times since with individuals I have cajoled to stand, some of whom have indeed ended up being elected, it was reasonable in this instance to assume that I would not. After all, the council ward was held by the Conservative leader of the council, Roy Robinson, and we had not even fought the seat for some elections past.

So, under Gordon's guidance, I set about my short campaign. This involved producing my own leaflets, under the generic Liberal banner of 'Focus'. In the days before word processors, these were produced by typing up sections of text to fit the allocated space on the folded A4 piece of paper that was to be the leaflet. The sections were then cut out and attached to the A4 paper with gum, and the leaflet given a modicum of interest by the addition of generic artwork supplied by the Association of Liberal Councillors – drawings of pound notes slipping down drains, or buses, or traffic signs. Anything really. The range was endless. It took absolutely ages to produce what would now take less than half an hour.

The council ward was called Ouse Valley, and encompassed the villages of Glynde and Firle, together with the small settlements of Beddingham and Tarring Neville, and a place called South Heighton, which was either a village adjacent to Newhaven or a suburb of it, depending on your point of view.

Glynde and Firle were both estate-owned villages, and indeed still are, where virtually every house is owned respectively by the

Hampden family or the Gage family. A certain frisson exists between the villages going back to the English Civil War, when Glynde was parliamentarian and Firle royalist, which nowadays is largely for effect, but not entirely.

Firle is now a dead end, since the old coach road to Eastbourne was superseded by the A27 a long time ago, and in the 1980s, visitors to the pub, the Ram Inn, tended to be relatively rare. So when a rep arrived one lunchtime, the pub went quiet as he entered. To break the silence, he said brightly: 'I came through a nice village on the way here. It was called Glynde,' whereupon the landlord suggested he might go there for a drink – I paraphrase.

Later, after I had been elected to Glynde and Beddingham Parish Council, there was a serious discussion as to whether residents of Firle ought to be allowed to use Glynde's swimming pool.

I am happy to say that the Ram Inn is much more accommodating these days, though the semi-feudal nature of the villages persists. Lord Hampden and Lord Gage have each majestically let it be known that they do not approve of Lib Dem posters appearing on estate houses, though it has not always stopped residents from displaying them.

There used to be an unwritten deal, at least in Glynde, that rents were kept low but maintenance was pretty non-existent, though one year, with unfortunate timing, rents in the village were jacked up shortly after it had been revealed that Lord Hampden had donated £39,000 to the Satanist conman Derry Mainwaring-Knight to enable him allegedly to buy some satanic regalia for the purpose of destroying it. In the event, it was used to buy a Rolls-Royce.

Nowadays, rents in both villages have increased significantly as they are opened up to DFLs (new, richer tenants Down From London).

So it was in Firle one bright morning that I began my canvassing. The second door I knocked on was opened by a friendly woman who beamed at me when she saw my shiny new yellow rosette.

'A Liberal!' she exclaimed. 'Do come in for a cup of tea.'

I now know that it is not a good use of canvassing time to spend too long at any one particular address, as it stops you meeting other people, and sometimes, I have discovered, people of different political views will even try to keep you talking precisely to stop you getting round.

A liberal-minded friend of mine living in a predominantly Tory area in London has taken this one stage further by inviting a Tory canvasser in, and then making a series of increasingly right-wing propositions to see how far right he could go – castrating sex offenders, for example – before the Tory disagreed with him. Alarmingly, he got rather a long way before this happened, by which time almost half an hour had been lost to the canvasser.

In my case, no such duplicity was intended. The woman was genuinely nice, and, after my initial reluctance, I began to think that canvassing might be quite a pleasant activity after all. But as I was taking the cup of tea to my lips, she ventured: 'Yes, I've always been a Liberal. The sooner they bring back hanging, the better.'

What should I do? Tell her that was not Liberal policy and lose her vote? No, I changed the subject. And there was my first political compromise.

April came and Gordon, who I think must have been quite pleased with the way I was approaching the election, told me that he had access to some butter from the EEC butter mountain – excess production kept in cold storage – and perhaps I could make some available to pensioners in the villages.

I do not think I was clear how this was to be done, but, duly armed with boxes of butter, I sought out the good pensioners of Firle to hand this out. I must have been naive, for I was taken by surprise by that headline in the *Sussex Express*.

I read the story glumly:

> Three boxes of butter from the EEC mountain are at the cen-
> tre of a political storm raging in the village of Firle.
>
> Parish councillors claim that the Liberal Party candidate in
> the forthcoming district elections has been vote-catching by
> distributing packets of butter to pensioners in the village –
> and then announcing he was their local candidate.

The story also correctly reported that the voluntary bodies that
had been given the task of distribution – the WRVS, Age Concern
and the Salvation Army – did not have the structure to get the butter out to some villages, which was why others had got involved.

The story appeared on Friday 24 April, less than two weeks before
polling day, and I thought I had blown it. So it was with trepidation
that I went back to Firle the next day to continue my canvassing.

To my surprise, I received a warm reception all round. Eventually
I asked one villager if he had not seen the local paper. 'Oh yes,' he
replied. 'Of course you were trying to get us to vote for you, but
at least you gave us something. More than the Tories ever have.'

In Glynde, a wizened old resident told me confidently: 'You're
going to win.'

It turned out his certainty was based on the fact that I had managed to persuade the residents of two opposite houses in the village
each to display a poster for me. He explained that one was social-
ist in tooth and claw, and the other very right-wing. 'Anyone who
gets the same poster up at them two houses will win, sure as I'm
standing here,' he said.

It was true that I had talked them both round, one tactically
because he hated the Tories, the other because she thought I was
a nice young man. She had even invited me into her house, where

I was alarmed to see a small signed photo of Adolf Hitler in a silver frame on her dresser.

And so to the count, which took place in a draughty South Heighton village hall – a straight contest between the Conservatives and the Liberals.

On one side of the room stood the Tory council leader, Roy Robinson, surrounded by the great and the good – the men smart country types, the women not quite in twinsets and pearls, but almost.

On our side there was my partner and I, and just about the only other Liberal member in the ward, Brian Knight.

When I had asked for a list of members and was told Brian was my best bet, I set about finding him, which was no easy task. Brian lived in Keeper's Cottage in Glynde, a house about a mile or two down a track and literally in the middle of nowhere. I eventually did locate it, with the help of the local postman, and arrived one day and banged on the door. Nobody answered, but it was clear that someone was at home. I banged again with the same result. But having found the place, I was not about to give up, so went round to the back and opened the kitchen door. The family were round the table.

I introduced myself as the Liberal candidate and explained I had knocked at the front. Brian was very welcoming and invited me in.

'Did you not hear me knock?' I asked, puzzled.

'Oh yes,' he replied. 'But when I saw you with your briefcase, I assumed you were a Jehovah's Witness. Nobody else ever comes down here.'

So we stood in the village hall, the two sides, hovering close to the table where the first box was opened, the one from Glynde. It was clear that the vote was finely balanced. The Tory Great and Good were muttering to themselves and gradually, almost imperceptibly, moving away from their candidate.

The Glynde box fell in my favour 120–108, the one from Firle 98–37, and the one from South Heighton 301–151. Only the handful of postal votes went to the Tories.

By the time the result was declared, the Tory Great and Good had physically abandoned their candidate and moved well away in a huddle. I was shocked by this. Yes, he had lost, but Roy Robinson was, as far as I could tell, a good man who had in his own old-fashioned way done his best both for the Conservatives and for his electors over many years. How callous of them to walk away from him just when he needed their support. So it was left to us three Liberals to commiserate with him after the declaration.

And so, at twenty-nine, I found myself on two councils: Lewes District, and Glynde and Beddingham Parish, the election to which was on the same day and where I had put myself forward on Gordon's advice, and not on a party label.

The parish council was a sleepy affair, comprising three local farmers, two old Sussex boys and me. Lord Hampden got himself co-opted onto the council after the election. Clearly, he had not wanted to test his support publicly, or perhaps being a member of the House of Lords he was averse to elections. I did not think it appropriate that the man who owned the village should also be on the council, but if anyone else shared that view, they did not say so.

The parish would meet about once every six weeks for about two hours. There was phenomenally little business to discuss. The odd bench to place, the occasional planning application upon which to comment, the odd district or county consultation to which to respond.

The council was technically two councils meeting together – Glynde and Beddingham. It met in those days in the old schoolroom in Glynde, but once a year, for legal reasons, was obliged to meet in Beddingham. This was a formality, and such meetings rarely lasted more than five minutes. The council was never one to want to waste money – indeed, its main focus appeared to be to spend as little as possible – so there was reluctance to hire a room for such a short meeting.

Accordingly, the annual meeting would often be held on the pavement outside the Reading Room, with the parish clerk conducting business as cars passed by, after which the members of the council would retire to the next-door Trevor Arms.

To begin with, there was undoubtedly a certain hostility towards me from some of the parish council, with the exception of a lovely old boy with a wonderful Sussex burr called Alec Mepham, who was secretly delighted I was stirring the pot. Alec was really a Labour Party supporter but always voted for me, and would have done even if Labour had ever stood in local elections there.

He once told me with some relish how he was canvassed by Sue Rathbone, the rather posh wife of the Tory MP Tim, shortly before the 1997 election which saw me gain my parliamentary seat.

'Will you be voting for Tim?' she enquired.

'Nope.'

'Oh,' replied Mrs Rathbone, in that rather strangulated voice only Tories of a certain class can manage. 'Why not?'

'Because I've lived here over thirty year and I ain't never once set eyes on your husband in this village.'

In the end, I think the parish council came round to accepting me and I was touched when, in 1999, I was asked if I would stand again for election. Having been elected to Parliament two years earlier, I had naturally planned to stand down, but I did carry on for one more four-year term, making me, I think, one of only two MPs at the time to also be a parish councillor. My sixteen-year stint ended in 2003.

The district council was naturally rather livelier than the parish. I was summoned to the council offices and had no idea what to expect. Indeed, I had no idea how councils worked or even who, with the exception of Gordon, the other Liberal councillors were. The election had seen a small swing to the Liberals, but still left the Tories firmly in control, with thirty-four seats against eleven Liberals and three Independents.

I stood in the members' room, alone amid a gaggle of people, none of whom I knew. A man came up to me. It was, I later learnt, Keith Moorhouse, the Tory councillor for Plumpton, who had been elected as Tory leader in emergency session following my defeat of their previous leader.

'So you're the man who defeated Roy Robinson,' he said to me, and I nodded. 'What a tragedy a man like that should fall a fence like this,' he spat out, then turned on his heel. Councillor Moorhouse and I would have many run-ins over the next few years.

The council members then made their way to the debating chamber, where it turned out membership and chairmanship of committees was to be decided. Rather than this having been decided between the groups beforehand, a cumbersome and somewhat farcical process ensued. This entailed all those who had been nominated by the two groups to sit on a particular committee coming together in a huddle to elect their chairman and vice-chairman. Given that the Tories had a clear majority and therefore took all the positions, what the purpose of this charade was I still do not understand. And as it was common for councillors to sit on more than one committee, proceedings had to take place almost sequentially to ensure that all members of the committee in question were in the relevant huddle.

I was asked at one point by a Conservative if I would be the Liberal representative on the Cinematographic Licensing sub-committee. There were three members, he explained, and proportionality required that there be two Conservatives and one Liberal. He further explained, in response to my question, that the sub-committee's job was to decide whether films should be approved for screening in the district.

This sounded like fun, and I readily agreed. It was only afterwards that I found out that there was no cinema in the district and that the sub-committee had never met.

I soon learnt that the council was not short of such unintentional idiocies. Although it had only been created in 1974, it seemed to belong to a much earlier era.

There was a council crest rather than a logo, all the offices shut for lunch between 1 p.m. and 2 p.m., and there was no real attempt to communicate anything the council was doing to its electorate or indeed to solicit any views they might have.

The council was run by its chief executive, Cyril Mann. He was a local government official of the old school who was very proud of his council and resistant to change. I rather liked him in a funny sort of way, though I am not sure the feeling was mutual.

He was somewhat short and it was noticeable that many of the chief officers he had appointed to his management team were of similar stature. He would sit in a high-backed swivel chair at meetings of the chief officers. It was the only such chair in the room. It was also the seat used by the Lib Dem group leader, David Bellotti, to chair group meetings.

I disliked this chair and the hierarchy it shouted out, and resolved to get rid of it if I ever got the chance.

At the first committee I attended, the wonderfully named General Purposes Committee, Cyril brought forward a madcap scheme to cut the council's traditional solid oak tables in half. For, while committee meetings took place upstairs in the town hall, then a district council building, the room was too small for full council meetings, so the council had to use the county council's debating chamber.

The county council premises was almost literally across the road, but Cyril, fiercely independent for his council, objected to having to use it, and I did get the impression that the county would sometimes make it difficult for the hire to be arranged, probably just to annoy Cyril. The final straw for him, it appears, was when district members were refused use of the county councillors' members' room and the heating in the chamber was switched off halfway through a district council meeting.

So Cyril's answer to this situation was to make the cramped town hall room work by slicing all the council's oak tables in half, lengthwise. That way, he argued, there would be just enough room for the full council to meet in its own premises. The cost of this, and for improved ventilation, was to be around £25,000.

I wondered what sort of mad organisation I had joined. On a practical point, I did not understand how a table which had been cut in half would actually stand up. Nor did I understand how the tables would be narrow for council meetings, but restored to full width for committee meetings, as the plan envisaged.

What I did understand was that the council was planning to spend a lot of money to cut up attractive old tables, and I told the committee that I thought those who supported the idea were 'vandals in suits'. Uproar ensued and the chair of the committee demanded I withdraw the word vandal, but I refused. In the end, the tables were not sliced, and the district continued using the county council's chamber.

About six months into my first term, south-east England was hit by a very violent storm that saw trees blown over and much damage done. As a keen new councillor, I thought I would come into the council offices to see what I could do to help. Living on the main A27, the road into Lewes was clear, unlike many other roads, where fallen trees made passage impossible.

I arrived and headed for the main back office. I opened the door and was greeted with the sound of telephones ringing every-where and the sight of one poor employee in the corner looking very harassed. I picked up the nearest phone and said in my best voice: 'Lewes District Council. Can I help you?'

It was a local resident, furious that her rubbish had not been collected that morning.

Unknown to me, David Bellotti had also decided to come in to help, and he had headed for the nerve centre set up by Cyril to co-ordinate the council's response. This was based in one of the temporary huts the council used. In the hut, Cyril had laid out piles of paper neatly and methodically on the table. Unfortunately, when David opened the door, all the papers blew off.

I enjoyed my opposition years on the council, from 1987 to 1991. The Tory administration was flat-footed, hidebound and sluggish. It was the fun of a speedboat dancing round a container vessel.

They would tend to react to any radical idea with spluttering apoplexy, never more so than to the motion I tabled to full coun-cil requiring all councillors who were members of a Freemasons' lodge to declare this.

I make this sound like a wheeze but I genuinely felt, and still do, that those who take decisions on our behalf need to be open about any outside interests they have that might influence the decisions they take. It is the same reason I would commit much time sub-sequently to campaigning for freedom of information legislation, and for the publication of MPs' expenses.

Naturally, the ruling Conservatives wanted no truck with a motion put forward by the Liberals. In fact, I do not recall them ever accept-ing any proposal we put forward on anything, even if they secretly agreed with it. Every vote went straight down the party line. They had even contemptuously rejected my suggestion that the council should use recycled paper, with the Tory leader stating that he had no intention of using 'toilet paper' for council business.

Publicly, council leader Keith Moorhouse slammed the idea of requiring masons to make themselves known, calling it a 'witch-hunt'.

But then something happened. The Tories were advised by chief executive Cyril Mann that, while they could of course vote the motion down, any who were masons would have to declare an interest in that specific item of business and not vote. In other words, even if the Tories rejected the motion, we would find out who all the masons were. It was a delicious ruling.

The Tories were furious and even took the unprecedented step of ringing the Liberal group leader, David Bellotti, to urge him to get me to withdraw the motion before the council meeting the following Wednesday. David told them, quite correctly, that even if he were to ask me, I would not withdraw it.

So the meeting came, and council leader Keith Moorhouse went into orbit, variously accusing me of being 'Machiavellian, impudent, mischievous' and guilty of 'sheer wickedness'. One by one, the masons dramatically stood up to declare their membership before walking out, eight of them, all Conservatives. The mood was tense, broken only by Tory councillor Trevor Bennett, an undertaker, who stood up to declare an interest as a 'monumental stonemason'.

Keith Moorhouse was a curious chap. He had been on the council since its inception and was soon to retire from his post at Plumpton Agricultural College in his ward. He had a habit of writing down everything that was said in council and committee meetings, for what purpose nobody knew. He never seemed to refer to his copious notes at any subsequent point. Allegedly, he stored them all in a shed in his garden.

He appeared to have no sense of humour and little self-awareness.

At one council meeting, when we were protesting about Clause 28, the Tory prohibition on gay material being properly discussed in schools, he made a speech that began veering towards the homophobic. This led to disapproving noises from our side, and he felt the need to explain that he was not against people being gay, merely the promotion of homosexuality.

'I've nothing against homosexuals,' he told the council. 'I just don't want it forced down my throat.'

At another meeting, the council met shortly after a town council by-election in the Lewes Bridge ward which we had won and where the Tories had come last, in fourth place. David Bellotti made a gently amusing speech to mark the event, which culminated in him leaving his seat, walking over to Keith Moorhouse and gently placing in front of him a wooden spoon adorned with a yellow ribbon. He then quietly walked back to his seat.

Nothing happened for what seemed like ages, but was probably merely a few seconds, then Keith Moorhouse grabbed the spoon, stormed across to the Liberal side of the chamber, and smashed the spoon down in front of our group leader, now back in his place.

There was no question, however, of his diligence and commitment to his role. Cyril Mann told me of an occasion when he was arm-twisted by Keith Moorhouse into attending a very dull meeting in Plumpton village hall, one which in no way justified the attendance of the council's chief executive. At the end of this torrid evening, the Tory leader asked Cyril if he would like to stop by on his way home for a drink. Cyril brightened at the idea and readily agreed, and the two repaired to Keith's house, just down the lane from the hall.

Inside, with Cyril sitting comfortably, Keith rubbed his hands and asked: 'Cocoa or hot chocolate?'

Keith ruled his group with a rod of iron. The Tories seemed to accept this, though some clearly resented it. One such councillor was the member for Ditchling, a lovely old lady called Muriel Benham, who would always mutter amusing complaints about him to me. Muriel really regarded herself as an Independent, but had been forced to stand under the Tory banner to avoid an official challenge from that party in her ward.

Ditchling at the time contained two formidable women who vied for the unofficial title of Queen of Ditchling. One was Muriel and the other was Vera Lynn. Their approaches could not have been more different. While Muriel would always chat to me, and even invited me round for afternoon tea on one occasion – the only person I have ever known who had one of those three-tiered cake stands and actually worked her way up it – Vera Lynn would always ignore me, even after I was elected as MP and we ended up as the only two people in the back of a car together – presumably because I was a Liberal, she being a staunch Tory. Perhaps I was not regal enough.

Looking back, I can see that in my first two years on the council I pressed for a number of policies that have since won through, including free TV licences for pensioners and a universally available concessionary bus fares scheme, as well as an end to uncontrolled dumping of chemicals at sea, the banning of stubble burning, and improved efforts to clean up local beaches.

My first big campaign was against the aerial spraying of pesticides, and reflected my strong commitment to the environment, which, along with issues of civil liberties and justice, drove my political interest to a large extent.

It began when I received a complaint from a local resident who had been sitting in her garden in Denton, near Newhaven, when an aeroplane passed overhead, releasing spray doubtless intended for the fields close by. Within minutes she fell ill and was taken to hospital, where blood tests revealed traces of six different pesticides including the then banned DDT.

Another complaint produced a similar story. A woman accidentally sprayed in her garden was rushed to hospital with liver problems. Shortly afterwards, all the fish in her pond were found dead.

I raised the issue in the local press and this generated around twenty-five similar stories from the Lewes area. This suggested to me that what I had uncovered was the tip of the iceberg and I resolved to look into the matter in depth.

What I found concerned me greatly. I discovered that there were thirty-eight pesticides on sale in the UK that had been banned or severely restricted elsewhere in the world; that the methods for applying the chemicals were highly inaccurate, leading to droplets so small they evaporated into the air or so large that they rolled off the target crop onto the ground; and that apparently significant numbers of people were having their health adversely affected and nobody seemed to be doing anything about it.

My investigations led to my producing a 57-page report, which I launched at a well-attended public meeting in Lewes. Other speakers included Tony Monnington, a local farmer, a representative from the agrochemical industry and one from Friends of the Earth.

The agrochemical industry seemed intent on denying that there was any sort of a problem. They even argued that more people were injured each year by deckchairs than by pesticides. They were able to do so, I suppose, because if a person was injured by a deckchair, it was clear what the cause was, whereas linking a condition to pesticide exposure was more difficult to prove.

Back in 1988, I was naive and had not yet come to understand the nuances of politics or the drivers of behaviour. I think I must have believed that I was the first to unearth the scale of the health implications of pesticide use at the time, and that having demonstrated beyond reasonable doubt that there was a problem, action would of course follow. I failed to understand what I would later learn – that in society there are vested interests that do not necessarily want to correct problems, and those interests may well use their influence with elected politicians to ensure action is in fact not taken.

In this instance, there was some support for change from the farmers themselves. Firstly, they were in the front line for any complaints, and secondly, inefficient use of pesticides was expensive.

I sent my report to the government via MP Tim Rathbone, which elicited the reply from employment minister Patrick Nicholls that I was being 'unduly alarmist'. I countered by suggesting that he was being 'dangerously complacent'.

Notwithstanding the minister's response, aerial spraying was banned soon afterwards, and today, the substances available tend to be safer and applied far more accurately. I like to think that I played some part in this, however nebulous.

Certainly, individuals with commitment, a good idea and fortunate timing can make a difference, and they do not have to be ministers or even MPs.

Take the case of the Lewes Lib Dem councillor Ian Eiloart. It was he who first suggested that it would be a good policy to raise the threshold at which income tax became payable. That was subsequently adopted by the Lib Dem conference, made its way into the 2010 manifesto, then the coalition agreement, and became the most widely recognised and popular Lib Dem achievement of the coalition.

The whole pesticides episode had made me even more interested in the environment in all its manifestations, and this has remained with me as a constant ever since.

Incidentally, my pesticide campaign also generated my first ever TV interview, on what was then TVS, predecessor to Meridian. I was quietly pleased with the piece and how I came across, and even more so when I wandered into Lloyds Bank in Lewes the following day. There, the cashier eyed me quizzically from behind the screen and asked: 'Weren't you on TV last night?' I beamed and nodded.

'TVS about half six?' I nodded again.

'You're the weatherman, aren't you,' she exclaimed, and before I had a chance to say anything, added: 'What's the weather going to be like today?'

Taken aback, I mumbled something that corresponded roughly to what I had heard on the radio that morning, completed my transaction, and left the bank, thinking the exchange mildly amusing.

I thought no more of it until the next time I went into the bank and the same woman saw me and again asked me for the forecast for that day. Again, I offered something short and relatively meaningless, and left, this time a bit more worried.

On the third occasion she asked me, I came clean and explained the situation. She was terribly disappointed that I was not the weatherman, not a celebrity, but merely an elected local councillor. Thereafter, whenever I sensed that I might get carried away with myself, I recalled that episode, and that politicians come below journalists and only just above estate agents in the public's estimation.

Much of my time in my early days, as it was throughout my time in politics, was spent on pursuing a myriad of issues raised with me by those I was elected to represent, whether personal to them or general to the community in which they lived. In the case of the latter, I would dutifully feed back both the issue and what I had done about it in my regular Focus leaflets.

One issue I took up was the need for speed limits in the villages I represented. Incredibly, the national speed limit applied through Glynde and Firle, despite their being settlements with houses packed closely together. As part of my campaign, I asked the county council for the accident record for Glynde. The county replied, deadpan, to inform me that there had only been one reported accident in the previous four years, when a 61-year-old man on a bicycle had collided with a bullock.

One campaign that has sadly not yet come to fruition is the one to reopen the Lewes-to-Uckfield railway line, which I began in 1988, supporting the work of the Wealden Line campaign.

The line had been closed in 1969, not by Beeching or indeed by British Rail, but by East Sussex County Council, who wanted to build a new road into Lewes, the Phoenix Causeway: the railway line was in the way. British Rail actually opposed the closure, as the line was profitable, but it went ahead anyway.

One of the last steps I took as an MP was to persuade Danny Alexander, as Chief Secretary to the Treasury, to include £100,000 in the last coalition Budget for a further study, which I hope will finally lead to the line reopening.

However, it was another transport campaign around that time that would lead to more interesting developments for me, involving MI5 and a test case several years later in the courts. It was during the early 1990s that the then Conservative government decided to embark on 'the biggest road-building programme since Roman times'. This included highly controversial schemes such as the Newbury bypass and a proposal to replace the single-carriageway A27 from Polegate to Lewes with a new, off-line dual carriageway. This was particularly controversial and led to the formation of a well-organised and effective opposition called the A27 Action Group.

I was clear that the scheme was a bad one, and the more I looked into it, the more convinced I became. Firstly, it proposed to cut a swathe through some of the most beautiful countryside in Sussex, an effect worsened by the unsympathetic design of the scheme. In particular, I was horrified by the intrusive, clunky bridge that was to replace the level crossing at Beddingham. This was high, ugly and would clearly detract from the familiar landmark of nearby Mount Caburn, notable for its shape rather than its height.

It also became established that 40 per cent of the traffic was local and would stay on the existing unimproved road, probably at higher speeds, thereby worsening the accident rate overall.

The public outcry was substantial, aided by another public meeting in Lewes at which the Department's plans were advanced by a sour and bad-tempered official, only helping to solidify the opposition to the road.

The scheme was eventually dropped and I began to pursue an alternative approach, namely of on-line improvements to make the road safer, and encouragement to use the parallel railway.

I am pleased to say that this approach proved effective and the accident rate improved markedly over the following years. Moreover, when the level crossing at Beddingham was finally replaced by a bridge, the new section of road was carefully designed and fitted the contours of the landscape very well.

None of this stopped the siren voices, from Eastbourne in particular, rather arrogantly and with scant regard for the views of local people continuing to demand a dual carriageway with monotonous regularity. They professed concern about the accident rate, but really were only interested in knocking a few minutes off the journey time from Polegate to Lewes, at whatever cost to the taxpayer. They seemed singularly uninterested in the A259 from Eastbourne to Hastings, which had a much worse accident record.

In terms of the other element to the strategy, namely promoting the parallel railway, I eventually succeeded in persuading Southern that they should cut their fares between Eastbourne and Lewes, on the basis that they had to run long trains to pick up London commuters at Lewes and Haywards Heath, and so ought to try to attract onto rail the many white-collar workers who were based in Lewes, the administrative centre and county town of East Sussex.

Accordingly, Southern cut their season ticket fares by about a third, and saw an increase in passenger traffic along the corridor of about the same amount. The managing director, Chris Burchell, told me the company had actually made a small profit from the initiative.

So the rail company gained, the rail passengers gained, and indeed the road users along the A27 gained, as traffic volumes decreased slightly. And all this at no cost to the public purse, unlike the alternative proposal to spend over half a billion pounds of public money on a new and highly destructive road. The £75 million subsequently announced by the Chancellor in the 2014 budget for on-line improvements got the balance right.

Later, when I was a transport minister, I persuaded my colleague Mike Penning, the roads minister, to install two unconventional signs along the road, which read 'Lewes to Eastbourne 20 mins by train', on a blue background adorned by a red National Rail sign. This reinforced the attractiveness of the rail option – the journey by road was at least half an hour and generally longer in the rush hour – and as a bonus annoyed the unreconstructed road lobby in Eastbourne.

Chapter 2

My first two years as a councillor had been stimulating and enjoyable and I resolved to widen my political field of activity. The changes came thick and fast.

I put myself forward for election to East Sussex County Council, for the Telscombe division, which included my district ward, and the villages on the other side of the Ouse in another Liberal ward, Kingston. But two-thirds of the division was in unpromising territory, in Telscombe Cliffs and East Saltdean. So it was a good result to turn a Tory majority of 512 in 1985 to a Liberal one of 211 in May 1989 and take the seat.

The same week, I received the news that I had been successful in my application to become the Liberals' environment campaigner, based in the party's Whips' Office in the House of Commons. This is despite the fact that I had berated the party's then environment spokesman, Malcolm Bruce MP, for holding interviews in London just a week or so ahead of the county elections.

The *Evening Argus* conflated the two events, declaring I was 'just green with joy' and running the story next to a photo of me looking as miserable as sin.

The county council proved to be rather less rigid than the district in its approach to matters. Although it had a Conservative majority, it was more willing to look at issues on their merits. The council unanimously agreed, for example, to a proposal I put forward to oppose an EU move to require compulsory testing of cosmetics on animals. That such an idea could even be seriously considered by the EU shows how far we have moved in a quarter of a century.

It also agreed to my suggestion that the council should only use dolphin-friendly tuna in its catering.

My new job in the House of Commons was based upstairs in the Whips' Office, just off central lobby. We were a small team of fewer than ten, but it was to prove to be a good intake. Three of us – Ed Davey, Adrian Sanders and myself – would go on to win parliamentary seats in 1997, while Tavish Scott and Liam McArthur would end up as MSPs in the Scottish Parliament.

My areas of responsibility were very wide. On my own, I had to cover environment, energy, animal welfare and food and agriculture. I remember bumping into a Labour researcher who told me his area of responsibility was wind power. I am sure that he knew more about that area than I did, but I doubt if he was able to create the broader context into which to place what he knew, as I was forced to do.

Interest in the environment was in fact at an all-time high. The Green Party had just scored almost 15 per cent in the European elections and, in those first-past-the-post days, had won no seats.

My party, suffering from the fallout of a painful merger between the Liberals and the SDP, with David Owen insisting on maintaining a 'continuing SDP', suffered badly, and in East Sussex, where I was agent for our candidate Delia Venables, we came fourth. The rump of the SDP staggered on until they fell behind the Monster Raving Loony Party in a by-election, whereupon David Owen mercifully pulled the plug.

In my first week in the Whips' Office, in spring 1989, Paddy Ashdown, our new leader, came round to say hello to all the staff.

He was remarkably cheerful given that, as I learnt shortly afterwards, we were within a week of going bankrupt.

On top of that, there were continual wranglings about matters as basic as what we should call ourselves. 'Liberal and Social Democrats' seemed an obvious runner, until someone acidly pointed out that LSD was not necessarily a helpful abbreviation. I preferred 'Democrats', which gained some currency in the media, but it was a term that was banned in the Whips' Office, with fiercely old-school Liberals like the Welsh MP Geraint Howells insisting that the word 'Liberal' should always be used. I think in retrospect he was right. So we settled on the cumbersome and rather ridiculous 'Social and Liberal Democrats', which predictably ended up with us being known as 'salads', until such time as we were able to ditch the first two words. Nor was the 22-strong parliamentary party particularly cohesive. Indeed, being part of two council groups that functioned well, I was dismayed that the MPs seemed to be largely a group of individuals only loosely linked.

The most detached member was David Alton, who seemed to have fallen out with his colleagues some time earlier. David would never come into the Whips' Office, even to the extent that I would observe him shouting to be heard into the phone immediately outside the office in Members' Lobby, against the hubbub of countless MPs of all parties. I wanted to ask him why he did not simply step into the Whips' Office and make his call in peace, but never did.

At this time, all the parties decided they needed to show a bit more interest in the environment, some being more convincing than others. For the Tories, John Gummer showed early enthusiasm, even if at the outset he did confuse climate change with the ozone layer, and Chris Patten showed genuine concern.

Of course, this new-found attention to the environment was something I very much welcomed. I hastily put together a project called Campaign Earth, to keep our long-standing green credentials up front, and to give our council base something to campaign on locally. Malcolm Bruce and I launched it together in a room in the House, complete with organic vegetarian food. I am not sure the journalists who attended were very impressed with this aspect.

The launch did not get much coverage, but then, prior to the successful Eastbourne by-election, nothing we did at that point did, even when it produced a good story.

I had, for example, written round to each of the water companies to establish their leakage levels, something that to my knowledge had never been done before. The results were startling, with leakage levels up to 40 per cent. Amazingly, they had all replied and I was able to produce a table – a nice, strong story, all parcelled up for a journalist.

But nobody wanted to bite. As far as the media were concerned in late 1989, we were an irrelevance. Eventually, the BBC, conceding that the story was a good one, agreed to run it, but they would only do so if it was fronted by Paddy Ashdown rather than Malcolm Bruce, despite our protestations.

So Paddy trundled over to the BBC. The first question they asked him was:

'Mr Ashdown, aren't you a one-man band?'

I mentioned that my researcher's brief was wide, and energy policy also featured prominently during my time as the party's environment campaigner.

The country was seeing the tail-end of the big pit-closure programme that had followed the ill-fated 1984 miners' strike. In late 1989, Malcolm Bruce got involved in the campaign to save Betteshanger Colliery in Kent. The pit, like so many, was marked for closure, but unlike others, the workforce had put together a plan to keep it open as a sort of miners' co-operative.

Malcolm thought this was a good idea, and tried to help, but his enthusiasm was not shared on either the right or the left. The Conservatives were still vindictively trying to close as many pits as possible, and Labour did not want to be seen to be opposing the National Union of Mineworkers (NUM), especially after the controversial creation of the Nottinghamshire-based Union of Democratic Miners during the strike.

Both were content, therefore, for the plan to fail and when, despite their opposition, it looked like it was gaining legs, the National Coal Board, presumably with the tacit consent of the NUM, went in and smashed all the equipment in the pit. This was hard politics and it was not attractive.

Each of the parties decided it needed a solid document on the environment, and I was charged by Paddy and our new environment spokesman, Simon Hughes, with producing ours.

The result was a weighty tome called 'What Price Our Planet?', which covered just about every environmental issue going. Reflecting the title, there was an economics section, tying together the environment and the economy in a way that was at least fifteen years ahead of its time. That section was written largely by the party's economics researcher, Ed Davey, later to be Energy Secretary in the coalition government, and the local government section at the back by one Paul Burstow, from 1997 MP for Sutton, and from 2010 a minister at the Department of Health.

Although inevitably now somewhat dated, 'What Price Our Planet?' was ahead of its time, dealing with such matters as genetic engineering, then barely heard of.

The document was finished right on publication deadline, about six o'clock one morning after an all-night session. Simon, who had essentially left me and Ed Davey to get on with it, seemed pleased with the result, with one exception. Reflecting his Christian beliefs, he disliked the Gaia approach I had written into the document, preferring one where man has dominion over all other forms of life. Having worked myself almost to a standstill to meet publication deadline, I did not appreciate this philosophical discussion in the middle of the night.

Checking through my old cuttings for the research for this book, I came across a piece from the *Local Government Chronicle* from 1994 in which Simon had said: 'My motive is to serve the person I believe to be the Creator of our world and to make the world more like He intended it to be,' so perhaps I should not have been so surprised.

The same article, incidentally, revealed that he liked Iron Maiden and was on *Top of the Pops* once, presumably as an audience member.

Generally, Simon cut an inspirational figure, and not just for a new researcher like me. He seemed, and was, a different sort of politician. He was, however, also intensely irritating about 5 per cent of the time, including his terrible punctuality. He once arrived almost twenty-two hours late for a meeting with me in the Whips' Office, and kicked off the conversation in blissful disregard of this.

Even then, he had an old taxi, painted orange, which was idiosyncratic but also, he told me, an electoral asset. Everyone knew it was his when he drove around his constituency. Many years later, towards the end of my time as MP, I indulged myself by buying a red Triumph Herald convertible and although I used it relatively rarely, it was astonishing the number of people who recognised it, so I suppose Simon was right on the recognition factor.

Simon's taxi was not in good condition and took a long time to start, accompanied by copious plumes of black smoke from the exhaust. It was with concern, therefore, that I learnt that a national newspaper wanted to compare the vehicles of each of the three environment spokesmen from the main parties. Astonishingly, Simon's came out greenest.

One night shortly after my election in 1997, when the House of Commons was sitting very late, Simon offered a lift home in his taxi to two MPs who looked adrift when business had ended – me and Ann Widdecombe.

We duly got in the back of his taxi. Ann and I had never really spoken to each other and were in many regards poles apart, and Simon was separated from us by the taxi driver's screen. Conversation was both surreal and challenging.

Ann was dropped off first and Simon drove me round to the corner of Bateman Street in the West End, where my flat was. As I got out, offering my thanks, two girls got in, clearly thinking his was a taxi for hire, and asked for Bermondsey, which was of course Simon's constituency, and off he drove, as I stood gaping from the pavement. He told me the next day he had not charged them.

Working with Simon back in 1990, I learnt that it was not just Lewes District Council that was full of arcane procedures. In fact, it had nothing on the House of Commons.

At the time, there was some interest in the movement of nuclear material, particularly by road, and one day, we discovered that a Private Member's Bill on the subject had been quietly introduced and was making its way through the legislative machine. These Bills, of which there are a great number, stand little chance of becoming law unless they have government support, as time is limited and it just requires one MP, typically the government duty whip, to shout 'object' for the Bill to be delayed and indeed normally lost.

This particular Bill, however, seemed to be making progress, and it became clear to us that this was in fact a government Bill masquerading as one from a backbench MP. But that also meant that it only needed one MP – Simon, for example – to stand up to shout 'object' for the Bill to be stopped in its tracks.

Here was an opportunity for us to secure beneficial changes to the Bill in return for allowing its passage into law. Accordingly, a meeting was set up between the relevant minister and Simon, which I was also to attend.

We descended to the bowels of the Commons and opened the door into a dimly lit, windowless room. There sat the minister with about fifteen civil servants. Simon set out what we wanted, knowing we were in a strong position. In the end, we negotiated some good changes, which the minister seemed philosophical about but his civil servants clearly hated.

And so it came to the Friday when the Bill in its amended form was due to go through, but as its title was read out, a Labour MP, who had wandered into the chamber and looked as if he had had a good lunch, shouted 'object' and the Bill fell.

On the food front, a party reshuffle had seen responsibility for food issues removed from Geraint Howells, who was seen to be too wedded to the producer interest, and shared between the Southport MP Ronnie Fearn, our health spokesman, and Matthew Taylor, the young MP for Truro.

Ronnie was a lovely guy and popular in the wider party, not least because of his camp stage appearances at party conference, but he lacked the killer instinct. I groaned when he fluffed a line I had written for him – 'the Tory government has put the botch into botulism' – by delivering it as if he were John Inman.

Matthew was altogether sharper and had what it took to make an impression and make a difference. He did not really need me to help him, although I did manage to get him onto the front page of the *Daily Telegraph* with a rather gruesome story about 'super-glue meat'. This was the revelation that, in order not to waste any of the animal, all the bones were scraped clean, added to the gristle and anything else that could be found, and reconstituted with a blood gel to look like prime steak.

It is worth remarking that my research role occurred in a time before the internet, almost before desk computers. I had only a very simple word processor. This meant a lot of my time was spent in the House of Commons library, laboriously trawling through newspapers and magazines, and ordering books from the ever helpful librarians. It also meant keeping a lot of paper files in the Whips' Office.

Generally, my role was going well and we were regularly scoring hits on the government. Then one morning I came in to find my filing cabinet open. As far as I could tell, the only file that was missing was one entitled 'Conservatives/Environment'.

In late 1989, my local party decided to set in train the process for selecting its parliamentary candidate to fight the next general election. The Liberals had firmly established second place behind the Conservatives back in the 1970s when Gordon Hook – he who persuaded me to stand for council back in 1987 – had been the candidate. He had flown the flag in 1974 and 1979, and David Bellotti had contested the seat for us in 1983 and 1987.

I was enjoying my politics and being successful. In just two years, I had won elections to three councils and secured a post in Parliament. I decided I wanted to put myself forward for the parliamentary seat.

I told David Bellotti of my decision, which he did not welcome. He thought he should be allowed a third go at the seat, which did not strike me as a very good argument. In fact, given that not much headway had been made into the Conservative majority, if anything, the opposite was true.

In the end, he decided not to seek the nomination again and I was selected to be the parliamentary candidate, with 87.5 per cent of the vote in a two-cornered contest with Uckfield councillor Mike Skinner.

In the curious way events unfold sometimes, this outcome was good for David, as it meant he was free to contest the Eastbourne by-election, which became necessary later that year.

The Eastbourne local party in fact sounded me out at an early stage, but I told them I was committed to Lewes. The other factor was that I love Lewes and the towns and villages in the constituency, but I felt no such emotion for Eastbourne. I also feel strongly that an MP should live in the seat they hope to represent.

The Eastbourne election was caused by the appalling assassination of Conservative MP Ian Gow. The Tory had been a very popular MP, but that did the Tories no good in the by-election, which just goes to show that in politics, gratitude is the expectation of things to come.

David had actually stood in Eastbourne once before, back in 1979, before then contesting Lewes twice, but our private polling at the start of the campaign showed just 4 per cent of the Eastbourne constituency knew who he was. By the end, that figure had risen to 96 per cent, which is some testament to the famous Liberal by-election unit of the time.

The Tory candidate in the by-election, one Richard Hickmet, was completely unknown, and had the misfortune to be photographed on his own in an Eastbourne street consulting a map of the town. It did not help his campaign.

So Eastbourne fell to the Lib Dems, which did wonders for morale, not just locally but across the country. After the horrors of the merger and all the fallout that had generated, we were on our way back.

David's election meant there was now a vacancy for our group leader on the district council, and I put myself forward for the post. My enthusiasm knew no bounds. The district group accepted me as David's replacement.

It was an enormously busy time, not least in my own council ward. In the summer, I had been summoned to Cyril Mann's office in the district council. He wanted to brief me personally on a planning application about to be submitted in my ward.

It turned out that this was for a major £30 million project to build a brand-new opera house adjacent to the existing one at Glyndebourne, and he excitedly showed me the plans.

I looked at them dispassionately.

'It looks like a gasometer,' I remarked provocatively.

Cyril went visibly pale, and dropped his voice.

'You can't say that. This is a major investment in the district, a matter of pride.'

Now, I did not really object to the concept of building a new opera house, and recognised the unique reputation of Glyndebourne and its role in the cultural life of the country. I did, however, object to the way in which the application was being progressed, with the special treatment afforded to it, which seemed to me to prejudge proper consideration of the scheme by the planning committee. I particularly objected to the chief executive shortly afterwards writing round personally to all forty-eight members of the council to 'explain' the scheme.

The application was of course approved, and construction began. This involved a large number of lorries trundling through Glynde village, and I thought it would be a good gesture if Glyndebourne were to recognise the disruption, and make a small financial contribution to the village.

As I have mentioned, Glynde was estate owned and many of the residents were actually quite poor. The 1981 census showed Glynde with a higher percentage of properties dependent on outside toilets than anywhere else in East Sussex.

The children's playground was in a particularly poor state, with some pieces of equipment out of action, and broken concrete under some others. The estate showed no interest in rectifying this, and the parish council, as usual, was not keen to spend too much money, so I hit upon the idea of asking Glyndebourne to contribute, and wrote to Sir George Christie accordingly.

I pointed out that Glyndebourne was spending £33 million on its project, construction was causing disruption to the village, and it would not be unreasonable to make a financial contribution to the children's play area. I had in mind about £10,000.

The reply I received was abruptly dismissive, giving short shrift to the idea, and annoyed me. Sir George told the *Daily Telegraph*: 'If it was known that Glyndebourne allowed some of its supporters' money to be siphoned off for the benefit of an unrelated local scheme, our supporters would quickly withdraw.'

£10,000 out of £33 million? I resolved not to give up, and contacted a journalist on TVS to help. The channel at the time had an arts programme, and we concocted an idea to make progress.

Accordingly, TVS contacted Sir George Christie to ask him for an interview about his project, only for him to have to face questions on camera about the children's equipment in Glynde recreation ground. He was not best pleased, but did as a result send me two opera tickets to auction – a result of sorts, I suppose.

However, there is a happy ending. The children's equipment today is in a much better state, and Glyndebourne's new opera house has been a great success, with superb acoustics. And it does not even really look like a gasometer.

As well as my normal council duties, now on three councils, I had to prepare for a full set of district council elections the following May, and for a general election that could come at any time. Michael Heseltine had effectively ousted Margaret Thatcher, only to see John Major take over. As was wryly observed at the time, in the contest between the lion, the witch and the wardrobe, the wardrobe had won.

It was not certain how long the government would last. On the one hand, the Tories were unpopular in the country, not least as a consequence of the self-inflicted wound of the poll tax – or community charge, as ministers, and virtually nobody else, preferred to call it. On the other hand, John Major could present himself as a new face and might just go early to ask for a mandate.

I also had to secure an income, having left the Whips' Office, so accepted David Bellotti's suggestion that I act as a caseworker for him in Eastbourne.

Another person who worked for David at this time was Paul Elgood, who went on to become our leader on Brighton and Hove Council. He was walking along Grove Road one day towards David's office when the then largely unknown Tory candidate Nigel Waterson literally bumped into him, sending him flying into the gutter.

Nigel looked down at him and said: 'Mind where you're going!' before walking off.

David had won Eastbourne with a comfortable majority of 4,350 but the time he would have until the next election was an awkward one. Had it been six months, it is very likely the people of Eastbourne would have given him another chance. Had it been three or four years, there is a strong possibility that he would have dug himself in. As it was, he had eighteen months.

In the event, Nigel Waterson captured the seat from David Bellotti in the 1992 election with a majority of 5,481 and held it until Stephen Lloyd won it back for the Lib Dems in 2010. It was one of only two seats to switch from Tory to Lib Dem at that election and it could not have happened to a more deserving case than Nigel.

Chapter 3

It was clear in the months preceding the all-out district elections in May 1991 that there was a real chance the Lib Dems would take control of the council. On the face of it, this was a tall order. We went into the election with only twelve seats, compared to thirty for the Tories. But dig beneath the surface and the omens looked good.

First, we were on a roll, having won the Eastbourne by-election and followed that up in March with an even more remarkable victory in Ribble Valley, where a Tory majority of almost 20,000 in their sixth-safest seat turned into a Lib Dem victory by almost 5,000.

Second, the Tories had badly lost the argument over the poll tax and were for the time being stuck with a hugely unpopular policy.

Third, the Lewes District Council area was clearly a straight fight between the Tories and the Lib Dems. Labour had not won a council seat at any level – county, district or town – anywhere in the Lewes constituency since the 1970s, a trend that was to continue at successive elections through to 2015.

I knew that if we were to win the district we would have to make gains on the coast, and in particular in Seaford, which returned twelve of the forty-eight councillors. I also recognised that there was considerable disquiet in the town about how local affairs were being handled.

Seaford was one of only five large towns in the country not to have a town council, although there had been five local referendums between 1980 and 1995 asking whether one should be established. The definitive poll in 1995 would produce a clear Yes vote, and Seaford eventually got its town council in 2001.

Before we took control in 1991, the functions such a council would normally undertake were instead performed by Lewes District Council on its behalf. A semblance of local input was provided by a curious body called the Seaford Consultative Committee. This comprised simply the town's twelve district councillors meeting together, the same twelve who were then subject to the iron rod and group discipline of Keith Moorhouse when they got to Lewes.

In my view, this so-called committee was nothing but a charade that did nothing for the town and might as well not exist. Nor was it representative of the views of the town at large. The previous election had seen 58 per cent of the town's votes go to the Tories, and 36 per cent to the Lib Dems, which in my mind suggested that the make-up of the committee, if it was to mean anything, should be seven Conservatives, four Lib Dems and one other.

My approach in those days was rather more acerbic and tabloid than it later became, and I issued a press statement calling for reform, and labelling the committee 'a creaking, undemocratic, unrepresentative self-appointed body of yesmen'.

Naturally, the response from the Seaford Tories was one of angry indignation, but there was a good deal of spontaneous support in the letters pages of the local paper, the *Seaford Gazette*, for what I had said, including from some Conservatives. The local paper itself pointed out that the Tories on occasion said one thing in Seaford on their committee, then voted the opposite way when they got to Lewes.

In one editorial, the *Gazette* flagged up how one councillor, Irene Hyde, had spoken against a planning application in Seaford, but then voted for it in Lewes. It suggested that when people had voted for Hyde, they had not expected to get Jekyll as well.

Encouraged by the reaction, I worked with local people in the town to establish what became known as the Seaford Alternative Committee. This was composed, it has to be conceded, largely of Lib Dems, but did include a couple of Independents and at least one Tory voter.

It was only ever intended that this should be a short-term arrangement, and I announced at the same time that if the Lib Dems took control in May, we would move to establish a neighbourhood council.

Looking back through the local papers for the early months of 1991, I surprise myself by the sheer range of stories I managed to get covered, whether positive ones about our plans, or negative ones about the Tory administration at Lewes District. I sense that the local press felt it would be more interesting to break the blue hegemony in East Sussex. They were certainly helpful to me.

The stories covered everything from recycling rates to interest rate swaps, where I accused the Tories of playing Monopoly with taxpayers' money, and recommended that they return to Old Kent Road without passing Go and without collecting £200. It was a good sound bite, but in truth, I probably understood what was a complex issue as little as the Tories I was criticising.

John Eccles, a veteran reporter on the *Sussex Express*, was always receptive to a good news story. On one occasion we were facing a twin resignation by two Lib Dem town councillors, Ruth Sheen and David Drabble. I asked John on the Monday how he intended to cover it, and he confirmed my fears that this was to be the main front-page story on the Friday. I tried to persuade him that the story did not merit this, but he insisted, rightly in fact, that it did. But he made me an offer that if I came up with a better story, he would put that on the front page instead. I duly brought forward a story I was working on, namely the use of the landfill site at Beddingham as a disposal point for low-level nuclear waste, and the resignation story was duly shunted off the front.

I liked John, who was a character, but he was not averse to cutting corners if he could get away with it. In one edition, he suggested that a house occupied by a woman called Molly had been knocked down, which generated a furious letter from said Molly the following week, from a house still standing. The awkward moment was avoided by a bright sub-editor who titled her letter 'Good Golly, Miffed Molly'. John was to be crucially helpful in the run-up to the 1997 general election.

As election day 1991 approached, the Lib Dems were buoyed up by a visit to Newhaven and Seaford by Lib Dem leader Paddy Ashdown, which received extensive local and national coverage. The Tories could only manage an unknown junior minister, Baroness Blatch.

I had spent the previous few weeks briefing the local papers that we were on course to take control, and that was reflected in the positive coverage we received in the run-up to election day, with headlines such as 'Lib Dem Push On Lewes'. I did actually believe we could take control, but would of course have looked rather foolish if we had made but little progress, so positive had my assertions been.

My honest assessment was that it was touch and go whether we would take control, and that it would depend on Seaford, as I had always thought. Then we were given a gift just before the election.

The Conservatives had been amassing a reserve to build the council a new office block, and had managed to put by £1.2 million. They believed that it was inefficient for the council to be operating out of seven different buildings, a view my colleagues and I did not share.

We made it clear in our election literature that we would cancel the office block and spend the reserve more usefully on what the public wanted.

The Tories were forced onto the defensive, and began to back-track, but then their leader, Keith Moorhouse, issued a leaflet featuring a story headed 'Creaking Floorboards Face the Chop', while his colleagues in Seaford were saying the opposite. The contradiction made the front page of the *Seaford Gazette* on the day before the election.

The results were very good. In what the *Brighton Argus* called 'the great Lib Dem landslide', we went from twelve to twenty-seven seats, and the Tories dropped from thirty to eighteen. In my own ward, in a four-cornered contest, I won 86 per cent of the vote.

And so I found myself leader of the council and, at thirty-three, by some distance the youngest councillor on the authority. I had proven my ability to campaign successfully, but leading an administration of twenty-seven Lib Dems would require a different skill set, and not one I had had very much preparation for, something that would cause problems down the track.

There was, predictably, no formal training available to people in my situation, although I did have a conversation with Martin King, the Lib Dem leader of Adur District Council, along the coast west of Brighton. In due course, there was also help for the group from the Association of Liberal Democrat Councillors, based in Hebden Bridge.

We all assembled in a room at the town hall on the Saturday morning to work out what to do next. I had optimistically booked a large room for this meeting about two weeks earlier, but when we arrived, I was taken aback by the way the room had been laid out. There was a top table with three chairs behind it, facing three or four rows of seating, reminiscent of a schoolroom.

I asked the caretaker why he had set out the chairs as he had. He replied that that was the way Councillor Moorhouse had always required it. We therefore spent the first few minutes reorganising the room, forming a square.

I was determined that the group should operate in a democratic manner, so we then embarked on a long and laborious process to elect chairs and vice-chairs of committees.

I ran into trouble early on when there was a robust contest for chair of the Personnel Committee between two Lewes-based councillors, Mike Chartier and Robert Evans. I personally favoured Mike, who had been a town councillor for four years, while my experience of Robert had led me to conclude, rightly as it turned out, that he might be hard work.

To my dismay, the vote was tied and I had to use a casting vote. Robert made it very clear he thought he was better qualified, which on paper he was, and in the end I reluctantly supported him, but I had not handled the matter well and it showed.

I suspect my arrival as council leader was greeted with horror by Cyril Mann. Here was a whirlwind who was keen to make sweeping changes, whether or not he understood the consequences.

And changes aplenty there were in the first month. I told the chief executive that I wanted to change the hours of the council offices so they were open at lunchtimes. To my great surprise, Cyril enacted this from the very next day. I was not sure if he was being ultra-helpful or trying to stir up anger amongst the staff as a way of encouraging me to slow down.

I also acted to abolish the rather pointless Seaford Consultative Committee, replacing it in the interim with a Seaford sub-committee, constructed, as every other committee or sub-committee was, in proportion to the council result. This meant it would have four Lib Dems and three Conservatives, as well as non-voting representatives from outside groups like the Residents' Association and the Chamber of Commerce.

Keith Moorhouse called the decision 'scandalous' and accused me of establishing a 'junta'. Independent councillor Graham Mayhew called it 'a fairly astute political move'.

In line with our election manifesto, we also decided to shift committee meetings from afternoons to evenings, to help councillors in employment, and encourage a wider group of people to stand in future. The average age of our group was much lower than the Tories', including working-age councillors with children. The Tories were nearly all retired.

Like every other change we made, the Tories complained about it, and it is true that the odd meeting did run very late, even to midnight. However, this was only partly down to our initiatives and quite a lot down to the opposition put up by the Conservative group, so it was a bit rich for them to complain about finishing times.

The Tories could not get used to the changes at all. One of their leading lights, Alf Deats from Newick, had grandly told Mike Chartier a couple of years earlier that we would never take control and never have a Lib Dem as chairman. Now the Tories were frozen in disbelief, matched for its effect only by the sheer sense of wonder many in the Lib Dem ranks felt.

As council leader, I chaired the Policy and Resources Committee. Most of the business we discussed had already been through topic-based committees, but some material, particularly financial matters, came here first. Some of these items seemed rather abstract, such as setting the council's annual borrowing limit, which I recall being somewhere in the order of £73 million. No doubt this was terribly important, but nobody on the committee really seemed to understand how it worked, what it meant or whether it should be changed, so it tended to go through every year on the nod.

By contrast, decisions about whether to spend £300 on a particular item would elicit many comments and much heated debate, presumably on the basis that everyone had a handle on the concept.

Our ruling group had a relatively thin majority on these committees, and on one occasion we were left in a minority, with one member fewer than the Tories. Whether the Tories did not realise – quite possible – or they were too flat-footed to take advantage of the position I do not know. I did know, however, that the last item on the agenda was controversial and they were bound to oppose it. I also knew that one of our missing number, Graham Mayhew, who by that time had moved from being Independent to joining us, had indicated that he would arrive by a particular time.

I had thought that the meeting would be some way from the final item before he arrived, but for some reason, we made speedy progress that evening and were about to reach the penultimate item about forty-five minutes before his expected arrival time.

That item was one of those that was on every agenda, and normally nodded through without discussion – the Write-Off of Irrecoverable Debts.

I passed an urgent note to the council's deputy leader, Gordon Hook, telling him he had to keep the item going until Graham Mayhew arrived. Gordon was fantastic and turned in a virtuoso performance, raising points, asking questions, casting doubts. So effective was he that the Tories joined in too, as did other committee chairs, and the debate sailed along until the door opened and Graham Mayhew entered, whereupon I declared, after a minute or so, that I thought we had given the issue sufficient airing and it was time to move on.

We began a series of chief officer appraisals, to measure performance and set targets for the following year. One involved the estates manager, David Brown. David was a smooth, elegant, silver-haired man of about fifty-five, who never saw the need to break out of a walking pace. I got the impression he was a competent officer but was not really going to change his approach in any way as a result of the appraisal process. He was humouring us, in a rather attractive way.

Cyril was somewhat more impatient than I was and at one stage put a rather sharp question to David Brown. A moment's silence followed while David Brown mused over his reply, and then I suddenly burst out laughing before desperately trying to stifle this outburst.

The rest of the room quite understandably wondered what on earth I was laughing at. The truth is that I had just realised that the interplay of the two officers in front of me – Cyril Mann and David Brown – was not unlike that between Captain Mainwaring and Sergeant Wilson in *Dad's Army*, both in physical appearance and temperament. I could not of course share this, so explained it away, not very convincingly, as a coughing fit, though I could not get the *Dad's Army* image out of my head for the rest of the meeting as I tried to concentrate on the task in hand.

More controversially, an issue blew up affecting the council's deputy chief executive, Peter Oldfield, in July, less than three months into the new council. A company of which he was a director and company secretary, the Home Trust, came under heavy criticism by Adur District Council when it was accused of 'preying on the elderly'. It operated a scheme whereby council tenants were offered cash to buy their homes cut-price, and so live there rent-free for the rest of their lives. Upon their death, the property would transfer to Home Trust.

Adur launched an investigation after an 83-year-old widow was approached by the company. She agreed to the deal and qualified for the highest discount on the property, so the council was paid £13,000. Four months later she was dead and the property was valued at £45,000.

The then leader of Adur District Council, Martin King, told the *Brighton Evening Argus* that it was important, in his view, for Peter Oldfield, who had acted for the widow, to be named publicly, telling the paper: 'This whole rigmarole of making money at the loss of housing for the public stinks.'

Adur Council decided to refer the matter to the Law Society.

It turned out that Peter Oldfield had negotiated a contract with the previous Conservative administration to allow him to take part in private ventures. I was not made aware of this when I became council leader, and while I accepted that the activities of the Home Trust were perfectly legal, and that Peter Oldfield had secured permission to undertake private work outside the council (though it was not clear whether anyone was aware of the precise nature of this), I regarded what the Home Trust was engaged upon to be unethical. I also thought it wrong in principle for an officer in such a senior position to have such outside interests, and was furious that I should learn about such arrangements from another authority and a local paper.

There followed an electric meeting behind closed doors involving Peter Oldfield, Robert Evans as chair of the Personnel Committee, and myself. The upshot was an agreement that the deputy chief executive would with immediate effect take extended leave until his contract with the council expired the following June. This was endorsed subsequently by the Personnel Committee.

Following the meeting on 24 July, Peter Oldfield issued a statement defending the activities of the Home Trust, which he said he believed were in the public interest, but also expressing regret for any embarrassment caused to Lewes District Council.

In my response, I accepted that the Home Trust was acting perfectly legally, but added: 'I regret, however, that Lewes District Council has been sucked into this matter, as I believe it reflects badly on local government. On a personal basis, I regard the activities of Home Trust as distasteful, exploitative and contrary to the spirit of the right-to-buy legislation.'

Following the meeting of the Personnel Committee a few days later, Peter Oldfield and I issued a joint statement saying departure terms had been agreed and that the arrangement was entirely amicable. Cyril Mann told me privately that he thought we had been over-generous with public money.

Cyril, in fact, took the opportunity to announce his own retirement after thirty-three years in local government, and this was noted at the same Personnel Committee meeting.

I was slightly surprised by his decision and indeed worried what the public would conclude from the announced departure of both the chief executive and his deputy within three months of us taking control.

I think Cyril probably did not relish the pace of change, or indeed its direction, from what he had seen since the elections in May and concluded that this was a good time to go. He had in fact had health problems, having suffered a heart attack three years earlier, and I understood that his doctors had advised retirement for some time.

It is also the case that he relied quite a bit on Peter Oldfield and I suspect he knew he would feel Peter's departure, and certainly, between then and the following June, when his retirement took effect, this was noticeable.

Cyril Mann therefore duly retired on health grounds the following June, but I am happy to say he was still to be seen round Lewes in 2015. Although Cyril and I were from very different moulds, he believed in public service and in the importance of the council, and I respected him for it.

In due course, we appointed a new chief executive, John Crawford, who had been a senior legal officer for Brighton Council.

John was professional and very competent and a good choice. He stayed with the council until his retirement in 2011.

I recall his first day in post when I arrived in his office overlooking the lovely gardens at Lewes House, where the council was then based. I had walked up through the garden, eating mulberries off the old tree that had rested in the far corner for so long, and picking mushrooms from the lawn. I was wearing an old T-shirt and jeans, and my hands, holding mushrooms, were purple with mulberry juice. He looked at me slightly askance.

'John, you're in a Liberal council now,' I said, and he laughed.

Amid all the internal reorganisations and preparations for the general election, one major external challenge arose with doubts over the future of the Newhaven–Dieppe ferry. It was to be a running issue throughout the decades ahead.

The ferry crossing is actually the oldest established between Britain and France, having originally begun in 1850. It boasts some interesting associations, including the fact that the father of Vietnam, Ho Chi Minh, served as a pastry cook on the boat in the years following the First World War, having earlier worked on a French steamer from 1911. The Vietnamese government picked up on this and by 2015 they had made plans for a statue near the quayside. To that end, I attended a rather delightful if somewhat surreal celebratory event hosted by the Vietnamese embassy and Newhaven Town Council.

Another association is with Lord Lucan, whose car was found in nearby Norman Road following the death of Sandra Rivett, and the assumption is that he left the country via the ferry to Dieppe.

Newhaven port was owned by British Rail but sold off to Sea Containers in the 1980s by Margaret Thatcher's government. During their tenure, the company did little with the port, but ascribed to it a high value, presumably to enable them to borrow money against it.

The immediate threat in late 1991, however, came from striking French seamen, with the French press speculating about permanent closure. Cyril Mann and I went to Dieppe to meet the various partners, including the mayor, Christian Cuvillier, and the president of the Chamber of Commerce, Jean-Paul Lalitte, and lobbied ministers on both sides of the Channel, as it looked possible that a decision to end ferry operations might be imminent. In the event, a deal was reached in December to give the ferry a guarantee for six months. Such hand-to-mouth arrangements would sadly become all too common from then on.

Throughout the year I continued to serve as a county councillor, though that inevitably took a back seat to my district role and my preparations for the general election. I could not, however, resist the open goal presented by the Conservative administration's decision to invest in a new logo, spurred on by the possible reorganisation of local government that was in the air, with the suggestion that county councils might be abolished.

I say new, but in fact, the only change to what had gone before was to change the words 'East Sussex' to 'East Sussex County Council', and move them from below the wavy lines image to above it. For that, the council paid £20,000, £30,000 or £43,000, depending on whether you believed the *Evening Standard*, the *Daily Telegraph* or the *Evening Argus*. More than £10,000 of this would be spent on changing stationery.

The wavy lines were to remain, though a survey in Lewes showed only 20 per cent recognised it as belonging to the county council, with the same percentage associating it with the water authority. Five per cent thought it was something to do with a hairdresser's perm.

I reported the matter to the district auditor, calling it a grotesque waste of money. Nothing resulted from this, of course.

Subsequently, I put down a written question at the county council, asking how much money had been spent over the previous twelve months on improving the image of the county council. The answer was £220,329.

As it happens, I had concluded that we ought to update the district council's logo, to get away from the rather 1950s crest that adorned our notepaper. I thought it would be a good idea to hold a competition, both to involve the public in their council but also frankly to save money. We offered a £500 prize for the winning entry.

We had an encouraging response and a few of us, including our excellent, recently appointed arts officer Carole Buchan, gathered in a room to survey the huge number of entries we had received. I had forgotten to specify that we did not want crests, which made up about a quarter of the entries, and I felt rather bad at sweeping these away perfunctorily, recognising the painstaking time some people had put into their creations.

We settled on a simple design, with two green wavy lines above a slightly less wavy blue one, symbolising, or so we assumed, the hills of the South Downs and the coastline, above the name of the authority. The logo, designed by a Ted Brewer from Newhaven, was introduced gradually, as existing stocks of paper were used up. The whole exercise cost less than £2,000. The logo is still in use today.

Come the New Year, Lib Dem efforts were focused almost exclusively on the general election. Nationally, it was expected that the Tories would lose their majority and we could end up with a hung parliament. In Sussex, the Lib Dems were aiming to hold Eastbourne and win Lewes, with Hastings an outside chance for a third seat.

In my experience, candidates often think they are going to win, even if a rational assessment would suggest otherwise. I suppose, as a candidate, if you do not think you can win, why should any-one else think so?

We knew Lewes would be an uphill struggle – Tim Rathbone was defending a majority of almost 14,000 – but in those heady days we thought anything was possible. After all, we had won the dis-trict council convincingly the year before, and I had had a pretty good run in the media since then. In addition, we had clearly estab-lished in the electorate's mind that only the Lib Dems could topple the Tories. Our organisation was keen as mustard, if a little naive and inexperienced.

A poll carried out by the *Sussex Express* in March put the Tories only 5.5 per cent ahead of us, which corresponded to our own internal assessment.

I challenged Tim Rathbone to a head-to-head, a debate which made the main story in the *Seaford Gazette* with pictures of the two of us, thereby helpfully reinforcing the two-horse race mes-sage. Unsurprisingly, he rejected my call, but coming hard on the heels of two hustings meetings which he, alone of the candidates, had failed to attend, it made him look evasive.

The papers were talking up our chances, and a number of key Lib Dem MPs visited the seat, including Paddy Ashdown and Simon Hughes. Then, in early April, Tim and I were given a free £25 char-ity Grand National bet by Ladbrokes. Tim chose Auntie Dot, which struggled in fifth from last. I chose Party Politics, which romped home, raising several hundred pounds for a cancer charity.

The newspaper reports were predictably helpful, about the out-sider winning. I took it as a good omen and said I was looking for a double on the following Thursday, election day.

Sadly, it was not to be a good omen. It was the nearest I got to winning that year.

The week before the election, we had thought we were in

with a chance, though the ranks of Tory posters along the A259 through Seaford suggested we would have to do very well in Lewes and Newhaven.

But in the last few days the mood changed. It was almost tangible in the air. The catalyst, if there was one, was the dreadfully misjudged Sheffield rally held by Labour leader Neil Kinnock, which seemed to swing the public mood back to the Tories. Certainly, the public seemed more comfortable with bank manager John Major and his improvised soapbox than with the strident garishness of Neil Kinnock.

The Tories had run a largely negative campaign and this intensified after the Sheffield rally. The Lib Dems were really bystanders in all this, until the Tories successfully attached us to Labour in the public's mind, and appealed to the public to hold onto Nanny.

From the last weekend onwards, the requests for poster boards stopped coming in and I could feel our vote softening. When the votes were cast on the Thursday, I had managed a swing of just 2 per cent from the Tories, and reduced the Tory majority from 13,620 to 12,175. The fact that we suffered the same fate across the country, missing most of our targets except for the odd seat like Bath, and the fact that Lewes produced one of the best Lib Dem percentages in the country, was little comfort to me.

What it did do, however, was prepare me mentally for 2015, when a not dissimilar set of circumstances applied, and I was able to handle defeat then with a genuine degree of equanimity.

In 1992, however, the result poleaxed me and I felt humiliated. I had been ready for defeat, but not for the huge gap between the two parties. I remember being at the count and staring in disbelief at the two piles of votes, a towering one for Tim Rathbone and a much more modest one for me.

If you have not been a parliamentary candidate in a seat you hope to win, and then crushingly failed to do so, then there is no way I can effectively convey what it feels like. The nearest I can get to it is to say that I felt as if a huge lump of me, from my neck to my waist, had been cut out and thrown away, leaving a huge hole.

The feeling only intensified over the next fortnight. I felt I had let my Lib Dem colleagues down. I had to face a barrage of nasty letters in the local press. And I was out of a job with no income stream beyond what were then modest council allowances, totalling probably no more than £4,000 a year, even being on two major councils and leader of one.

I suppose I was to an extent feeling sorry for myself. What stopped the rot and got me back on my feet was a local Lib Dem member, Dawn Davidson, who had been an agent up in Lancashire. In her brusque northern way, she told me: 'You're not a Liberal until you've lost an election.'

For some reason this cheered me up and I put the 1992 election behind me.

Chapter 4

Soon after the election, I walked into a storm. It was called Lewes Bonfire.

A bonfire? You mean fireworks and so on? Blank looks greet any discussion of Lewes Bonfire for those outside Sussex or those who have not been to witness it. It is quite unlike anything else in the country.

Ostensibly, it marks the burning of seventeen Protestant martyrs in the town in 1557, which helps explain the annual burning of Pope Paul V, the incumbent during the Guy Fawkes plot of 1605.

It is for this reason that it appears superficially to be anti-Catholic, but it is not. Rather, it is anti-establishment and marks the annual right of the ordinary people of Lewes to take over the town for a night. It is a grass-roots event in which those who have offended the various Bonfire Societies are paraded through the streets in effigy form before being burnt at one of the bonfire sites. In that sense, it is more akin to a satirical cartoon.

A huge amount of planning and fundraising goes into the preparations of the Bonfire Societies in Lewes – there are seven in all – and they are joined in a huge procession through the town on 5 November by societies from elsewhere in Sussex, mostly villages nearby.

The long procession parades through the town's narrow streets, flaming torches in hand, bangers going off, while the pavements are crowded with onlookers, on one occasion as many as 80,000, according to the *Sussex Express*, in a town with a population of 16,000.

In our health-and-safety-conscious country, it is the sort of event that would never be allowed to start, and indeed there have been more than a few in the police and fire service over the years who have arrived in Lewes and wanted to sanitise it to remove what they perceive to be the inherent dangers of the event.

So it was in 1992 that the police identified steps they wanted to take to make Bonfire safer. This involved the police producing a new code of conduct, bitterly opposed by the Bonfire Societies. The district council had no choice but to be involved as we were the authority responsible for granting street closures for the event.

Accordingly, I chaired a meeting which took place in late June, attended by representatives of the police, the district council, East Sussex County Council as the highway authority, and the Bonfire Societies. At this meeting, the police demanded that certain roads in the town traditionally used by the societies for their procession route be kept completely clear for emergency vehicles.

The atmosphere between the police and the societies was hostile, and I found myself trying to hold the ring. I had no wish to get on the wrong side of much of the population of Lewes, for whom Bonfire is almost a religion. On the other hand, I did not relish the consequences of something going badly wrong on the night when we as a council had overruled the advice of the police. However, in trying to straddle the two positions, we ended up stranded in the middle.

It was not helpful that a full meeting of the council was due shortly, and even less so that Graham Mayhew, at that stage still an Independent, had tabled a motion criticising the draft code of conduct as 'unnecessarily prescriptive and detrimental' to Bonfire. We would have to come off the fence.

A difficult group meeting of the Lib Dem councillors followed, when it was suggested and agreed that those of our group who were Bonfire Society members should absent themselves from the discussions. In retrospect, that was a wrong call and I think I should have used my position as group leader to insist they stay. Pushing them out of the tent was not sensible.

We decided to vote down the motion and instead vote for our own amendment that confirmed the council's commitment to both Bonfire and safety. In other words, we were still hopeful that we could straddle the fence. Graham Mayhew insisted on a recorded vote to try to embarrass our group, and particularly his Lib Dem ward colleague Mike Chartier, but Mike, with his strong Bonfire connections, had perforce had to declare an interest so could not vote anyway.

I would have loved to have walked away from the whole thing, and left it to the police and the societies to sort out between them, but we were tied in very firmly because of our street closure and land ownership responsibilities.

In the end, we came down broadly on the side of the police, after advice that to do otherwise would leave us legally very exposed if anything did go wrong. But because our street closure order specified vehicle and crowd control barriers and special emergency routes through the town – in other words, the key police demands – we were then bang in the firing line.

Fortunately, a late bit of fudged give-and-take meant that Bonfire Night was able to proceed in a way that both sides could live with, and passed largely without incident. There was just one drink-related arrest, and forty minor injuries.

I was grateful to my Lib Dem colleague Paul Mockford, a key

Bonfire member, for his supportive letter in the local paper, which probably carried more weight than anything I could have said.

It did not, however, stop a number of locally elected Lib Dems appearing as effigies on 5 November. I first saw my head coming down the street, next to that of the Chief Constable Roger Birch, as I was leaning out of the town hall window.

My first reaction was quiet admiration for the artistic quality of the papier mâché head, which had achieved a very good likeness. Above the generic rectangular plaque that read 'ENEMIES OF BONFIRE' and accompanied each head, there was a line of description added. Mine read 'Storming Norman', which was certainly preferable to that for my deputy Gordon Hook, who had 'Hook, Liar and Stinker' attached, while the mayor of Lewes, Ann De Vecchi, had 'Interfering Old Mare'.

Then, on 9 November, the Chief Constable stunned everyone by calling for a new safety clampdown. He wanted to see a ban on children carrying flaming torches; a curb on the throwing of bangers; road closures; and restrictions on the sale of alcohol.

Having tried to do my best to bring the two sides together and only succeeding in getting my fingers burnt, I wanted nothing to do with this. I told the local press that if the police were determined to push for change, they would have to do so in co-operation with the societies.

A couple of years later, when I was in Dalarna in Sweden, I witnessed the traditional Midsummer's Day ceremony, when something like a maypole is raised from the ground to an upright position using the traditional method, namely forked branches of increasing size, and rope. I sat on a grassy bank, on a lovely sunny day, next to a councillor from Newcastle. He observed that this sort of ceremony would not be allowed in England, referring to the fact that we were all well within the radius of the circle described by the pole were it to topple over. In England, we would all be well back behind a boundary rope, and those carrying out the raising of the pole would doubtless be in hard hats and luminous jackets, rather than in normal clothes as these Swedes were.

It was at that precise point that my views on health and safety moved, and I reflected that, at least with adults, it was up to the individual to make their own risk assessment in situations like this, rather than some official body playing safe on your behalf. So I now take the view that, yes, there is a risk associated with being on the streets of Lewes on 5 November but, within reason, people should be free to make up their own minds whether they want to take that risk, rather than have an official body decide it for them.

Several years later, in 2009, as an MP I would introduce a Bill in the Commons to address the wider issue, the Personal Responsibility Bill. This sought to establish the principle that an individual is responsible for their own actions and the consequences of those actions, unless there has been 'a clear breach of a duty of care' or injury or damage is suffered as a deliberate act of another person.

It added: 'Nothing in this Act shall impose any liability on any person for any accidental injury or damage suffered by any other person (P) which could have been averted if P had used common sense.'

In other words, if a workman leaves a hole in the pavement without guard rails or warning signs, they would be liable. If someone sells a cup of hot coffee to a person who then spills it on themselves, they would not.

It was, in my view, a short and thoroughly sensible piece of legislation and I hope someone will revisit it. The over-zealous obsession with health and safety is one of the worst aspects of British life. When children are prevented from spending their lunch break in the playground because it has been snowing and they might slip over – this actually happened in my time in a primary school in Lewes – something is seriously wrong.

Incidentally, I do not in any way blame the Health and Safety Executive, who do apply a sensible balance and are as exasperated as I am by children being banned from sitting under conker trees and all the other nonsense rulings.

While all the Bonfire business was going on, another process was unfolding that would prove very helpful to the local Lib Dems. The Boundary Commission was finalising its proposals for new parliamentary constituencies. Helpfully, they were suggesting that Peacehaven and Telscombe, coastal towns between Newhaven and Brighton, should transfer to the Brighton Kemptown constituency, and East Dean should move from Lewes to Eastbourne. In return, Lewes would gain Polegate and Willingdon from Eastbourne.

The areas projected to leave the constituency were ones which predominantly voted Conservative, whereas Polegate and Willingdon tended then to be much more Lib Dem-inclined.

Naturally, we were amenable to these ideas, although we from the council did suggest that instead of gaining Willingdon and Polegate, we instead took Uckfield and the surrounding villages. In the end, Willingdon, which was hugely against the proposals for good geographical reasons, stayed with Eastbourne, and Polegate alone transferred to Lewes. The areas proposed to be moved out of Lewes were duly transferred.

The consequence of the moves was that the notional Tory majority in the Lewes constituency fell from 12,175 to around 6,500, in what would numerically be the smallest constituency in East Sussex. The *Sussex Express* ran a story headed 'Tory Fears', which predicted that the changes would make the seat potentially vulnerable at the next election. It was highly prescient.

In politics, you are never far away from an election, and those for East Sussex County Council came round again in May 1993. I was defending a majority in my Telscombe division of just 211 over the Conservatives, but it was a bad night for the Tories generally and my majority increased to 1,524.

So bad was the result, in fact, that the Tories lost control of the council for the first time, and a joint administration was formed between the Lib Dems and Labour.

Our group leader was the Newhaven councillor David Rogers, who was a senior member of our district council team, as chair of the Leisure Services Committee. He had also been our finance lead.

David was a super campaigner who had carved a seat on Brighton Council out of nothing as far back as 1977. When he moved to Newhaven about ten years later, he determined to take on the incumbent Tory for the county seat in 1989. This was a rather pompous individual called Colonel Peter Harwood, who would describe himself as Mr Newhaven. He held a central role in the local Tory constituency organisation and, at the time, was the most prolific of the Tories criticising me in print, even more so than Keith Moorhouse.

David ran a brilliant campaign and won the seat, which helped set the scene for 1991, when we won all six district seats in the town from the Tories. He had a great political brain and knew just how to wind the Tories up, but he could also be prickly on occasion.

My relations with David had always been reasonably cordial, and indeed he undertook the role of agent for my general election campaign in 1992. But our working relationship on the district council had not always been easy. In particular, he had a habit of writing rather tiresome letters to me and circulating them widely, when it would have been much easier and more productive to have just picked up the phone.

Following the successful county elections, David called a group meeting and presented the results of his negotiations with Labour, including the allocation of chairs and vice-chairs. While I thought that the overall package was a good one for us, I did not like the fact that the group was being presented with effectively a *fait accompli* in terms of who would do what. This was in stark contrast to the group votes that the district council group always had for such posts.

I was, of course, particularly upset that what I was offered was only a very junior role, as vice-chair on the Public Protection Committee under a Labour chair, Terry Randall. The committee handled matters relating to the fire service and trading standards.

No doubt some of this was bruised ego on my part, but I did genuinely think that my record to date merited something better. And I strongly felt that David, if he was not going to go down the route of group elections, should have had a conversation about his intentions with me, and indeed every other member of the group, on a one-to-one basis before everything was set in stone. He clearly had talked to some.

We exchanged frank letters and I wrote that, having made my point, I regarded the matter as closed. Nevertheless, it did worsen relations and presaged a very bumpy internal time for me in the Lib Dems, particularly at district level.

When I came to prepare a skeleton for this book, I realised that my memory of the period from 1993 to 1995 was sketchier than for any period before or since. When I consulted my notes and press cuttings for the period, I think I found the explanation. The period in question was so horrible I must have tried to wipe it from my memory.

As well as a number of personal disputes between individual councillors, there was growing disenchantment with my leadership from a sizeable minority in the district council group.

There was a feeling that I was too interested in getting coverage in the press, and that I should adopt a lower profile. I thought that this criticism was fundamentally misplaced. The coverage prior to 1991 had only been helpful to the council results that year, and my own results at each local election had only got stronger.

I was set to fight the next general election, having been swiftly reconfirmed as the candidate, and I was clear in my own mind that if I was to win, I would need three elements to work together: a natural Liberal vote, a tactical vote and a personal vote. A sitting MP could become known relatively effortlessly. If I was to climb the hill to challenge him, I had to become equally well known.

This, to a degree, was happening. Back in late 1991, after we had been in control of the district council for a few months, a local free sheet, *Freetime*, undertook an amusing vox pop with a photograph of me.

'Who Is This Man?' the published article began. 'A Cabinet minister? A comedian? A singer/songwriter?'

Five respondents were pictured and quoted. Lilian Knight from Lewes said: 'He's MP for Lewes. Or is he a comedian?'

Wendy Gray also from Lewes, spookily offered the following: 'Has he something to do with transport … the minister for transport, perhaps?'

She was almost twenty years ahead of that becoming true.

Two of the five thought I might be the local MP, and two thought I might be a government minister.

In 1993, I was also taking on board the training I had received as a parliamentary candidate, which is that the public have to hear a message many times before it sinks in. Those inside the circle, in other words the Lib Dem activists, will become sick of the message before it has sunk into the public consciousness.

But some in the group found the number of column inches I was generating to be a bit, well, tasteless. There was also, no doubt, a certain amount of irritation, perhaps even jealousy, that I was commanding the headlines while others were doing a good job without the same public recognition.

In October 1994, I asked for an analysis of the press releases issued by the district council in the previous six months. This showed that, of 139 releases over the period, I had been quoted as council leader in twenty-two, with other Lib Dems quoted in fifty-one releases.

I am sure that there were well-founded and justifiable criticisms of the way I carried out my role as leader. I was, after all, learning on the job, as we all were. But what disappointed me was that, with some colleagues, this led to mutterings behind the scenes, plotting even, rather than a more constructive approach, which would have been to try to help. I suppose the fact that I was head-strong made this less easy.

The situation was not helped by the loss of Gordon Hook, who had decided to move to the West Country, and so stood down as deputy leader from the end of 1992, although he would remain on the council until his term was up in 1995. (Gordon being Gordon, he naturally got stuck in down in Teignbridge and remains a coun-cillor to this day, topping the poll in his ward in 2015.) I had lost not just a good friend, but someone who was never afraid to guide me when he thought I was getting something wrong. Perhaps my losing Gordon was like Cyril Mann losing Peter Oldfield. Unfortunately, no such close relationship existed with my new deputy, the Telscombe Cliffs councillor Neil Commin.

A flashpoint came when the issue of cannabis arose again in 1994. I say again, because my views on the subject had had some expo-sure in the local paper two years earlier. At that time, a number of officers in Sussex Police had questioned the accepted approach to cannabis and suggested that minor possession cases should be overlooked. Tim Rathbone, who was chairman of the all-party parliamentary committee on drugs misuse, had issued a statement criticising this, which was when I weighed in.

There was a case for decriminalising cannabis, I said, to separate it from harder drugs that were more dangerous, and I suggested that the tobacco in a joint might be more dangerous than the cannabis. It would be an interesting prelude to my time as drugs minister more than twenty years later.

Peter Lindsay, the sparky editor of the *Sussex Express*, wrote an editorial next to the news piece, saying I had got it all wrong, that cannabis was a gateway drug to other more harmful substances, and that I should back a crackdown against all kinds of drugs.

I knew I had put forward a viewpoint that was controversial, and one I anticipated would not be shared by the majority of the public, but it was my honest view and I thought I should not hide that. One reason was that my views were based on personal experience. I had smoked cannabis at university, as indeed at that time had most of the student population, or so it seems now. I stopped short in 1992 of announcing that to the world, for fear of the electoral consequences, but did take the opportunity, shortly after I was elected as MP, to put this on the record, under cover of the other various MPs who were making similar disclosures. I also insisted on reiterating this when I became drugs minister in 2013, to the horror of the Home Office.

To my surprise and quiet delight, the letters page the following week was broadly supportive, with six letters in favour and three against. One letter suggested that if the editor wanted to clamp down on all drugs, we should turn our attention to alcohol, tobacco and indeed tea, coffee and aspirin.

There was, in any case, little adverse reaction within the local party, indeed quite the opposite. The same was not true two years later, in 1994.

The catalyst on this occasion was a motion to the Lib Dem party conference to decriminalise possession of cannabis, which was carried on a card vote by 426 to 375. I voted in favour. There was also majority support for a royal commission to examine the whole drugs issue.

While the latter was supported by the leadership, they wanted nothing to do with the cannabis vote, and Paddy Ashdown abruptly stormed off the stage.

My support was picked up nationally, and locally this led to Peter Lindsay, who had clearly not been persuaded by the earlier letters page, running a front-page story with the headline 'Has Norman Gone Potty?' I imagine that this was an attempt at a pun.

The story also threw in, for good measure, my calls for drastic changes to the civil list, interpreting this incorrectly as a call for the abolition of the monarchy. (Interestingly, this coincided with an opinion poll undertaken for the *Sunday Mirror* in which 73 per cent of respondents answered yes to the question 'Do you think the Queen should be our last monarch?')

Again, the letters page the following week was overwhelmingly positive, deploring the 'shock horror' comments of the editor and of MP Tim Rathbone, which, according to one letter writer, smacked 'of irrational self-righteousness'.

However, the timing of our conference overlapped with the fallout from the dramatic resignations of Anne Harberson and Robert Evans from the group and from their elected positions on Lewes District Council and Lewes Town Council – each had sat on both. Anne and Robert were a couple and both had been elected to represent Lewes Priory ward in 1991. Anne had chaired the Planning Applications (North) Committee, while

Robert chaired both Personnel and the Contracts Works Board. This latter body handled the in-house services provided direct by the council through an arm's-length body – services such as refuse collection.

I had had to call an urgent group meeting on 20 July, just forty-five minutes before a full council meeting. An issue had blown up over pay increases to council staff, with Robert disagreeing with the group's position. Matters had come to a head when he had spoken vehemently against the agreed recommendation for increases at a meeting of the Contract Works Board and at the recent Policy and Resources meeting. At the latter he had failed to vote with the group on any issues.

Neil and I had tried to secure assurances from him as to his future behaviour but received none. The chief executive had written to me formally to make it plain that the management team had little confidence in Robert's continuation in post, I informed the group. Furthermore, Robert had been given every opportunity to attend this meeting or have his views read out, but he had made it plain he would do neither.

The town council group also had issues with Robert's behaviour and, in September that year, the council asked the district auditor to investigate allegedly *ultra vires* acts, specifically buying a photocopier without a mandate and altering several parts of a consultant's report on staffing. He denied the accusations.

Naturally, the group was concerned at what this meant for Anne Harberson's position. Neil and I had spoken to her and made it clear that she was an individual in the group and would be treated as such, irrespective of her relationship with Robert.

The group agreed to support in principle a motion before council that congratulated the Contract Works Board on winning the contracts for refuse collection and street cleaning and sought to change the membership of the Board, including appointing a new chair in David Fitton, a Newhaven councillor.

When the meeting reached the item in question, Robert Evans stood up to oppose the motion, following which he publicly announced his resignation from both the Lib Dems and the council, tendering his letter of resignation to the chief executive.

The walkout was quite theatrical. It was followed at the beginning of August by the formal resignation of Anne Harberson. In February the next year, Paul Mockford, having passed me his resignation letter in the middle of a council meeting, was to try the same trick, but executed it with rather less panache than Robert.

So, that autumn we faced four by-elections across two councils in difficult circumstances (caused by two Lib Dem resignations and set against the backdrop of my forthright remarks at conference), a local ward issue that had flared up – the fencing or otherwise of the council-owned land at Landport Bottom – and a resurgent Labour Party benefiting from their recent choice of new leader, Tony Blair.

The results were not great, though far from the catastrophe they might have been. After six hours' counting and two recounts, the results were announced at 3 a.m. We held one of the two district seats, the other going to probably the best-known Tory in Lewes, Frances Tufnell, who had been chairman of Lewes District Council in the run-up to the 1991 election at which she had lost her seat to us. She and another Tory, Isabelle Linington, took the two town council seats, but we only missed out on the second of these by twelve votes. Had it not been for an increase in the Labour vote, we would have held all four seats. The turnout was an impressive 47 per cent.

We had in fact not expected to win both district seats. Our second candidate had been Maureen Messer, who lived in Lewes Bridge ward and would subsequently win a district seat there the following year. As the votes were being counted, it looked at one stage as if she might actually be elected, so she dashed off to ring the Chief Constable. This was because, as the wife of a serving policeman, she was supposed to have secured permission to stand, and having failed to do so, she thought at least she should let him know that she might shortly be elected.

Eight days later, on 7 October, I woke up to a damaging edition of the *Sussex Express*. On page three, the page lead was a report on the by-elections under the heading 'Tories Burst Lib Dem Bubble'. This was a straight and predictable piece. But this report was innocuous compared to the front page.

The headline read: 'Lib Dem Allies Attack Norman'.

'Top politician Norman Baker is reeling from a blistering attack by his Lib Dem colleagues,' the paper reported. 'Seven of his so-called allies faxed us a letter early Wednesday, slamming Norman's call for cannabis to be decriminalised.'

It went on to quote extensively from the fax, and named the seven district council signatories: Mike Chartier, Neil Commin, Ann De Vecchi, Graham Mayhew, Judith Ost, David Rogers and Diana Stiles.

The story quoted David Rogers, who called the by-election results 'very disappointing' and said he felt particularly sorry for 'our unsuccessful candidates, and many ordinary hard-working Liberal Democrat helpers and supporters who are NOT in the limelight' (his emphasis).

The editor concluded: 'Privately, Cllr Baker will know he has the political fight of his life on his hands – from within. There are ambitious Lib Dems who would like a chance to stand for a winnable seat like Lewes.'

I recognised that the way my remarks on cannabis had been blown up by the *Sussex Express* in a somewhat hysterical manner had not been helpful, but I did not think that could in any way justify the sending of a fax of that nature to the paper. I regarded that action as disloyal and stupid in equal measure.

That was also the view of a number of my council colleagues, who put their own thoughts on paper. Seaford councillor Rosemary Collict wrote: 'It seems some of my colleagues are determined to commit political suicide ... This is not the first time the knives have been out within the District Council group. I believe our loss of seats in Priory has its roots in group bickering and loss of discipline.'

She went on to say that while she did not necessarily agree with my views on cannabis, she had 'complete confidence' in me.

Mary Hurst, our hugely well-respected Kingston councillor, called the action of sending a fax to the paper 'self-destructive'.

Patrick McCausland, another Seaford councillor, said he was 'appalled' by the fax, adding: 'If anything was designed to seal our fate next May, that was.'

May 1995, of course, was when the council was up for re-election.

To add to the mix, I received an anonymous card posted to my home in Beddingham. On the front were lilies surrounding the words 'With Sympathy'. Inside was printed the phrase 'Thinking of you', to which had been added 'on the way down. 10 July 1994 – consequences.'

As nothing in particular happened on 10 July, I assume this was meant to refer to the charged group meeting ten days later.

The group, clearly, was badly split, and things would get worse before they got better.

On 18 November, a letter appeared in the *Sussex Express* from one 'Abigail Baker – no relation – thank goodness', which purported to report comments I had made at a recent Policy and Resources Committee meeting.

I was alleged, during a debate on animal welfare, to have asked from the chair whether it was possible to be cruel to an amoeba and whether it would be right to intervene in a confrontation between a rabbit and a fox. My interest in animal welfare was extensive, but did not stretch that far.

It seemed the black arts were at work. The following week, the editor, Peter Lindsay, confirmed in his column in the paper, 'My Word!', that the 'Abigail Baker' letter was a fake. It had what appeared to be a genuine name, address and telephone number, but no such person existed at that address.

He revealed that he had also intercepted a second fake letter, purportedly from a G. Taylor in Chandler's Mead in Cooksbridge, a village just outside Lewes. The tone was the same as that of the first. This time, the name appeared to have been lifted from the electoral register, as a Gordon Taylor was living in Chandler's Mead, but through his local councillor Mavis Clark, Mr Taylor absolutely denied he had sent the letter.

The editor wrote that conversations he had had with Lib Dems suggested the letters in question may have originated from within the party's district council group, a suggestion denied in the following week's letters page by Graham Mayhew, though how he would know is not clear.

In any case, the letters were passed by the paper to the police for possible action under the Malicious Communications Act 1988. The County Trading Standards Officer at the county council, Paul Allen, confirmed that in his view, an offence under the Act had been committed.

On 17 November, all group officers received a letter from the group's secretary, Newhaven councillor Jan Marshall, tendering her resignation from that post. This followed an acrimonious four-hour group meeting the day before. It was left to me to produce the minutes of the meeting.

Jan wrote that, while she had always tried to be impartial, she did not feel she had the support of a number of committee chairs. She also resented the 'deputy leader's lack of support for the group's properly elected leader' and the lack of protection from the chair he had afforded her when she was attacked. (It had long been the practice for the deputy leader to chair group meetings.)

The next day, on the same day the Abigail Baker letter appeared in the press, I received a personal letter from Neil Commin.

In it, Neil, who had been one of the seven signatories of the fax to the *Sussex Express*, informed me he was resigning as deputy leader. He said that while he had hoped that Monday's meeting had produced a 'truce' and a common purpose to work together, the criticisms made of him by the group's secretary rendered his position untenable. He also resigned from the Lewes '95 campaign group that had been set up to put together a winning strategy for the following May's local elections.

The meeting on the Monday had, after much blood-letting, resolved 'that the group should act in a united fashion with Norman as leader in order to achieve the best possible result in the May elections'. The proposal, from Newhaven councillor Jo Lewry, was carried 25–0 with one abstention. The unity had lasted only a matter of hours.

In response, I wrote to both Jan and Neil, thanking each of them for their contributions and expressing sadness that matters had ended as they had.

However, it was not entirely without surprise that I then read a report of the resignations in the *Sussex Express*, which contained a great deal of detail that could only have come from someone at the meeting.

In December, I received a Christmas card from Anne Harberson and Robert Evans, liberally sprinkled with hateful personal comments. At least they had the decency to sign it.

Chapter 5

The early months of 1995 passed without major public incident, helped by the election of a new deputy council leader, Newhaven councillor Peter Harper, who had support from across the group.

It was painfully clear, however, that trust had broken down in key relationships between councillors. Matters were particularly bad between myself and the vice-chair of the policy committee responsible for handling finance, Ann De Vecchi, and we barely spoke to each other for weeks on end. This was not helped by a difficult relationship mirroring this at officer level between the chief executive and the director of finance, Julian Kearsley.

I was also wary of Graham Mayhew, who seemed to me to enjoy the internal machinations of the group a little too much. Graham had been elected as a Labour councillor in Lewes in 1979, the last year Labour won anything in the town, but had gone Independent soon afterwards.

In the spring of 1993, Graham contacted Gordon Hook and expressed an interest in joining the Lib Dem group. The matter was discussed at some length at a group meeting.

The general view was that Graham wanted to join in order to play a bigger role in the council, specifically as a committee chair, but, in a sense, there was nothing wrong with that. The question was whether he was really a Lib Dem at heart, and thus whether he could be trusted.

There was a general consensus that he was left of centre, and that therefore he was broadly in the right place. Vic Tomkinson, one of our Ringmer councillors, would often describe himself as really Labour, but that did not stop him being a loyal and effective member of the group.

I was broadly in favour of taking a gamble with Graham, with Gordon being more cautious. In the end, we agreed to accept him. I think in retrospect Gordon's caution was well placed. The Lib Dems were a flag of convenience for Graham.

Later in 2002, Graham announced he was joining the Conservatives, to some incredulity both in our group and in the town. Indeed, in the Conservatives as well.

The Lib Dem district council leader at that time, Ann De Vecchi, observed: 'Becoming a Tory gives Graham a full house. He's now tried every party except the Greens.' She added acidly: 'He shares the Tory principle in self-interest above all else.'

It was, on that occasion, one move too far and he lost his Lewes Priory seat a year later at the 2003 elections before resurfacing as an Independent again and winning a town council by-election in March 2014.

I should add that Graham, throughout all this, tended to support me at general elections, displaying a poster on his fence and occasionally canvassing for me, which I appreciated.

There were other issues in the group as well, such as the antagonism between our two leading Seaford councillors, Diana Stiles and Rosemary Collict. In order to try to help here, I took them both out to lunch at Seasons, a Lewes restaurant. My sympathies were very much with Rosemary, but I tried hard to stay neutral. In the event, they ended up arguing all through the meal, to the extent that I could hardly get a word in. As I paid the bill, somewhat brain-dead, I concluded that trying to solve that one was a lost cause.

It seemed that the project that had started so brightly in 1991, and in my view had achieved so much in transforming the council beneficially, was sinking into the mud. I felt rather helpless. I recognised that I had made mistakes, got some things wrong, but I had also got a lot right and I did not think I deserved the vitriol that was regularly thrown at me by my own side.

So, for the early months of 1995, I largely left the day-to-day work of the council behind and concentrated on trying to ensure that we won in May. I was conscious that if we lost control, and were seen to do so due to acrimony and animosity, the public were unlikely to give us another chance for a long time. And, of course, we could kiss goodbye to any hope of winning the parliamentary seat.

The strategy paid off and we not only held the council in May but increased our number of seats by one, taking twenty-eight against just sixteen Conservatives and two Independents. Labour also managed to gain two seats in a part of the district outside the Lewes parliamentary constituency, in Peacehaven East.

Given the run of bad headlines and the general dysfunctionality of the group, this was a super result, and I felt to a large degree vindicated for the approach I had taken. The electorate seemed to like it, even if not all my council colleagues did.

My happiness was short-lived, however. At the first group meeting of the new council, just three days after the election, I faced an election for group leader. I was taken aback, as I had thought that the election result was such that no such challenge would be forthcoming. I wondered how the electorate would feel if they found a coup had taken place. I remembered a reaction of that sort when, a while before, Ken Livingstone had seized control of the Labour group on the Greater London Council immediately after an election.

In retrospect, I should not have been surprised, given the level of animosity that had existed over the previous year.

As soon as the niceties of welcoming new colleagues were out of the way, Graham Mayhew proposed that we go straight on to the election for group positions. It was obvious that a core of colleagues determined to remove me had prepared well, whereas I, naively, had made no preparations and spoken to no colleagues.

I was proposed by Rosemary Collict and seconded by Jo Lewry. Neil Commin was proposed by Christine Tester and seconded by Judith Ost.

The format saw each candidate speak for five minutes then answer questions. Each would leave the room while the other spoke. I was propelled into going first, with no time to prepare my remarks.

A secret ballot was then held and the result declared. I had won by 14–13.

It was clear that Neil Commin and his supporters were not expecting this result. They had thought they had it sewn up. What I think they had failed to factor in was the fact that many of the new councillors knew me, but did not know Neil. Indeed, I had been active in helping them get elected in their wards, knocking on doors, delivering leaflets. Secondly, Neil's support had been strongly Lewes-based, and there was always a general Lewes tendency to think only about Lewes, and pay too little attention to the rest of the district, particularly Seaford.

That vote was crucial for my political future. Had one vote gone the other way, I doubt if I would have won the parliamentary election in 1997. I might not even have stood, or been allowed to stand.

Neil, to his credit, stated that he unequivocally accepted the result and that I should now be allowed to get on with the job without further challenge. For my part, I gave notice that I would only do the job for a further two years, which would probably coincide, as it in fact did, with the general election in May 1997.

While I had broadly enjoyed the first two years of my time as leader, from 1991, the last two had been torrid and I had no wish to repeat them. I resolved to take more of a back seat and adopt an all-or-nothing strategy for the general election. I made up my mind that this would be my last parliamentary election if I failed to win – apart from anything else, I was living on virtually no money – and, win or lose, it would also be my last term as a district councillor. I would stand down as leader two years out and, if I lost the general election, I would, with the group's agreement, take on the ceremonial role of vice-chairman and then in the last year chairman of the council. Fortunately, it never came to that.

The group vote for leader had lanced a boil, but the backwash from the year before was still there. Further to a decision by the group, I had written to the two colleagues from the previous council who had lost their seats, Diana Stiles and Gavin Keegan, thanking them for their contribution.

Following my letter to Diana Stiles, she wrote back to me, beginning her letter 'Dear Unctuous Hypocrite', and making the ludicrous suggestion that I was pleased she had lost her seat. I took this to be a reference to the decision by the Seaford branch to target Seaford West rather than her ward of Seaford Central, admittedly not a good call. She had lost out to an unknown Tory called Edwin Tipping, subsequently known to us as Mr Pastry on account of his striking physical resemblance to that long-forgotten character.

I was of course sorry we had lost her seat, though when I read her letter, I confess I was not sorry we had lost her.

The position with Gavin Keegan could not have been more different. Gavin had in 1991 won over the solid Tory village of Newick, a feat never achieved before or since. I was very sorry when he lost in 1995, by the agonisingly small margin of nine votes, largely due to the intervention of a Green candidate who polled only forty-five votes. Undoubtedly most of those would have gone to Gavin had she not stood.

Over the years, Green candidates would cost us quite a few seats, which all fell to the Tories, including, of course, my own parliamentary seat in 2015.

My pop/rock band, The Reform Club, was gigging around that time and, as fate would have it, we were due to play Newick village hall the weekend after the election. I always kept my music and my politics separate, notwithstanding that our lead guitarist at the time, Rod Wilson, was also a Lib Dem district councillor. On this occasion, however, I inserted into our set a cover of the Spencer Davis Group hit 'Keep on Running', which I publicly dedicated to Gavin, who was there for the evening. Sadly, he did not.

In my own Ouse Valley seat, I polled 571 votes against 103 for the Tory.

One of the most colourful results was in the Hamsey ward. This was the smallest ward in the council in population terms, covering the small settlements of Hamsey, Cooksbridge and East Chiltington.

The ward had been won in 1991 by the new Tory councillor Mavis Clark. She was a short, stumpy woman who would invariably sit next to Keith Moorhouse in council meetings. She was Tory through and through in a rather two-dimensional way, but not out of the usual Tory country mould. On a personal level, she was always happy to have a chat outside the formal council setting, which some of her colleagues were not.

One night she rang me at home at about a quarter to midnight to complain that I had been interfering in her ward. As I was the parliamentary candidate at the time, it was not inconceivable that I had picked up some casework from her patch, so asked her what the issue was. I had not yet gone to bed, so I was more bemused than anything else by this late call.

The nub of her complaint was that, the weekend before, I had got involved with an abandoned car, which she told me she was dealing with. I asked her if it was still there, which she confirmed it was.

'Well then,' I told her, 'I can't have been involved otherwise I would successfully have had it removed by now.'

I thought this rather neat.

For the 1995 election, I had persuaded Andrew Clarke to stand for us in Hamsey. Andrew ran, and runs, a shop called Potts in Cliffe High Street in Lewes, selling china and ceramics. Over the years he was a leading light in the Lewes Chamber of Commerce.

I cannot recall how I persuaded him to stand, for I do not think he is a natural Liberal, but stand he did, and threw himself into the contest. When the votes were counted, he had won by 237 to 214, a majority of just twenty-three.

Mavis was far from pleased, and issues were raised about the arrangements for the polling station at East Chiltington. Because no public building existed in the parish, the district council used the local pub, the Jolly Sportsman. There was some suggestion that voters, either on their way to vote or on their way back, were offered a pint by one of Andrew's friends, who was telling for us.

Though this was never proven, there then followed an extended period of hostility between Mavis Clark and Andrew Clarke, generally centred around low-level acts of irritation. The police became involved on more than one occasion, sometimes rather heavy-handedly in my view. Certainly, a large amount of police and indeed district council time was spent on East Chiltington matters for some months thereafter.

The new council proceeded in a much better frame of mind than its predecessor had. If anything, there was a lethargy in some quarters, and in July I had to write round to the group to remind them of the need to attend meetings.

There was, however, a flare-up that month, when one of our councillors, Jim Cook, hit a colleague, David Fitton, outside the Newhaven Town Council chamber in Fort Road. Distressed witnesses called the police from the direct-line phone outside the nearby police station at 11.30 p.m.

David Fitton is a slight figure, and Jim Cook a beefy type. This made the incident even more unacceptable in many people's eyes. David had to been taken to the Royal Sussex Hospital in Brighton to deal with his injuries – a nose bleed, double vision and two black eyes. He maintained that Jim had tried to strangle him and had punched him in the face.

Jim Cook immediately had the whip withdrawn and David Fitton made an official complaint to the local party about the assault. Jim did apologise quickly after the event but, perhaps understandably, this did not satisfy David.

Some time after he ceased being a councillor, Jim Cook was tried and convicted of a financial offence. His Lib Dem ward colleague David Neighbour, with whom he did not get on, came along to watch the case and ended up being evicted from the court for heckling. He would have his own police problems, with an assault allegation at a beach hut.

Early in 1996 came the sad news that Mary Hurst had died. In 1980, Mary had been only the second Liberal elected to the district council, after David Bellotti the previous year, and had served until 1995.

When we took control in 1991, the first thing we decided, literally within five seconds, was that Mary would be our first chair. She was a person who was universally liked and respected for her humanity, her modesty and her tireless work for her community.

After one council meeting that she had chaired, I found Mary, who was over seventy, preparing to walk home to Kingston, more than two miles away, because her husband Cyril was unable to pick her up that day. She would not dream of costing the council a taxi fare. In the end, the chief executive took her home himself.

Although physically small, she would stand her ground when there was a point of principle she wanted to defend, even if surrounded by those hostile to her views.

She had a habit of calling Keith Moorhouse 'Councillor Moorhen'. I never knew whether this was a genuine slip or Mary being mischievous, and neither did Keith Moorhouse.

I was delighted that we were able to get her an MBE before she died, and honoured to have been asked to read the eulogy at her funeral. She was a really lovely person. To this day, nearly twenty years on, I cannot pass through Kingston village without thinking of her.

At this time, I was busier on the county council than I had been. Back in 1993, David Rogers had created an Economic Development sub-committee and asked me to chair it. There was of course a crossover between the work of my sub-committee and what the district and borough councils in East Sussex were doing. On one occasion, I was mandated to write to each of the district and borough leaders about a certain matter, so had to write to myself at Lewes District. As it turned out, the request from the county was out of line with district policy, so I had to write back to myself, disagreeing with myself.

I discovered, with the kind of delight that comes from receiving an unexpected present, that the county council was a member of the Assembly of European Regions and that I was, by dint of my position on the sub-committee, the official representative. Indeed, I appeared to be vice-chair of the Tourism Committee.

The chair was a rather loud man from the Balearic Islands who was very keen to secure funding from the committee for a publication to support, yes, the Balearic Islands. He did finally secure this and a glossy, weighty publication followed. It was unclear to me who the target audience was, and it looked suspiciously like a vanity project to help secure his re-election.

Every now and then, therefore, the representatives from the various regions would meet up for a few days, taking it in turns to host the event. The meeting in Dalarna in Sweden, mentioned earlier, was one such event. On another occasion, I hosted the committee in Eastbourne. But my favourite time was when the French decided that the next meeting should be on Réunion Island.

Réunion is a *département* in the Indian Ocean, close to Madagascar. It had been unoccupied by humans until 1638, when the French moved in. One of the first things they did was to shoot all the native birds, so birds are a rarity on the island now.

The journey there was terrible – a long trip in economy from Paris, stuck between two fat people with screaming children behind me.

The island itself was fabulous, though, particularly the interior, where people were speaking a kind of Creole. We had the chance to visit an area where vanilla pods were growing, and to taste various vanilla-based products, also fabulous. How anyone can call vanilla ice cream 'plain' is beyond me.

There was also a variety of small banana growing there, the taste of which was out of this world. The first time I came across them, I think I ate about eight in a row. When I returned to England, I brought jars of banana jam back with me.

As for the business, we certainly had an agenda and passed resolutions, but I was never very clear what happened to them or whether they had any impact anywhere.

The decisions, insofar as any were required, tended to be reached the night before the meeting over dinner or in the bar, and when, at my first meeting, I moved an amendment on the day, the others present seemed to think that this was not only rather peculiar but not quite cricket, or whatever the equivalent is in non-cricket-playing countries.

I recall on one occasion trying to promote the idea of animal welfare and had proposed a form of words to the effect that we should recognise animals as sentient beings. It turned out that the concept was alien to many who were there and we had to have a break while someone came up with a French translation for the phrase and checked it with me. They suggested *êtres sensibles*, which I hope is accurate, since I agreed to it.

One presentation that attracted me came from a Chris Bowers, representing the European Federation for Transport and Environment. He made a brave speech about the unwanted environmental consequences of road building, and how more roads simply generate more journeys. It was music to my ears, as I had been making a similar case back home. My arguments fell on stony ground in East Sussex, and his were met with stony silence here, although his presentation had been professional and factually compelling.

I caught up with Chris afterwards and congratulated him on his speech, and we struck up a friendship. We kept in touch and eventually Chris came down to Ringmer and stood successfully for election as a Lib Dem to Lewes District Council.

A few months on from Réunion, a reporter from the *Evening Argus* asked the county council for details of which councillors had been overseas and where. I recorded my destination for this meeting as 'France', since the French insisted it was part of France and indeed a *département* in its own right.

David Rogers gently teased me about this.

'France?' he asked.

'Well, south of France then,' I replied.

Chapter 6

The Tories were not in a good place. It is true that John Major had pulled off a surprise win in 1992 but, as time went by, that looked more and more like a blip in their support, an aberration.

Gradually, he lost his majority as by-election after by-election went against him. Black Wednesday destroyed the party's reputation for economic competence, and a worrying number of his backbenchers were behaving very badly over Europe.

Allegedly he kept a book of what he called these 'bastards', though for what purpose was not clear. It did, however, inspire Rod Wilson, the Lewes councillor and lead guitarist in The Reform Club, to hand me a cheap, lined exercise book one day with a sticky label on the front on which he had typed the word 'bastards' in capital letters. It was 1994 and he had concluded I might need my own such book.

It was far from certain when the general election would be. It was a reasonable assumption that the Prime Minister would want to leave it as long as possible in the hope that something, anything, would turn up. Certainly the polls consistently suggested he would lose heavily if he called an election. On the other hand, things were so volatile that he might be forced into one at any point.

I was in a hotel in Sweden in June 1995 having a rare break from campaigning when I came down to breakfast one day and caught a glimpse of the front page of the paper, on which there was a photo of John Major.

My Swedish is very limited but I was able to make out that John Major seemed to have called an election – and there I was, stuck in Sweden. I rushed over to my Swedish friends for a translation, and discovered that there was indeed an election, but bizarrely, it was one John Major had called for the leadership of the Conservative Party.

I had a degree of sympathy for the Prime Minister, but I could not see what he could gain from such a manoeuvre, and so it proved.

Somehow, he managed to struggle on into 1997, then called an election some six weeks out, hoping that a long campaign would work in his favour, and perhaps he could turn it around as he had done in 1992.

The Lewes constituency Lib Dems were firing on all cylinders. There was, for the first time, financial support and serious professional input from our national campaign team in London. We had had good-quality literature going out on a regular basis across the constituency, and literature that integrated the county council campaign with the general election one very well. We had a team of almost 400 deliverers.

I wanted our campaign to be roughly 80 per cent positive about our own actions nationally, and mine locally, and about 20 per cent critical of the Tories, with a bit of tactical message thrown in.

For the general election literature itself, I hit upon the idea of producing a contract with the electorate, where I made a number of promises, for example to hold regular surgeries and not take on any second jobs. The idea was noticed and well received by the voters.

By and large, our literature did not attack Tim Rathbone, except in two regards. One was his voting record in the House, which looked to me to be poor.

When I became an MP myself, I soon realised that there were many good reasons why an MP might be absent from a vote, and indeed, it was not necessarily the best use of time to be sitting in the chamber all day, listening to debates about matters of no relevance to your constituency. I think in retrospect that this line of attack was unfair.

I had no regrets, however, about our other line of attack. As mentioned earlier, the sword of Damocles seemed always to be hovering over the Newhaven–Dieppe ferry, requiring constant engagement with the operators and the port owners on both sides of the Channel. Prospects had not been improved by the opening of the Channel Tunnel in 1994, which provided a quicker and more comfortable way to cross. While the ferry operators in Dover and Folkestone were most vulnerable, there was a knock-on effect in Newhaven as well.

It was therefore with some astonishment and anger that I discovered that Tim Rathbone had become a public affairs consultant to Eurotunnel. As far as I was concerned, they were the competition, and to actively work for them was a betrayal of Newhaven.

The public seemed to think so too, and the revelation of his Eurotunnel links went down badly not just in the town, but also more widely, including in Tory circles.

Shortly after this all came out, I was due to visit the *Evening Argus* offices in Hollingbury in Brighton. I liked to keep in touch with the local editors and journalists, and on this occasion, I was planning to make a gentle complaint about stories I had provided to the paper but which they had not covered.

As I waited in the offices for the editor to appear, the first edition rolled off the press. Emblazoned across the front page was a picture of Tim Rathbone, accompanied by a pithy headline accusing him of betraying the ferry, referring to his Eurotunnel links. I decided it would be prudent to shelve my complaint about coverage.

Of the three elements that needed to work together to give us victory in the Lewes constituency, the first, the base Lib Dem vote, was higher than before. The party had recovered from the nightmare of merger, and Paddy Ashdown was popular across the country with voters from right, left and centre. Our local councillors were performing well and enhancing the party's reputation at the grass roots too.

The personal vote was also going well. I had set a target of being as well known as the MP by the time the election arrived. Our private polling a few weeks out from the election asked constituents whether they could name the Tory MP and his Lib Dem challenger. Tim Rathbone, who had been MP for twenty-three years, was named by 84 per cent, and I was identified by 69 per cent, which I regarded as a very creditable result, particularly given the net positive that went with it.

In terms of the tactical vote, those of Labour and Green persuasion were desperate to see the back of the Tories and more open to voting tactically than ever before. Our polling showed that for tactical voting to work, people had to see the removal of the Tories as the most important issue; they had to believe that we could win; and they had to believe that their team could not. All three criteria were met in Lewes in 1997.

I was immensely helped by a segment of the Labour Party locally that decided to stick its neck out and openly recommend voting for me. I was also immensely helped by the sympathetic reporter on the *Sussex Express*, John Eccles, who splashed with the story and the headline 'Labour 13 Say Vote Lib Dem'. The Labour rebels even went as far as producing their own poster, with the slogan 'Labour Voting Lib Dem'.

The reaction was electric, with the news reaching far and wide. Just as it all looked like it was dying down, Labour publicly expelled its rebels, thereby breathing new life into the story.

While all this frenetic activity was going on, the Tories were proceeding as if nothing had changed. They cannot say that they had not been warned – the district elections in 1991 and 1995, and the 1993 election for county councillors in the constituency, should have told them there was a problem.

Yet Tim Rathbone appeared to think that he was safe as houses, an impression reinforced, I suppose, by the 1992 result, which, after all, had come hard on the heels of the loss of council control in 1991. He even spent some of the 1997 campaign in Northamptonshire helping a friend with his election battle.

Even when he was down in Sussex, his campaign appeared somewhat stumbling. On one occasion he arrived in the very sleepy village of Telscombe, a settlement with a population of less than fifty at the dead end of a long country track off the back road from Lewes to Newhaven.

He was in his rather dirty brown estate car, equipped with loudspeakers on top, which were broadcasting to anyone who would listen that he was arriving. But Telscombe being particularly sleepy, when he got out of his car, he could see but one individual. He strode across, introduced himself and asked whether he could count on his support for the general election.

'I'm afraid not,' came the reply. 'Firstly, I'm David Neighbour, the Lib Dem county council candidate, and secondly, you're in the wrong constituency.'

Telscombe had indeed been in Lewes but had been transferred to Brighton Kemptown with the recent boundary changes. This of course made a wonderful story for the local press, aided by the Tory agent Jeanette Allen, who maintained that all Tim Rathbone had been doing was driving up to the boundary before turning round again. That was clearly not true, but if it had been, what on earth was the point of driving miles along a lane with no houses only to turn round, doubtless with a difficult three-point turn, in the middle of nowhere?

The response I was receiving on the doorstep was generally positive, and we had about four times as many posters up as the Tories, but after 1992, I was counting no chickens.

We kept up the relentless campaigning with an eye-catching visit from Paddy Ashdown, arriving by helicopter near Tesco in Lewes, and addressing a self-assembled crowd of Tesco staff and employees of the county council's highways department. Other visits followed, including Shirley Williams and Peter Thurnham. Nobody had heard of Peter, but he had the cachet of having just defected from the Tories to the Lib Dems, obviously very helpful in a seat like Lewes.

Election day came and the mood felt good, quite different from 1992. Like many of my helpers, I had been up before it was light to deliver 'Good Morning' leaflets, a last chance to get a message across and remind our supporters to come out to vote. I did not stop until after the polls had almost closed at 10 p.m., still chasing people who had promised to support me but had not turned out to vote.

For a few, it was a helpful reminder, as they genuinely seemed to have forgotten. For others, it was an unwelcome call as they had settled down for the evening, but nevertheless, with the offer of a car, we did get some along. Others protested indignantly that they had already voted, but I suppose, cynically, it mattered less if we annoyed those who had already been down to the polling station.

I stayed at home and well away from the count, intending only to arrive there when we had a good idea of whether we had won or lost. It was a practice I adopted for all subsequent elections.

The first thing that happens at a count is that the ballot papers are verified. In other words, there is a check to ensure that the number of papers issued corresponds to the number of papers in the relevant box.

This process gives the various party representatives at the count an opportunity to see how the votes in each area have been cast and by the time all the boxes have been checked, it is possible to hazard a rough guess of the final result.

This time was more nail-biting than ever, so I rang the key Lib Dems at the count, Judith Ost and Ann De Vecchi, a couple of times to find out what was going on. Patiently, they told me that they would call me when they knew.

About 2.30 a.m., as I recall, Judith rang to say that the result was not certain but looking good, a fair assessment as it turned out. The final count gave me a majority of 1,300, representing a swing of 7.4 per cent from Conservative to Lib Dem. Turnout was high at 76.6 per cent, and even higher in the town of Lewes itself, at 80 per cent, with the voting here more solidly Lib Dem than anywhere else.

Unsurprisingly, I was very emotional and my voice came close to breaking as I gave my acceptance speech. From 1874 to 1997, the seat had returned a Conservative, and now it was Liberal again.

The result had finally been declared at around 5.10 a.m. and, after the formalities, my team and I left the count and headed for the only place we thought would be open, the White Hart hotel, where we had a cup of coffee. It seemed absurdly normal after all that had gone before.

It may sound fanciful, but the air in Lewes was tangibly different that day: cleaner, fresher, with a lightness I had not felt before. The whole town seemed happy and content, lifted by the removal of the Conservatives from government after eighteen years, and as a bonus, by the election of a Lib Dem MP.

Local Firle artist Charles Fox-Wilson was enthusiastic enough to produce a painting within three days, showing me turning up at the House of Commons in a car bearing the number plate L18 DEM, which duly appeared that weekend at the Firle art exhibition.

On that Friday morning, after a spot of breakfast at home and a plethora of phone calls, I returned to Lewes and wandered around, still in a daze, accepting congratulations every few yards. It took me over an hour just to walk up the High Street. I finally grabbed about an hour's sleep just after two in the afternoon.

This had been an all-or-nothing election for me. I had already made a decision not to recontest my county division, not least because two-thirds of it was now stranded outside the Lewes constituency. I ceased being a county councillor the day after the general election.

On the Saturday, I resigned as leader of Lewes District Council, as I had said I would, win or lose, and henceforth I would play very little role on the district. In fact, I came off all the policy committees, limiting my role to being a member of the quasi-judicial planning applications committee and to attending full council, until such time as my term in office ran out in 1999. I remained a member of Glynde and Beddingham parish council, which meant that for a very short period, I represented the villagers at four levels: parliamentary, county, district and parish.

It was, of course, also an all-or-nothing election for Tim Rathbone, who had held the seat for twenty-three years and announced shortly afterwards that he would not stand again. On the night of the count, it was clear that the result was totally unexpected for him, and he was seen holding his head in his hands. However, when it came to the declaration he was dignified, saying: 'It is an extremely good win for Mr Baker and I wish him well. I shall miss representing Lewes constituency. Bless you all.'

Sadly, he seemed to have a change of mind. About ten days later, he rang up the *Sussex Express* and asked to speak to John Eccles. When John answered the phone, Tim Rathbone said he had a statement and John should write it down. He duly reeled off a very different statement from the one he had made on election night and then rang off before John could ask him about it.

He told the paper that our electioneering methods locally had been 'contemptible', presumably referring to our exploitation of his Eurotunnel employment, and that his defeat and that of his party nationally was down to a 'misjudgement on the part of the British people'.

He also suggested, inaccurately, that the swing against him, 7.4 per cent, had been 'far below the national average'. In fact, nationally the Lib Dems had scored 1 per cent less overall than in 1992.

He added that people 'in the constituency deserve the very best representation. At the next general election they will get it once again, I am quite certain.'

I was genuinely sad for Tim that he had chosen to make this statement and I declined the opportunity to comment on it. His parting shot was in stark contrast to the elegant way in which John Major had announced his going, referring to a visit to the Oval in time for lunch and some cricket that afternoon.

Tim Rathbone would, after a short while, join a new, short-lived, pro-European grouping called the Pro-Euro Conservative Party, leading to his expulsion from the Conservative Party by William Hague, which I personally thought was rather unkind and unnecessary. The last time I saw him was at a pro-European event in Lewes. He had lost his impressive head of hair entirely, the result of chemotherapy. The hosts carefully sat us at different tables. I had no objection to sharing a table with him but it seems the feeling was not mutual. He died not long afterwards, in 2002, of cancer. He was sixty-nine. I always wondered to what extent his ill health had been brought on by his 1997 defeat. I think the public sometimes forget that politicians are human too. I think we forget it ourselves sometimes.

I was sorry he had taken defeat so personally, though I understood how that might be. His parliamentary career had not been the success it might have been. He was a left-leaning Tory, pro-Europe and against the poll tax, who must have found himself increasingly out of line with the strident tones of Margaret Thatcher. His party had moved away from him until finally it expelled him.

Chapter 7

I was surprised over the weekend to receive no communication from either the party or the House authorities telling me what I should do now I was elected. This was in sharp contrast to both the district and county councils, each of whom had by now a good induction process for new councillors.

In the absence of any guide to the contrary, I made my way to Westminster and headed for the Lib Dem Whips' Office. At least I had worked in the Palace of Westminster before, so had a head start on the majority of other colleagues who had been elected on the tide. In terms of seats, it had been the best Liberal result since 1929.

I knew many of the MPs from when I had been environment campaigner for the party, and was delighted to meet up again with my old Whips' Office colleagues Ed Davey and Adrian Sanders, now also both MPs.

In those first few days, it all felt a bit like *Tom Brown's Schooldays*: you were left to sink or swim. All I was given on day one was a locker, a key for it, and a pink ribbon. When I asked one of the House staff wandering round the place what this was for, he looked at me askance and replied: 'That's so you can hang your sword up.' Obviously I should have known.

The allocation of offices, I subsequently discovered, was a long, drawn-out affair, with the House authorities working laboriously through the MPs by seniority. Thus, for several weeks I was camped out in the Whips' Office, jostling with other MPs, phones ringing everywhere, while I tried to find a corner of a desk to open a post-bag of already in excess of fifty letters a day.

I had been given a temporary desk in a committee room some two floors away, shared with about ten other MPs, but without a telephone or computer it was of little use.

Furthermore, I had as yet no office in the constituency and no staff, bar Liz, a friend of mine in Ditchling who was helping out with correspondence (and who later became my wife).

The first parliamentary task was to swear the oath of allegiance. No MP can take his or her seat until they have done this. It is this oath that Sinn Féin MPs refuse to swear and which thus prevents them from attending the Commons.

I do not like the oath as a matter of principle. It requires an MP to swear to 'bear true allegiance to Her Majesty the Queen, her heirs and successors'. In my view, my authority for being in the House arose from the democratic vote that had taken place in my constituency, and my allegiance, if it had to be stated, was there-fore to my electors, not to whoever happened to be monarch at that particular point.

And what if an MP had campaigned for an end to the monarchy and then been elected? If that was what had been voted for, why should that mandate be thwarted?

An earlier run-in over the oath, back in Victorian times, had led to the requirement to swear allegiance on the Bible being with-drawn in the Promissory Oaths Act 1868, with a non-religious alternative being allowed, but no such escape clause has been pro-vided for republicans.

In a later parliament, I read out the prescribed wording but then added my own oath, pledging to uphold democracy and serve my constituents. Curiously, this was not recorded by Hansard, allegedly the verbatim record of everything said in Parliament.

In 2005, having again had to swear the oath, I did make a half-hearted attempt to secure change, raising the matter on the floor of the House with the then Leader of the Commons Geoff Hoon.

> Does the Leader of the House agree that, in the twenty-first century, it is somewhat anachronistic, not to say objectionable, that Members of Parliament who arrive here with a proper democratic mandate, having been elected, are not allowed to take their seats unless they have sworn an oath of allegiance to an unelected institution? Would it not be more appropriate in these days for an oath to be taken to follow the law, to uphold democracy and to serve one's constituents?

I expected a brush-off but, to my surprise, the Leader replied that he recognised that there were concerns and if there was 'a substantial body of opinion in the House in favour of change' he would be willing to discuss it with ministerial colleagues. He said this was a 'fair offer', which indeed it was, but it was putting the ball firmly back in my court, and I assessed that to win this particular battle would take an enormous amount of time and energy, and I did not wish to commit this. The issue was a matter of principle for me, but it was way down on my list of priorities.

I determined to make my maiden speech as early as possible, on the basis that if I made a mess of it, it could be put down to inexperience, whereas a poor speech some weeks or even months in would not be excused so readily.

It turned out that I was the first of around 200 new MPs to be called, on the first day proper of the new parliament. (The House had sat for one day previously to elect a Speaker and to allow members to take the oath.)

My speech was non-controversial, following the standard practice of being nice about your predecessor, talking about your constituency and making some general points about what you want to do.

I did say I had been listening to Queen's Speeches since I had been in short trousers. I do not know why I said that because it was not true. I think it must have been a colourful way to say I had long had an interest in politics. To my annoyance, the line was pulled out and quoted a number of times over the years, and made me realise the importance of being careful with words.

On re-reading the speech, I am pleased to note that I stressed the importance of freedom of information legislation and action to protect the environment.

The first Commons battle was, on the face of it, a rather childish one. As Lib Dems, we were still on the opposition benches, but now with the Conservatives rather than Labour, as had been the case prior to 1997. Because the electoral arithmetic had changed significantly, it was felt that we should no longer be relegated to secondary benches but have a front bench of our own, especially given that the Tories had been reduced to 165.

Unsurprisingly, this was not the view of the Tories, and an unseemly jostling then went on to determine who should have the second opposition front bench – in other words, the one not opposite the Prime Minister and Cabinet ministers.

There is a curious method of reserving your seat in the Commons, which involves filling in a 'prayer card' and placing it in the slot provided for a particular seat. This has to be done before the House begins sitting for that day, and you have to be there for prayers, always held at the start of business, in order to bag your seat.

I thought this rather ridiculous, and could not see why the House authorities could not simply allocate places for individual MPs, or at least for the parties, as there are not enough seats for every MP, by some distance.

I also objected to the fact that the ability to reserve a seat was inextricably linked to an act of worship, whether or not you were a believer. Moreover, the fact that many present were there not for the purpose of worship but to bag a seat could only trivialise the daily event. But under instructions from the Chief Whip, Paul Tyler, I duly reserved a seat one day.

Prayers are for MPs only and are not televised. They might change if they were. MPs stand solemnly while the Speaker's chaplain launches into a monotonous drone – the words are identical every day. And then, after about a minute, something bizarre happens. The MPs all turn round and face the wall, before part two of prayers begins.

I asked one of the door attendants what the purpose of this strange behaviour was. He told me it was so your sword did not pierce the bench. But leaving aside that no MP was wearing a sword, the fact that the first half of prayers had taken place with MPs facing forward presumably meant that any unintended bench-piercing would already have taken place, or might well be occasioned by the very act of swivelling round. However, I did not see any value in making these points to the attendant.

The Tories' resistance to making way for us on the second front bench had led to a decision to take some direct action to force the matter. Accordingly, five of us, including me, were sent to sit on the main opposition front bench where the Conservative leader and his shadow Cabinet would normally be. We had queued from early in the morning to reserve the seats. It was, in fact, to be the only time I would ever sit at the despatch box on the opposition side.

Inevitably, our direct action led to uproar when the House began sitting and we refused to move. A barrage of Points of Order from Tories and Lib Dems were put to the Speaker, Betty Boothroyd, inviting her to adjudicate on the dispute. Eventually, she ordered the five Lib Dems off the official opposition front bench, saying of both the Lib Dems and the Tories, 'I have never known such grown-up people behave in such a crass, childish manner. I think it is time that members of this House grew up.'

Childish it may or may not have been, but having got nowhere up to that point, it was effective, and henceforth the second front bench became ours. With one exception.

The seat at the end nearest the Speaker's chair was traditionally occupied by the Father of the House, if an opposition member. In 1997 this was Ted Heath, the former Conservative Prime Minister, who had resisted the invitation to retire to the Lords. It was said he had wanted to outlive Margaret Thatcher in the Commons. So Ted stayed with us, the lone Tory on the Lib Dem front bench, next to Paddy Ashdown for Prime Minister's Questions. Many in the House thought in any case that he belonged more with us than with the party for which he had been elected.

I dived into my Commons work with the enthusiasm of a child for a new favourite toy. Suddenly I could pursue all those issues that had interested me for years. I covered the entire remit of government, tabling questions to every department, just as I had done when first elected to the district council, but magnified many times. In my first three months, I would table more parliamentary questions than Tim Rathbone had done in twenty-three years. I also spoke in as many question sessions on the floor of the Commons as I could.

Within my first month, I wrung an admission from the Agriculture Minister, Jeff Rooker, that cattle infected with BSE had been buried at Beddingham landfill site; called for dangerous pesticides to be

banned; came out against hunting; called for a review of unnecessarily long and complicated benefit forms; and demanded an
end to misleading descriptions on ballot papers, such as Literal
Democrats, or the Conservative Party.

My enthusiastic, scattergun approach caught the attention of
Matthew Parris, then sketchwriter for *The Times*. He devoted an
entire column to me just two months into the new parliament, on
8 July.

According to him, and I have no reason to doubt his arithmetic,
I had tackled ministers forty-nine times in some thirty-four sitting
days. He wrote, reasonably fairly in fact, 'None of Baker's thoughts
are without merit, but assembled, they do seem unmarshalled by
any sort of presiding logic. There is no theme to the pudding.'

Rather less fairly, I thought, he concluded: 'Mr Baker should go
far. A bore is born.'

I felt chastened and a touch embarrassed that my enthusiasm
should have been interpreted in this way. Bob Maclennan, the Lib
Dem MP for Caithness, Sutherland and Easter Ross, stopped me
on the stairs to sympathise and tell me not to worry about it and,
to my surprise, later that day I received a very supportive handwritten letter from the colourful Tory MP Alan Clark.

Matthew Parris returned to the fray as the House broke up for
summer recess, noting that I had asked exactly 300 questions in
the fifty-five days Parliament had sat since the election, sixteen on
the floor of the chamber and 284 in written form.

I replied by letter to *The Times*, writing:

> His complaint appears to be that I am too active, certainly an
> unusual charge to level at an MP. I am working on the basis
> that my electors expect me to be full-time and raising in Par-
> liament the issues they raise with me. Is that so extraordinary?

Can I thank Mr Parris for his kind wishes for a relaxing holiday. I shall be off all August.

I suspect that the trigger for Matthew Parris might have been my opposition to the Plant Varieties Bill, mentioned in his articles. This was a Bill that the previous government had lined up and which was regarded as uncontroversial by the incoming Labour government. I did regard it as controversial.

For me, it was about whether we were prepared to allow multinational companies like Monsanto to buy up seed companies as they wished and gain an undue influence over agriculture, and specifically if they were to be allowed to patent naturally occurring strains.

This was some time before genetically modified crops were in the public psyche, and virtually nobody could understand why I was making a fuss over the Bill. I had, however, included a section on what was then generally called genetic engineering in 'What Price Our Planet?' way back in 1990.

I was to pursue GM issues for quite some time, and a couple of years later I made a speech in the Commons about genetically modified organisms that was memorable for me, and must have seemed mad to everyone else.

I had decided in my own mind that companies like Monsanto were behaving in a way that was highly damaging to the environment and the interests of small farmers in the developing world, and I had decided to attack them full on, including labelling them Public Enemy No. 1.

The Independent was up for giving this a front-page splash but wanted to protect itself from possible legal action by reporting exactly what I said in the Commons, so both the paper and I would be covered by parliamentary privilege.

There was a debate taking place into which I could seamlessly work such a speech and, as the Lib Dem environment spokesman at the time, I was bound to get called by the Speaker, but because this would be well into the evening, I agreed to write out my speech in full – which I never normally did, preferring to busk from a few notes – and give them a copy well in advance.

Then a problem occurred. The Deputy Speaker called the wrong Lib Dem to speak, notwithstanding that I was occupying the spokesman's place on the Lib Dem front bench.

I went to have a quiet word with the Deputy Speaker, who apologised for the error, but said he did not think there would now be enough time to get me in.

I rang my contact at *The Independent*, the journalist Marie Woolf. Marie was an old friend who had been researcher for Ming Campbell while I had been working in the Lib Dem Whips' Office back in 1989. Despite, or because of, the fact that she was lacking in stature, she had sharp elbows and I recall one occasion when she literally pushed two or three burly male researchers out of the way to get to the photocopier, on the basis that her MP was more important than theirs.

'Can we postpone the story?' I asked her. 'I don't think I'm going to get called.'

'You'd better,' she told me firmly. 'The presses are rolling and you are on the front page with your Commons speech.'

Frantically, I invoked the help of the Lib Dem duty whip, who went to plead on my behalf with the Deputy Speaker, without revealing the whole picture, of course. This worked after a fashion, in that I was to be given about three minutes at the end of the debate before the formal responses from the front benches.

I rang Marie back to tell her we were on track, though I sensed she was keeping her powder dry for an explosion the next day if this did not work.

The trouble was my speech was about ten minutes long and I

had no idea which sections *The Independent* had used, so when my three minutes arrived, there was no alternative but to deliver my speech at three times the normal speed – which, bearing in mind my normal delivery is quite fast, was really very fast indeed.

Other MPs gaped at me as if I had gone mad, but I got through the speech, giving a copy to the stressed-out Hansard reporters, who had been trying to keep up with me.

My remarks duly made the front page the next day. They even got picked up for the front page of, I think, the *Wall Street Journal*, who had latched onto my 'Public Enemy No. 1' line, that seemingly having more traction as a phrase in the US than here at home.

Monsanto even asked to come to see me in my constituency office in Lewes, and after they left I was delighted to find a file on me which they must have left by accident, setting out tactics for dealing with me. I returned it to them.

The lack of knowledge about GM crops extended to the Hansard reporters whose job it was to record verbatim what MPs said. Except that they then applied their own house style. They said this was to eliminate the ers and ums that inevitably populated any MP's speech, but their intervention went much further than this.

So I was furious when, on one earlier occasion, having raised the issue of GM crops in the Commons, I checked Hansard to find that they had decided unilaterally to render what I had said, 'GM crops', as 'grant-maintained crops' – there was an issue at the time about grant-maintained schools. They told me they would correct it for the bound volume. Fat lot of good that was.

I would in fact have a continual low-level running battle with Hansard over their so-called house style, which I regarded not so much as a matter of style as a matter of incorrect English. They would, for example, insist on spelling my county 'east Sussex', and maintained that the Prime Minister lived in 'Downing street'.

Most irritatingly, they continually rendered 'the government is' as 'the government are', especially annoying in the early days of the coalition from 2010, when I was keen to stress the unity of purpose. They refused to report what I said accurately, even changing written parliamentary answers I had signed off as a minister, which I regarded as improper.

In the end, I took to inserting into my speeches in the Commons variations of the following: 'The government is, and for the benefit of the Hansard reporters I have said is, not are...'

I finally won this little battle, though I expect Hansard was not sorry when I lost my seat in 2015.

Matthew Parris was really rather unkind to me for quite a long period, though, as the years went by, he did become more friendly in his judgements, at one point writing: 'You underestimate him at your peril. He has a habit of being right. He sticks to his guns and I think his constituents are very lucky to have him.'

I think he was softened by a question I had put in Prime Minister's Questions when I quoted Tony Blair having said something opposite to the policy he was now pursuing, and asked: 'Does the Prime Minister agree with himself?'

For my part, I grudgingly came to admire both his writing and his political insight.

Just after the beginning of August 1997, an article appeared in the *Sunday Express* under the byline of Simon Walters, then political editor for the paper. This began with the statement: 'Taxpayers will face a £500,000 bill by the time of the next general election if Liberal MP Norman Baker keeps bombarding the Commons with questions ... Mr Baker, 40, has been driving Labour ministers mad and now they want to stop his Commons paperchase.'

The article was fed to Simon Walters by Peter Mandelson, to whom a great many of the written questions were directed. Like many people, I found Peter Mandelson rather smarmy and too pleased with himself. That, of course, was a subjective view. What was factual was that he exercised huge power in the government, one of a triumvirate with Tony Blair and Alastair Campbell, but, as Minister without Portfolio, never appeared in the Commons to answer questions. I regarded this as unacceptable and arrogant in equal measure, so I had therefore been pursuing him through the only means available, the written question – hence his story.

Of course, it was nonsense to suggest I was costing the taxpayer anything, let alone £500,000. The fact was that the answers to my questions were drafted by civil servants and then answered by ministers, all of whom were already in post.

Naturally, his refusal to give me proper answers to even written questions only spurred me on further. For instance, I asked him to list the engagements he had undertaken in his ministerial role, a fair question you might think. He replied as follows: 'I do not propose to disclose details of conversations, meetings or other engagements undertaken in pursuance of my duties as Minister without Portfolio.'

I also asked him in November if he would list the occasions on which he had complained to the media since 2 May about reporting of the government, and was referred to an earlier answer to a Tory MP, Nick Hawkins five months earlier.

The complete reply he had received was this: 'No.'

And I asked him if he would list the details of journeys undertaken at public expense, a question answered properly by other ministers. He replied: 'I have travelled at public expense wherever this has been necessary to the fulfilment of my ministerial responsibilities.'

Mandelson himself became the story when a piece from Colin Brown appeared on the front page of *The Independent* on 9 August, following an interview on *The World at One* on Radio 4.

'Dozens of listeners' had phoned the BBC to complain of Mandelson's 'overbearing, arrogant, pompous' performance, reported Colin Brown, quoting a BBC source. In Tony Blair's absence on holiday, Mandelson had become the face of the government, even though he was not a member of the Cabinet, commenting on a wide range of stories: everything from Robin Cook's affair with his secretary through to the future of the royal yacht and the MI6 inquiry into Chris Patten that was then ongoing. He even chaired a press conference for Lord Simon of Highbury when the latter announced he was selling his BP shares.

It is sometimes forgotten that at this stage there was still talk of the Lib Dems and Labour working together. Before the election, Paddy Ashdown and Tony Blair had discussed how the split in the centre-left, which was seen as having kept the Tories in power from 1979, could be healed. Talks between the two started shortly after Blair succeeded John Smith in 1994. All that stopped a coalition being formed post-election, perhaps with Paddy Ashdown as Foreign Secretary, was the sheer scale of the Labour victory.

Actually, spin aside, I had been rather encouraged by the first couple of years of the new Labour government. I would have liked them to be more radical, but they were taking decisions I welcomed in a whole range of areas, a welcome change after the Tory years.

My enthusiasm stretched to the Prime Minister, who I thought achieved a notable personal success in his efforts to secure a lasting settlement for Northern Ireland. I wrote to tell him so and received a handwritten note back. I still think the Good Friday Agreement is perhaps his greatest achievement.

It is interesting, if sobering, to compare the Blair of the first Labour government, up to 2001, with the Blair of the Iraq War and its aftermath. It is as if he had been permanently damaged in some way.

My questioning of Peter Mandelson in 1997 was seen by him, and perhaps by some leading Lib Dems as well, as being an obstacle to the objective of pulling the two parties closer together.

At the press conference for Lord Simon, Mandelson publicly warned the Lib Dems that they should decide whether they were going to exercise 'a little responsibility' after being brought into the fringes of government.

Lib Dem sources told *The Independent* that this outburst was a reflection of the fact that he was 'deeply irritated' by my questioning, and in particular by my forcing him to admit that he had not spoken in the Commons for months.

Simon Hoggart, writing for *The Guardian*, had an explanation for Mandelson's silence in the chamber: 'Mr Mandelson functions in the same way as the Wizard of Oz. If he were to pull back the curtain and appear in public, his magical powers would vanish.'

If Mandelson thought he could frighten me off, or lean on the Lib Dems to rein me in, he was very wrong. For my part, having been targeted by his dark arts only strengthened my determination to make him properly accountable for the major role he was playing.

Along with many of my Lib Dem parliamentary colleagues, I never bought into the argument that we should cosy up to New Labour, the lazy argument being that they had moved back towards our centre position.

In fact, while I had welcomed the removal of the Tories at the general election, I had no particular enthusiasm for New Labour, and even at that early stage in the parliament I had come to dislike the media manipulation perpetrated by Mandelson and Campbell.

In December that year, I passed to *The Guardian* a letter leaked to me that had been written to the BBC by David Hill, Labour's chief media spokesman. It duly appeared on the front page on

13 December with a picture of John Humphrys under the headline 'The Man Labour Wants to Gag'.

In the letter, Mr Hill complained about the way Social Security Secretary Harriet Harman had been interviewed by the presenter on the *Today* programme.

He wrote: 'The John Humphrys problem has assumed new proportions. In response we have had a council of war and are now seriously considering whether, as a party, we will suspend co-operation when you make bids through us for government ministers ... we need to talk as this is now serious.'

I have reviewed the full transcript of that interview as part of my background research for this book, and I am bound to say that if there is a complaint to be made, it is about Harriet Harman not answering straight questions put to her. For example, the first question asked was this: 'Ms Harman, are you bringing in these cuts because you want to or because you have to?'

By the end of the interview, that question, despite being repeated, remained unanswered.

Like many in the Labour Party itself, I tolerated New Labour, as I understood that the party had had, after eighteen years in opposition, to make itself electable again. But while some good initiatives were taken early on, the whole New Labour concept always looked and sounded phoney.

Indeed, although they held many policy positions with which I disagreed, I felt more comfortable with what was disparagingly called Old Labour, who at least seemed to articulate what they believed in. These were the people who would have been marginalised by any Blair–Ashdown arrangement.

Chapter 8

Back in the constituency, peace had broken out. The fraught relations with the Lib Dem district councillors had improved as we all pulled together for the general election in 1997, after which the wounds healed completely, even if they did leave the hint of a scar or two. Thankfully, they would never open up again.

The fact that I had won, so my approach had been vindicated, coupled with the fact that I was now safely out of their hair, undoubtedly helped. Ann De Vecchi, with whom I had had a difficult couple of years, was now undertaking the role of my election agent and doing a superb job. She would also prove to be a good and well-respected leader of the district council for the next twelve years.

For my fiftieth birthday in 2007, Ann would buy me a year's subscription to *Saga* magazine, which I thought was a good joke. Rather worryingly, I found that it was actually quite a good read, and that most of the people featured appeared to be just over fifty, so perhaps it was less of a joke after all.

I had been having trouble sorting out an office. I had identified a premises in the High Street in a prominent location where the retail use had ceased. It was classified by the council as a secondary shopping area so I anticipated that securing a change of use would not be a problem.

I reckoned without the politics of the council's planning committee – Tories lining up for rejection, and Lib Dems bending over backwards, desperately keen not to be seen to be biased in favour of a colleague who was still a sitting district councillor. The initial application was rejected in July, but resubmitted with further information and finally passed in August.

A couple of years later, when my landlady, who lived upstairs, wanted to sell up, I decided for a number of reasons that it would be a sensible move to sell my cottage in Beddingham and buy the Lewes property.

My old cottage would be eradicated several years later when the level crossing was removed on the A27, prompting the *Argus* to produce a rather opportunistic insert for their news billboards announcing 'Lewes MP's House Demolished'. This was seen by my then near neighbour who was walking home and, horrified, broke into a run.

The move did of course mean I was then renting from myself and even though I had the rent independently assessed and set, the House authorities were queasy about this, and so I moved the office round the corner to the old library, where I stayed until I lost my seat in 2015. My wife, whom I had married in 2002, was not unhappy with the move, as she had understandably been far from ecstatic at having my office downstairs.

In the autumn of 1997, I was undertaking lots of visits around the constituency in response to a large number of invitations I had received. I suppose there was a novelty factor.

One visit I undertook was to a county council premises in Western Road in Lewes. This was not very far from my office – nothing in Lewes is very far from anywhere else – so I decided to cycle there.

When I arrived, I found there was nowhere to leave my bike safely, so I wheeled it into the reception area.

The receptionist behind the counter looked horrified: 'You can't bring that in here,' she admonished me. 'We're expecting the MP.'

I found quite quickly that there was a general expectation that, being the MP, I would arrive by car, and probably an expensive one. Being a supporter of cycling, and also being somewhat contrary by nature, I would cycle to many engagements. It was hard work. There were many places that made no provision for bikes, even educational establishments.

One issue I raised – the need for a new school for Wivelsfield, a village in my constituency – generated a surprising letter of congratulations from the local Tory councillor for the village, Jason Sugarman. Jason was to stand against me twelve years later, in the 2010 general election.

Also that autumn, the Lib Dem conference was held in nearby Eastbourne, highly convenient for me. As part of the programme away from the conference hall, I had agreed that my band, The Reform Club, would play in a venue in the town centre.

Although I had always loved music, my first live performance on stage was not until I was twenty-two, at The Goat in St Albans, when I sang a couple of numbers with a band called The Stripes. The first I belted out was 'Twist and Shout', which went down really well, so we moved on to 'Dizzy Miss Lizzy'.

The guitarist, one Mike Todd, told me I had to keep myself busy, and thrust a harmonica into my hands, which I gamely played, apparently successfully enough to get away with it, even though I think the only person who plays harmonica worse than me is Bob Dylan.

At the end, the barmaid came up and asked for my phone number and I decided that singing on stage was quite a good idea.

Even so, The Reform Club was not put together until the early 1990s, and we did gigs over the next few years, past the 1997 general election. I discovered that, unlike in politics, you either cut it in music or you do not – there is no middle fudge. Over the years, the band experienced both ecstatic enthusiasm and total disinterest.

Although the band was not political in any way, it became harder to just perform without people asking why I was doing it. When I answered, truthfully, that it was because I enjoyed it and it was time off from politics, that never seemed to satisfy them.

This problem became more acute after my election to Parliament, culminating in a whole page devoted to us in the *News of the World* following our Eastbourne gig. That gig was held upstairs in a cool venue called the Blues Bar. As well as members of the band, we had roped in Archy Kirkwood, the Lib Dem MP for Roxburgh and Berwickshire, on guitar, and Chris Berry, our Eastbourne candidate, on keyboards.

Archy was a competent rhythm guitarist and had been in a Scottish band in the 1960s, half of which went on to be part of the Average White Band, though not Archy's half. But that night he looked like a rabbit caught in the headlights. The room itself was small, with limited room for a stage, it was packed out with Lib Dems, and there were three separate TV crews filming us.

I learnt the power of TV from that evening, if I had ever doubted it. Each of the TV crews featured a different song in their coverage, and those who saw the extracts concluded, not unreasonably I suppose, that the extract in question was a fair guide to our performance.

Those who saw our rendition of 'Route 66' were impressed and complimented me the next day. Those who saw 'Be-Bop-A-Lula' told me it was quite good, but not to give up the day job. Unfortunately, the third crew waited until the early hours, when, buoyed by the good reception from the audience and not a little alcohol, I rather unwisely launched into 'Wild Thing'. This was not something that should have been captured for broadcast.

The *News of the World* piece was written up in a friendly way, but weaving the political and the musical inexorably. It suggested, for example, that by including Jimi Hendrix's bluesy number 'Red House', we were 'cementing the new relationship between the Lib Dems and Labour'.

There was much more of this, including suggestions for further tracks we might cover, such as 'What's the Story (Mourning Tories)', 'Have You Seen the Tories Baby (Standing in the Shadow)', 'Born to Be Mild (Lib Dem cut)' and 'Stand By Your Mandelson'.

Playing live became more difficult, in all sorts of ways, and shortly after, we pulled the plug. There matters rested until I thought it might be fun to record an album of our own material. I duly got back in touch with Mike Phipps, an old colleague from Our Price Records, where in the early 1980s I had been a regional director and he an area manager. Together we had actually put together and recorded a couple of numbers in about 1983. The result was *Always Tomorrow*, an album of entirely original songs written by the two of us, which we duly released in the spring of 2013.

For the cover, we used a striking folly as a backdrop for the band, a large pyramid to be found in the churchyard at Brightling Church, itself the title of one of the album tracks. The folly had been erected by 'Mad' Jack Fuller for him to be buried there. After the album was released, I was delighted to discover that between 1801 and 1812, Mad Jack had also been a Sussex MP, operating out of Lewes, and indeed owned the property virtually opposite my present house.

It probably helped that expectations of a politician producing anything vaguely listenable are inevitably low, so, this low hurdle overcome, the album was actually quite well received, bar a curmudgeonly report in the *Daily Telegraph*, and to date has sold well and clocked up over 30,000 YouTube hits for the single, 'Piccadilly Circus'.

There was quite a degree of media coverage when the album

came out, and my Department for Transport (DfT) office complained that they could barely get an answer out of me on anything for two weeks. They also found it rather amusing, listening in to a routine conversation between myself and Nick Clegg on the phone, that when he asked me for a complimentary copy of the CD, I told him he would have to cough up a tenner. Especially as Patrick McLoughlin had paid for one!

The recording of the album led to an invitation to join Noddy Holder and others on stage for a Christmas event, held in Islington in December 2012, where I sang the Wizzard number 'I Wish It Could Be Christmas Every Day'.

I would, over the years, also sing the occasional number with a local jazz band, the Jazz Caverners. This outfit featured a leading Lib Dem councillor in Polegate in the far east of the constituency, Roy Martin. Roy was a great character. He had been in the band since before I was born, and regularly played in places as diverse as Paris and New Orleans. Despite being over eighty, he still dressed as what he called a 'jazzer', invariably with a bow tie and a ponytail.

He was also a tremendous politician and represented the town at county, district and town levels, astute, and always doing his best for people.

I loved his sense of humour. We had a Lib Dem councillor in the town called Bob Hawkins, who, with his son, had a building business, H&H Builders. When there was a suggestion that the son might be prosecuted for assault, Roy raised this with the father: 'Hey, Bob, are you renaming your business H&GBH?'

I was very fond of Roy and managed to get a coach named after him, inviting him to do the unveiling. I had told him the coach was called Polegate, and it was only when he pulled off the cover that he saw his own name.

Sadly, he died a couple of years before the 2015 election, but the

town council, not a Lib Dem one, generously named a street after
him. I wanted the occasion to be one that Roy would have liked,
so a couple of us performed 'When You're Smiling' there and then
on the pavement, that being one of Roy's favourite songs.

Towards the end of 1997, I was invited to dinner with the German
ambassador. I assumed that the embassy had homed in on my
degree in German, and was inviting me, and others from the new
intake with similar interests, as a public relations exercise.

I duly arrived at the residence in Kensington. I was slightly late
and all the others were already seated. I should have remembered
that the Germans are very punctual.

To my surprise, it was a very small dinner, no more than ten,
and I was seated at the top end. The only other MP, Alun Michael,
a Labour MP in the government, was seated opposite at the far
end. All the other diners appeared to be Germans.

The man on my right began asking for my views on a range of
topics such as legal aid and the Office of Supervision of Solicitors.
I did my best but found the whole thing rather perplexing.

When I was able to, I caught Alun Michael.

'I don't understand. Why do they keep asking me questions about
legal matters?'

'It's a legal affairs dinner, Norman,' he replied.

'Oh. Then why are you here? It's not your portfolio.'

'The Lord Chancellor couldn't come so I'm substituting for him.'

'Oh. Then why am I here?'

'They think you're Kenneth Baker.'

In November 1997, I took part in an all-party visit to the United
Nations in New York. I told my local press that I was attending
as Paddy Ashdown's representative, which was not incorrect but
might have been termed 'economical with the truth'.

It was a fascinating visit. There was something uplifting,

aspirational and hopeful about the ideals of the organisation, writ large on the wall for all to see when we arrived.

The issues we discussed, including the money owed by nation states to the UN, and the make-up of the Security Council, have a familiar ring to them today. On the latter, I thought it indefensible that Britain and France should be permanent members with vetoes, whereas countries such as Germany, India and Brazil were excluded.

I asked our deputy permanent representative to the UN, Stephen Gomersall, when Britain had last used its veto unilaterally. He did not know, but sent someone away to check.

On examining the position further, it became clear that it was really only the US that regularly used a veto, with China and Russia doing so much more sparingly, and France, like Britain, not at all. Between 1986 and 2014, more than half the vetoes would come from the US.

Stephen confirmed to me that the last time Britain used a veto unilaterally was over Southern Rhodesia on 29 September 1972. France's last unilateral veto was in 1976. I suggested to him that there was little point in having a veto which the rest of the world would only tolerate us having provided we never used it. In a way, it was like the theoretical veto all British monarchs have if they choose not to give royal assent to an Act of Parliament. It exists, but would create a constitutional crisis if it were ever applied.

Would it not be better, I suggested to him, for the British and French to give up their seats as permanent members and instead have an EU member who could apply the veto? He went white and mumbled that this was an appalling idea, though I was no wiser as to why he thought so.

The briefing notes for the visit, supplied by the Foreign Office, noted that the Foreign Secretary had said that the UN Security Council had to be reformed if it was not to lose its legitimacy.

The briefing told me: 'In addition to permanent membership for Germany and Japan, we support proposals for one permanent seat each for Asia, Africa, and Latin America and the Caribbean … We remain committed to an early decision.'

By 2015, nothing had changed.

The most interesting meeting for me was the thirty minutes or so we had with Russia's permanent representative to the UN, Sergey Lavrov. He came across as super-intelligent, personable and generally deeply impressive. It is a cliché to refer to chess when discussing Russians, I accept, but this man was moves ahead of anyone else and his brain had got from A to B while ours were still starting up the electrical impulses.

Later the same month, I undertook a trip to Saudi Arabia. My only previous engagement with the country had when been the flight I had taken to Réunion had touched down to refuel. On that occasion, we had been warned to hide away any alcohol or racy pictures, and sure enough, while we were refuelling, the eerily smiling thought police boarded and checked all was to their liking. A Frenchman I mentioned this to told me that on the previous trip, the flight had been held up because the police had seen an art magazine with a picture of Cézanne's *Les Grandes Baigneuses*. The flight was held until paper and sellotape had been found to cover the image.

I had thought ours was a trip organised by the House, but I discovered on the plane that it was actually funded by the Saudi government. I would not have gone if I had known, given their human rights record. As it happens, it was an interesting trip, though perhaps not for the reasons the Saudis had in mind.

For one thing, we were effectively kept under luxurious house arrest in the diplomatic quarter, and warned to be careful what we said on the phone. As we gathered in the expanse of the hotel reception, my eyes wandered to the stairwell, where I saw a rather bad painting of King Fahd. I pointed it out to my fellow MPs, and remarked on the resemblance between the King and Captain Pugwash. The MPs chortled but our ambassador urged me in hushed tones not to repeat that. I could not see why. After all, it was hardly likely that the BBC cartoon of yesteryear was well known in the kingdom, and even if it was, so what?

We were due to meet Prince Saud, and I arrived downstairs in the reception area to find all the others in the delegation bar one Labour MP and myself had left about ten minutes earlier. The driver looked frantically worried. Clearly it was not going to be good for him to arrive late. I worked this out as he set off at break-neck speed for probably the most frightening car trip of my life, as he touched the equivalent of 140 mph in what we would see as a 30 mph area. Along the way, wrecked cars littered the side of the road. I mentioned this to the driver as a gentle hint that he might slow down. He simply replied that it was 'a matter for Allah' and put his foot down. We arrived on time.

Within a year of my election in 1997, I received an anonymous and somewhat curt note from *Who's Who*, requiring information about me for their publication. I had no wish to be featured in such a volume, which looked to me like an overblown exercise in vanity. I also thought it rather ironic that I was being asked to give details about myself by someone who had failed to provide even their own name.

I wrote back asking for the name of my correspondent, informing him or her that I did not provide information in response to anonymous requests, and indicating in passing that the draft entry for me was inaccurate in several respects.

Who's Who – who, indeed? – stood firm. They refused me the basic courtesy of providing a name, and I in return refused to tell them what the inaccuracies in my entry were. In the end, they must have done some more careful research, for they eventually produced an entry for me that was almost entirely accurate.

Over the years, I would also have minor disputes with other publications that expected me to provide information that was irrelevant to my public role, for example my marital status and details of children. My wife and our daughters are not public figures, they have never asked to be, and I saw, and see, no reason why they should be included in public reference documents.

For my part, I never featured them in any election literature and indeed did not even refer to them. I was standing for election on my political platform, not on whether I was married or not. I find it cringeworthy how American politicians appear to have to wheel out their extended family on stage at a certain point in their campaign.

I have always taken the view that politicians should be able to have a private life too, free from media intrusion, able to go home and shut the door on the world.

The corollary is that public figures should be fully transparent and held to account for what they do in their professional and public lives.

This thread has always run through my politics, from my council motion on freemasons onwards, and I pursued it with relish when I reached Parliament.

The first debate I secured in my own name, in July 1997, was on freedom of information and access to government papers. At the same time, I introduced my first Bill, the Public Records (Amendment) Bill, the effect of which would have been to reduce the period for which records are kept locked up from thirty years to twenty.

In the debate, I listed files for which the titles were known but the contents were still secret. They included the following:

- Census of industrial production 1907
- Taxi drivers carrying fares without depressing flags 1935–1952
- Dangerous driving conditions at hump-backed bridge on Beckenham Road, London 1935–1951
- Police fees for surgeons 1926–1953

The minister, Peter Kilfoyle, an Old Labour figure from Liverpool, told me that the files could not be opened as 'they contain information which could cause substantial distress (or endangerment from a third party) to the persons affected by their disclosure or their descendants'.

I could not see why, even if the files did contain personal information of a sensitive nature, such information could not be blacked out and the remainder of the file opened. The essential problem was that Whitehall made everything secret and a case had to be made to open it up, whereas I took the view that everything should be open unless a case could be made to keep it secret.

As part of my campaign, I asked each department what was the oldest record they held, and which had therefore not been passed to the Public Records Office in Kew. The results were interesting.

John Prescott's massive fiefdom, the Department of the Environment, Transport and the Regions, took first prize. It told me it was still hanging on to a 1771 map of the River Dee. The *Daily Telegraph* asked the DETR why this was still secret, and was given what the paper called 'a fine technical defence'.

'The department hadn't been founded back then,' a spokesman told the paper.

The Department of National Heritage, predecessor to today's Department of Culture, Media and Sport, had an unreleased drawing of a memorial from 1895, while the Home Office had a file, allegedly on a matter of national security, from 1876.

Even the transfer of material to the Public Records Office itself was no guarantee that records would be opened within thirty years. The oldest unopened file in its possession dated from 1873.

The 1876 Home Office file, actually covering the years 1876–1914, was in fact transferred to the Public Records Office and opened to the public by the then Home Secretary Jack Straw, alerted by me to the issue.

It transpired that the file revealed that British secret agents had been ordered to infiltrate Irish-American groups at the end of the nineteenth century due to concern about transatlantic support for Irish republicanism.

This was a welcome move from Jack Straw, even if some of the papers in the file were still withheld. It mirrored the positive response I had from Foreign Secretary Robin Cook to the papers relating to the notorious 1924 Zinoviev letter.

This was a fake letter, purportedly from the chairman of the Communist International in Moscow, Grigory Zinoviev, which called for intensified agitation in Britain. It ended up in the *Daily Mail* and helped the Conservatives secure a big majority at the general election shortly afterwards. It also damaged the Liberal Party very badly. It seems that, as in 1992 and 2015, when fear is in the air, it is the Tories who benefit and the Liberals who suffer.

In response to pressure from me, Robin Cook commissioned the Foreign Office's historians to produce a definitive memorandum on the letter, and this duly appeared in 1999.

In the spring of 2000, I sat on my first committee to consider a particular piece of legislation, the Utilities Bill.

A wonderful mix-up occurred when I moved an amendment to require the government to source 10 per cent of its energy from renewable sources by 2010. Although I strongly supported this idea, the motivation was partly mischievous in that the idea was contained in the 1997 Labour manifesto but showed no signs of being delivered.

When it came to the vote, the two Lib Dems cried 'aye', and both Tories and Labour abstained. The Labour whip, Greg Pope, had taken his eye off the ball, and the rest of his side were asleep, mostly metaphorically. My amendment was therefore carried by 2–0.

When the Bill then returned to the floor of the Commons, we had the entertaining sight of the Labour government instructing its own MPs to vote down the amendment and so actively reject a commitment in their own manifesto. It would of course have been simpler, cleaner and politically more astute just to have accepted the amendment and trumpeted their green credentials, but so controlling and humourless was the central Labour machine that this could not be allowed. Anything not in the approved grid had to be defeated.

My attendance at the various sittings of the committee was interrupted by the birth of my daughter. At my first meeting back, the minister, Helen Liddell, congratulated me and suggested I call my as yet unnamed daughter Neta, after the New Electricity Trading Arrangements being introduced in the Bill. My wife and I settled for Charlotte.

In August 2000, I was invited to open an art exhibition in aid of stroke victims. This was in the Lewes Constitutional Club, affiliated to the Conservative Party, but I took the view that it was a good cause and would have looked rather churlish to refuse, so I accepted.

However, the invitation had not, it seemed, been sanctioned by the Tory high command that ran the club, and their agent, Jeanette Allen, announced I was banned from the event. I thought this rather pathetic, but did show how super-sensitive the local Tories had become. Of course, their decision made them look petty and resulted in far more column inches for me than had they simply allowed me the low-profile opening I had anticipated.

Much more seriously, in October, disaster struck the county town. The River Ouse burst its banks and left a great deal of the town under water and hundreds of people homeless. The speed at which the water level rose was astonishing. Looking over the bridge at Cliffe, you could actually watch it rise.

If the speed was astonishing, so was the volume. Some houses had their entire ground floor filled, and water in the upstairs bedrooms too. The consequences of careless planning soon became apparent, as the operational rooms of the Sussex Ambulance Service flooded, along with the fire station and the new Royal Mail sorting office.

Many businesses were badly affected, including the totemic Harveys brewery next to the river, with the consequent sight of kegs floating downstream. To somebody's disappointment, no doubt, they were empty.

Given the scale and speed of the flooding, much worse than the previous occasion in 1960, it is a blessing that no lives were lost.

Apart from feeling sorry and concerned for the hundreds of my constituents who had been affected, I was angry that flood defence works that had been planned had subsequently been delayed. Back in 1998, the Sussex Flood Defence Committee had pulled the plug on the £2.5 million the Environment Agency said it desperately needed for Lewes.

I commented at the time: 'I am told that the river wall could last ten days or ten years. It is irresponsible of the Flood Defence Committee to take such an appalling risk with the county town.'

The Environment Agency had been planning to start work that year, so some of the devastation of 2000 might have been avoided had they not had their funding pulled.

The evening of the flood, I went to the town hall, where large numbers of people were being put up for the night. The atmosphere was calm, but this had been clearly been a traumatic experience for many.

The next day, with the flood water still present but subsiding, I walked round the town, popping into properties that had been flooded. There was not much I could do in practice except show moral support. People were torn between practical considerations such as the need to deal with their insurance company, and anguish at the loss of personal possessions, especially irreplaceable ones such as photographs.

My main task, as I saw it, was in the short term to help get life back to normal for residents and businesses, and then to get put in place the flood defences the town badly needed.

I wanted a town-wide scheme, but the Environment Agency insisted on adopting an approach that divided the town into cells and producing a cost–benefit analysis for each cell. This did mean that remedial action was relatively swift in the Malling and town centre areas, but it was slower elsewhere. In addition, I was concerned that protecting one area in isolation would simply divert any future flood water and increase the problems for other areas of the town. The Environment Agency said the displacement effect would be marginal. By the time I ceased being an MP in 2015, all bar one cell in the town had seen the investment necessary to provide much greater protection for the future.

Of course, whatever was happening locally and indeed nationally, my thoughts throughout the parliament were never far from the next general election, when I would have to defend a thin majority.

The official Tory line in Lewes took a bizarre turn. Jeanette Allen made a plea to Labour voters to end tactical voting and support New Labour. She told a meeting in Lewes:

What has happened to a once proud, fiercely independent Labour Party to allow itself to be enchanted by the Liberal Democrat Party with its puny powder-puff policies? Surely it's time for the Labour Party in the Liberal Democrat closet to be re-emerging to show their true colours here in the Lewes constituency ... Hundreds may have voted Liberal Democrat in the recent election but are we to assume that ... they must do this again and again and again and never be able to register their true allegiance or support for the Labour Party whose philosophy they allegedly believe in?

Her concern for the Labour Party was touching, driven of course by the fact that tactical voting had been crucial to the Tories losing the parliamentary seat. The Tories would have to wait until 2015, when Labour voters in large numbers abandoned tactical voting and so helped deliver the result she wanted: a Tory MP.

It was novel to hear a Tory agent urging people to vote Labour. What was dressed up as a principled stance was perhaps weakened by her suggestion that those who had voted for the Referendum Party, James Goldsmith's short-lived anti-EU outfit, should instead make their vote count by voting Tory.

The Tories were, of course, smarting badly from losing Lewes in 1997 and saw the result as an aberration. The former Cabinet minister Kenneth Baker, a resident of the village of Iford in the constituency, confidently predicted it would return to the Tory fold at the next election.

To spearhead their campaign, the Tories chose a thirty-year-old barrister called Simon Sinnatt, who had in fact been a Young Liberal in Ditchling when even younger than he now was. He was plump, fresh-faced and looked a little like an overgrown schoolboy, the sort Terry Scott would have played. The Tories ran him under the banner

'Simon Sinnatt – simply the best', which was in my view a pretty rubbishy slogan. He was in fact harmless enough, but did not convince.

The Labour candidate was one Paul Richards, who had just published a book entitled, satirically, *How to Win an Election*, having never won one himself.

I was buoyed during the campaign by a letter in the local paper from twenty-two constituents, many of them known Labour and Green Party members, urging tactical voting for me, echoing the successful 1997 pitch. This was also picked up in the nationals.

I was also delighted to welcome Ralph Taylor into the Lib Dems, and not just for the election boost this gave but because he was a principled and likeable man. Ralph had previously stood for Labour in Lewes in the 1987 general election, and just three months earlier had been on the Labour shortlist before losing out to Paul Richards. He would subsequently go on to be a Lib Dem councillor and mayor in Seaford.

Nevertheless, I was completely unprepared for the result of the 2001 general election in my seat. Nationally, I knew Labour would win, both because they had started well and because William Hague was not seen as a credible alternative. He had unwisely allowed himself to be photographed in a baseball cap, which somewhat detracted from the prime ministerial image he needed to create. As bad photos go, it must rank along Ed Miliband's bacon sandwich challenge, and the shot of Ed's brother David holding a limp banana and wearing a limper smile.

Locally, I thought I had done all right and might push up the majority from the rather precarious 1,300 to something around the 3,000 or 4,000 mark. When the votes were counted, I had won by 9,710. I could not believe it, and for about the only time in my life, I was left speechless. I struggled to give a short acceptance speech, so emotional was I.

Chapter 9

Shortly after the 1997 election, I began to take a close interest in the activities of Peter Mandelson and Alastair Campbell. It was obvious to all that these two, with Tony Blair, were running the show, bar the self-contained Treasury run by Gordon Brown. The Deputy Prime Minister, John Prescott, was there to provide a sop to Old Labour, and to stop them reacting negatively to the Blairite agenda. His role was equivalent to that of the old carthorse Boxer in Orwell's *Animal Farm*.

My concern was not so much about what Campbell and Mandelson were doing, although I took issue with some of that. Rather, I objected to the fact that these powerful people who were shaping the government were completely unaccountable, except in the loosest sense through Tony Blair, a problem made more acute because they were both highly effective in their roles.

I particularly disliked the fact that Campbell had been appointed as a special adviser with the authority to order civil servants around. I thought this was quite wrong, as was the fact that Campbell attended Cabinet meetings, a view shared incidentally and publicly by the Labour chair of the Public Administration Committee, Rhodri Morgan.

Campbell did not baulk at ordering Cabinet ministers around, either. The *Sunday Express* published an example of this, a stiff letter he had sent to Harriet Harman. The line 'I do not want to see interpretation of either in tomorrow's press' gives a flavour of the tone: telling off a naughty schoolchild.

There were clear attempts to remove those civil servants who were unwilling to bend sufficiently in the New Labour direction. Blair admitted to me in a letter in 1999 that sixteen out of the eighteen senior government press officers had been removed since the election. Heads of information were being replaced by heads of disinformation.

In April 1998, less than a year after the election, I called a debate on the Prime Minister's Press Office. It was given the graveyard slot as the last item on a Friday afternoon. As usual for this time, the House was empty, but the press gallery was not.

I thought that Mandelson should have taken the debate, but instead it was left to the Cabinet Officer minister Peter Kilfoyle.

In the debate, I made all these points, accusing Campbell of exercising 'untrammelled power', as well as slamming the close links between Blair and Rupert Murdoch, the favours Blair was doing Murdoch and the pitiful amount of tax paid by News International. The minister, in his reply, was dismissive. He maintained that there were no issues, and resorted to criticising the Lib Dem party for its Focus leaflets. I was misunderstanding the position, being political, making a mountain out of a molehill, he implied.

After the debate, our paths crossed outside the chamber.

'Well done, Norman,' he said quietly, patting me on the arm.

Peter Kilfoyle later became Defence Minister and would have to answer questions from me about American bases. Again, for me, this was a question first and foremost of accountability. I objected to the fact that all the various US bases were presented as RAF bases. Indeed, Menwith Hill in Yorkshire, the major listening operation, had been US Menwith Hill but was then renamed RAF Menwith Hill. I thought this was simply dishonest.

Perhaps this seems rather abstract, but in my view, it was symptomatic of a mindset that bigged up the British military capability, rather than baring the truth: that we were merely the back end of a penny-farthing to President Bush and the Americans. We were fooling ourselves.

The height of absurdity was reached when I discovered that the RAF was entirely absent from RAF Feltwell, leading to the following written parliamentary question in 2000, answered by the then minister John Spellar:

Q: For what reasons there are no RAF personnel at RAF Feltwell?

A: There is no operational requirement for RAF personnel to be based at RAF Feltwell.

Peter Kilfoyle later told me he had been refused access to RAF Menwith Hill when he was a defence minister. So much for the special relationship.

With Peter Mandelson, I began to take a much closer interest in the Millennium Dome, which he was championing, and effectively appointed myself as Lib Dem spokesman on the issue. Nobody seemed to mind.

This project, dreamt up by the Tories when they were still in power, had been discussed at a Cabinet meeting on 19 July 1997, barely two months into the new government. A detailed report of the meeting subsequently appeared in the *Mail on Sunday* in 2000 – so detailed that it seemed to have come from the transcript of the meeting rather than the far more anodyne official record that would have appeared in the minutes.

The leak from that meeting revealed that an overwhelming majority of the Cabinet wanted to cancel the scheme. John Prescott questioned its financial viability. Gordon Brown said the objectives were not clear. David Blunkett said the design had no vision, and he was deeply against. Jack Cunningham said he had no confidence in the management team.

Faced with this near-total opposition, Tony Blair and Peter Mandelson decided to go ahead anyway with a project costing £758 million.

In a press release from the Cabinet Office shortly afterwards, Mandelson justified the decision: 'Millenniums only come once in a thousand years.'

The release also stated that 'the Deputy Prime Minister ... is a great enthusiast for what we are doing'. This was rather at odds with the subsequently leaked report of the Cabinet meeting.

The questions raised at that meeting had been pertinent. What exactly was the Millennium Dome for? Normally, a concept is generated, and a building designed to deliver that concept. Here a building was being created with subsequent head-scratching to work out what the contents should be.

Various, seemingly random, ideas were floated for themes. One week it was Japan, another week Jesus, a third week Disney.

As Stephen Bayley, the Dome's creative designer, wrote shortly after noisily resigning: 'A formal audience with Mickey Mouse for inspirational purposes was, I felt, misjudged.'

As the clock ticked towards 1 January 2000, nobody had any clear idea what the contents would be.

As Mandelson initially would not appear in the Commons at all, I used the only method available to engage him: the written parliamentary question. I deliberately bombarded him with these, but let it be known that I would desist when he became accountable in the Commons, as every other minister was.

I was able to claim a victory of sorts in early November 1997 when Mandelson bowed to pressure and began answering questions in the Commons on the Millennium Dome, even if it was just for five minutes once a month. There was still no opportunity to ask him about his much wider role in government, co-ordinating government policy across all departments, or about his role in the eleven Cabinet committees on which he sat.

'At last the Prince of Darkness has been forced out into the light, even if it is only under a 25-watt bulb,' was my public response at the time.

I wrote to Rhodri Morgan to complain about Mandelson's lack of accountability and specifically his non-answers to my parliamentary questions. I suggested that the minister had broken the code of practice on access to government information, which said that ministers 'should be as open as possible with Parliament and the public, refusing to provide information only when disclosure would not be in the public interest'.

Mr Morgan, in reply, said he had asked officials to examine how previous holders of the post of Minister without Portfolio had been held to account, and that he would be writing to Mandelson to ask him to explain why he had failed to answer my parliamentary questions.

He added that David Clark, the minister who headed the Cabinet Office at the time, 'has taken a very strong line that, with Freedom of Information coming in, it is best for ministers and civil servants to get used to it and to get into that spirit now'.

David Clark was one of the good guys and genuinely committed to introducing a properly functioning and radical Freedom of Information Act. His enthusiasm was not, however, shared by all his ministerial colleagues, and Jack Straw in particular was said to be sceptical about the concept.

I knew, as I suspect David Clark also did, that the longer it took to enact legislation, the weaker it was likely to be, as ministers identified information from their time that they would rather not see the light of day.

Eventually, a watered-down version was enacted in 2000, with a long lead-in period of preparation, so that the Act did not become live until 1 January 2005.

David Clark, for his efforts, was sacked, it seems for the sin of trying to implement his party's manifesto. Tony Blair would later say that the Freedom of Information Act was his greatest mistake. In his memoirs, he wrote:

> Freedom of Information Act. Three [sic] harmless words. I look at those words as I write them, and feel like shaking my head 'til it drops off. You idiot. You naive, foolish, irresponsible nincompoop. There is really no description of stupidity, no matter how vivid, that is adequate. I quake at the imbecility of it.

Some might suggest the Iraq War might have been a more appropriate cause for self-flagellation.

Throughout my time in opposition I would regularly meet ministers to discuss issues of interest. Some, such as the various transport secretaries, were very open, especially Andrew Adonis.

The same cannot be said for Mandelson. He only agreed to meet me once, in the semi-public area just off central lobby. He came along with a female who looked about fifteen, who did not introduce herself and whose function was not revealed to me. He was as cold as a deep freeze, as taciturn as if every word uttered had to be paid for. It was an extraordinary performance.

Mandelson set about finding sponsors for the Dome, for various 'zones' that were to be created. Sponsorship of the Faith Zone looked particularly unattractive to commercial bodies, so it was with raised eyebrows that I learnt that two Indian brothers few of us had ever heard of had offered to put in a cool million. It looked too good to be true.

The two were Srichand and Gopichand Hinduja. The Hindujas were subsequently described by the BBC as 'one of the world's most influential families'. They had built their wealth through making deals under the Shah of Iran's regime, but entered the billionaires' league with oil deals in the 1980s. They were described by the *Eastern Eye* newspaper in 1999 as Britain's richest Asians.

On 22 January 1990, investigators at the Indian Central Bureau of Investigation named Gopichand Hinduja as a suspect in the Bofors arms scandal. It was less than a month later that the two brothers first applied for British passports. Their applications were turned down the following year, with Doug McQueen, the official who had been asked to adjudicate on the applications, finding multiple reasons for rejection.

The brothers had not been in the country for five years prior to their applications, as required under the British Nationality Act. More seriously, he wrote, 'there must be some doubt in both cases as to whether they can be said to meet the requirements of good character', adding for good measure, 'We do not usually grant citizenship to people who are known to be the subject of criminal investigation.'

In February 1997, the brothers expressed an interest in contributing to the Dome, then under the umbrella of Michael Heseltine, and the following month Gopichand reapplied for a British passport. This was speedily granted in November the same year, six months after the general election. This was despite a note from the British High Commission in Delhi, raising the Bofors scandal and advising that the application be treated 'unenthusiastically'.

In February 1998, the Hinduja Foundation, the brothers' charitable organisation, gave a verbal undertaking to underwrite the Dome's Faith Zone to the tune of a million pounds, an offer reiterated in June.

In October 1998, Srichand Hinduja made a second application for a British passport. This was granted in March 1999. Besides the fact that earlier decisions had been overturned, the process had taken a mere eight months for Gopichand and just five for Srichand. In March 1999, the average waiting time for all nationality applications was almost twenty months.

The Hindujas were astonishingly well connected. On their mantelpiece in Carlton House Terrace, itself one of the best addresses in London, they displayed various framed photographs of themselves with famous figures: George Bush, Margaret Thatcher, Tony and Cherie Blair, Al Gore, Indian Prime Minister Atal Bihari Vajpayee, Michael Jackson and Mother Teresa.

Perhaps the photo with the Blairs dated from the time shortly before the 1997 election when the Hindujas had entertained the then opposition leader, accompanied by Mandelson, at a private dinner at their Carlton House Terrace residence.

According to a report which appeared in *The Guardian* in February 2001, Gopichand Hinduja had spoken on the phone to Tony Blair before 8.30 a.m. on the morning of 18 October 2000, concerning the purported wish of the brothers to buy Express Newspapers. Downing Street denied the call had taken place.

The Blairs were not the only Labour figures to meet the brothers. Over the two years 1999 and 2000, Stephen Byers, the Trade and Industry Secretary, met them no fewer than eight times. They also met Patricia Hewitt three times, Clare Short (though she seems to have been quite careful), Chris Smith, the Lord Chancellor Lord Irvine and Keith Vaz, the latter many times.

Crucially, it was confirmed that they had met Lord Levy, popularly known as 'Lord Cashpoint', who brokered the deal to secure the £1 million contribution at the request of Peter Mandelson. That meeting took place on 29 October 1998, the same month in which Srichand Hinduja reapplied for his passport.

Lord Levy was appointed by Blair as his Middle East envoy. He visited a good many countries, but it was not clear exactly what he was doing and how this fitted in with the Foreign Office's objectives. There were concerns that these might be becoming confused with fundraising efforts for the Labour Party.

Nor had the Tories been reluctant to engage with the Hindujas. The brothers held a reception for William Hague, then Tory leader, in March 1999, as a fundraiser for the Tories. The following week, Conservative officials sent letters to some of those present, offering meetings with shadow Cabinet members in exchange for a £1,000 donation.

The former Tory MP Timothy Kirkhope was employed by the Hindujas as an adviser to the family after he lost his seat in the 1997 general election. He had been the immigration minister when Gopichand Hinduja applied for a passport in March 1997.

When Margaret Thatcher was Tory leader, the teetotal brothers paid £25,000 for a bottle of House of Commons whisky autographed by her. They also contributed thousands of pounds to Edward Heath's constituency office costs. Mr Heath was a referee on Gopichand Hinduja's passport application.

Thatcher did, however, on Home Office advice, decline an invitation to join the brothers for a Diwali party. Blair, however, seemed quite happy to attend a similar event in 1999.

During my time as an opposition MP, I would benefit from a series of really good researchers in my Westminster office, including Jana Sparks, Rob O'Halloran, Tom Fewins, Shaun Carr, Phil Bell and Stuart Bonar. With Stuart, I had carried out detailed research around the Dome and the Hindujas. Something smelt off.

I discussed the matter with the *Observer* journalist Anthony Barnett over lunch one day. Anthony presented a bit of a ramshackle image, with his unkempt hair, old-fashioned glasses and scruffy appearance. He reminded me of the comic poet John Hegley. But he was an absolutely first-rate journalist with a strong sense of where to go to find a story and was not afraid to go there. When we put together the information we had separately assembled, it seemed highly likely that Peter Mandelson had interested himself in Srichand Hinduja's passport application.

I was about to prove the value of the humble written parliamentary question. On 15 December 2000, I tabled a question to the Home Secretary for answer three days later, on the 18th.

I asked 'what representations he has received on the applications by G. P. Hinduja and S. P. Hinduja for British citizenship from (a) the Rt Hon. Member for Hartlepool [Peter Mandelson] and (b) the Hon. Member for Leicester East [Keith Vaz]'.

My researcher Stuart, trying to read my writing, actually copied the family name down wrongly as Hindiya, which is how the question was submitted. That would of course have given the minister a perfect excuse not to answer the question.

On the 18th, I received a holding answer, then nothing more for a month. It subsequently transpired that, behind the scenes, a heated discussion was under way as to how to answer this question. It would of course have been perfectly easy to have replied that it was not normal practice to comment on individual applications. Such a blocking answer would not have come as much of a surprise to me.

Peter Mandelson, predictably, did not want to be referred to in the reply, but Jack Straw, supported by his junior minister Barbara Roche, insisted that the question be properly answered. Whether he did this because he believed that MPs' questions should as a matter of practice be properly answered, as he told me subsequently, or because he was not unhappy to finger Mandelson, I cannot say.

In any case, the reply, issued by Barbara Roche on 18 January, included the following:

> Both Hon. Members, along with other Hon. Members, made enquiries about the cases. The Hon. Member for Leicester East … made enquiries about when a decision could be expected in the cases, and the Rt Hon. Member for Hartlepool … made enquiries about how an application might be viewed given the government's wider policy of encouraging citizenship from long-standing residents who fulfilled the criteria, but did not make representations that an application be granted.

The Observer ran an exclusive at the bottom of page one, but almost apologetically, and Anthony had to fight to get even that in. The Mail on Sunday picked it up in its later editions, but by the end of the day the story was dying away.

Then Jack Straw intervened again to insist on a correction to the line given out to the media by Alastair Campbell, a line based on information given to Campbell by Mandelson.

Alastair Campbell had to tell the lobby that, contrary to what he had told them on Monday, the day before, there had been involvement, in the shape of a phone call between Mandelson and Home Office minister Mike O'Brien. This came after a three-way phone call between O'Brien, Campbell and Mandelson, in which O'Brien had insisted that Mandelson had spoken to him on the phone about the passport application.

It also meant that Chris Smith, as Culture Secretary, inadvertently misled the Commons on the Monday, the day after the story appeared in the papers.

Mandelson then unwisely went onto *Channel 4 News* and was asked why he had told *The Observer* he was not involved and Alastair Campbell had that day said he was. Had he had a memory lapse?

'I didn't forget anything,' he told the programme, directly contradicting Campbell.

It was that interview that finally did for Mandelson. Jack Straw rang Blair and Campbell to say Mike O'Brien did remember the phone call and, what was more, he, Straw, had reminded Mandelson about it.

On the Wednesday morning, the 24th, Blair and Mandelson met at 10.30 in the Prime Minister's office for more than an hour. For the majority of the time, just the two of them were present, with Campbell also making an appearance. Blair put it to Mandelson that he had covered up the phone call to O'Brien, and told him he had to go. Mandelson objected but his resignation followed shortly afterwards.

It was his second resignation in a short space of time. In 1998 he had had to resign as Trade and Industry Secretary after the disclosure of a secret £373,000 house loan from the former Paymaster General, Geoffrey Robinson. He was reappointed as Northern Ireland Secretary less than a year later.

As luck would have it, I was on a parliamentary visit to Berlin when news of the resignation broke. I spent most of the next day being phoned by journalists about the matter. The *Mail on Sunday*, which must have hated Mandelson, went one better. I received the following message via the hotel I was staying at:

> Dear Mr Baker,
> Congratulations, you've got your man. My editor is sending me out to Berlin tonight to buy you champagne to arrive at the Westin Grand Hotel Berlin at around 23.00 o'clock local time.

See you then,
Jonathan Oliver

Jonathan, who was a good reporter and an honest one, duly turned up at the appointed hour and handed it over. We had a friendly five-minute chat, then he left again to get his flight back.

When I returned to London, I went to the BBC in Millbank for a pre-arranged interview, whereupon the journalistic equivalent of a plague of locusts descended on me, all from the BBC. It seemed each separate programme strand wanted to speak me, rather than my doing one clip for TV and one for radio. I did wonder at that point whether the BBC was making the best use of its resources.

In the Commons, Tory MPs came up to me to offer congratulations, one or two suggesting that their party should have been on the case. A few Labour MPs sidled up to me quietly to say well done – Old Labour, I should stress. One Labour Cabinet minister, I assume in jest, even offered to contribute to my constituency party, asking me, 'Where do we send the cheque?'

The one party that remained mute was the Lib Dems. I attended a meeting of the parliamentary party and was asked to give a quick résumé. It was met with near silence. I cannot recall a single Lib Dem who said anything half-complimentary.

There was a view that I had scored a terrible own goal, that Mandelson was a moderniser who was sympathetic to Lib Dem objectives, and that we had lost a friend. I thought this was rubbish.

The lack of enthusiasm was shared by the Lib Dem leader, Charles Kennedy, and his office, concerned, amongst other things, that the story detracted from a poster launch they had planned for that day.

At Prime Minister's Questions that day, Charles used his two questions pointedly to ask about something else, and was hammered in the papers the next day for not following through on my parliamentary question.

Given the level of criticism that followed, I offered to sit next to him the following week, which I duly did, but that only served to reheat the criticism that had been seen the week before.

I felt rather hurt and a bit bewildered by the way my party had reacted. I had secured the scalp of one of the key New Labour figures who, in my view, had been a malign influence in government, and while others elsewhere in the House had warmly congratulated me, I had been met with a chilled silence in my own ranks. I never quite forgave my party for this.

Not for the first time I felt I was working against the grain, on my own. If there was a Lib Dem family, I did not feel part of it.

Blair set up an inquiry into the Hinduja passport affair, and Sir Anthony Hammond KCB QC was selected to handle it. The terms of reference were 'to establish what approaches were made to the Home Office in 1998 in connection with the possibility of an application for naturalisation by Mr S. P. Hinduja and the full circumstances surrounding such approaches and the later grant of that application and to report to the Prime Minister'.

These were narrowly drawn terms and would not allow wider consideration of the contacts between the Hindujas and leading politicians. Nevertheless, I wrote to Sir Anthony to test how he was intending to interpret his role, and subsequently had a short meeting with him.

Sir Anthony, known to his friends as Wally, had been a Home Office insider, and was perhaps most famous for his role in the arms-to-Iraq scandal a decade earlier. He was the lawyer who encouraged ministers to use gagging orders to keep information from being made public.

He was also the official legal adviser to Hakluyt, a somewhat shadowy intelligence company with links to MI6, although this was oddly missing from his entry in *Who's Who*. Perhaps the anonymous author of that publication slipped up here too.

Hakluyt has also employed Rupert Huxter as deputy managing director. He was previously private secretary to Peter Mandelson and Michael Heseltine, the two politicians most closely associated with the Dome. The Tory MP Andrew Mitchell listed himself as 'a senior strategy adviser to Hakluyt & Company' in the 'Miscellaneous and unremunerated interests' section of the Members' Register of Interests.

Hakluyt, named after a sixteenth-century geographer, was started up in 1995, with a promise to find information for business clients that they 'will not receive by the usual government, media and commercial route'.

Meanwhile, in February 2001, a judge in Delhi turned down an application by the Hinduja brothers to leave the country. They had been questioned over allegations that they had received millions of dollars in illegal commission from Swedish arms manufacturer Bofors fifteen years earlier to facilitate sales of arms to India, something they denied. The brothers were finally cleared of the charges in May 2005.

In his report, published the following month, Sir Anthony made it clear that he had not seen it as part of his role to examine the reasons for Mandelson's resignation. Nor was it his role to look into anything to do with sponsorship of the Dome, nor to look into ministerial contacts with the Hindujas, nor to comment on whether ministers might have breached the code of conduct.

For good measure, he added that he had not interviewed either of the Hinduja brothers, citing 'practical difficulties in visiting them in India'. It seemed not to have occurred to him to use video conferencing facilities, or even a telephone.

Nor did he, either initially or in the subsequently reopened inquiry demanded by Mandelson, speak to Darin Jewell, Srichand Hinduja's former aide, who had made it known both that he had relevant information to impart and that he had sent it through to Sir Anthony Hammond, who told me, when I raised this with him, that he had not received it.

Lastly, just in case a chink of light might be left to escape, he reported that he had accepted the representations made by Jonathan Caplan QC on behalf of Mandelson to the effect that Hammond's approach should be to give Mandelson the benefit of the doubt. 'I will therefore take the facts in his favour rather than do an injustice which is without remedy,' Hammond wrote.

As they say in the transport world, the way you lay the tracks determines where the train goes.

Sir Anthony's report basically gave Mandelson a clean bill of health, though he did say that he thought it likely that the key phone call between Mandelson and O'Brien had taken place.

In 2002, the Parliamentary Ombudsman, Sir Michael Buckley, ruling on the disclosure of information by the government, breathed new life into the story when he publicly accused the Cabinet Secretary Sir Richard Wilson of preventing him, over an eight-month period, from having access to important papers relating to the Hinduja affair.

Interestingly, it was revealed in February 2001 that Sir Richard had also had lunch with the Hinduja brothers, though he insisted the issue of passports was not raised.

Pursuant to the Ombudsman's request, it turned out that documents relating to the naturalisation applications were missing from the Immigration and Nationality Directorate.

Sir Michael concluded:

They appeared to be withholding papers, which they readily

acknowledged existed, from my investigation ... Such a refusal strikes at the heart of my office's function. Together with the lack of co-operation from the Home Office it had made it impossible for me to corroborate the account contained in Sir Anthony's report.

The Dome itself got off to a shaky start with a cringeworthy opening event to see in the year 2000 and the new millennium, though for pedants that did not technically start until a year later. Visitor numbers were not great; there had been rows about the environmental footprint of the building; and then there were the contents.

I went in my official role to see the Dome shortly after its opening. I was deeply impressed with the new Tube station, which I thought was fabulous, and also decided I liked the Dome building itself as I approached it. The contents, however, were mildly interesting at best, junk at worst. Overall, it compared badly with BA's London Eye, which had been erected opposite Westminster at no cost to the taxpayer, was opened in March 2000 and was proving to be very popular.

Someone gave me a blue Millennium Dome teapot, which I still have. Like the building itself, it is quite striking. I kept it for cheap tea, however, so that the relationship between the teapot and the tea would mirror that between the Dome itself and its contents.

Drastic measures were needed, and a young Frenchman, Pierre-Yves Gerbeau, later known as PY, was brought in to rescue the attraction. I have always liked my politics to be fun, so it was with mischievous delight that I discovered that they may have appointed the wrong man by mistake, in the manner of the Evelyn Waugh novel *Scoop*.

M. Gerbeau worked for Eurodisney and was described on his

appointment as the man who had 'turned round Disneyland Paris', saving it from financial disaster. But within days, officials were forced to admit that the 34-year-old had only been a 'nuts-and-bolts operations man' at Eurodisney, on a salary of about £35,000, about a third of what he would now get at the Dome.

There was, however, another Eurodisney employee, a Jean-Marie Gerbeaux, the former director of communications there, who had transformed its public image, turning it from an expensive flop into a money-making success. This 52-year-old had a long track record of success, and was earning twice the salary of PY Gerbeau.

It reminded me of the incident when some Americans had bought the old London Bridge, thinking it was Tower Bridge, and only realised when they unpacked it back home.

I imagined the phone call that would have come from Bob Ayling at the Dome to PY.

'Is that M. Gerbeaux who works at Eurodisney? It is? Would you like to come over and run the Dome for us here in London?'

PY, when contacted by the press and asked how he was selected, replied that they would have to ask Bob Ayling, adding, 'I never met the gentleman before Friday a week ago.'

Mistake or not, the public decided they liked him and he did a pretty good job of breathing new life into the Dome. His was either an inspired appointment or a very happy error.

The same was not true for Bob Ayling, who, in June 2000, was forced to resign as a condition of the Millennium Commission throwing a further £29 million lifeline to the Dome to stop it going under.

In the meantime, it was clear that the part I had played in removing Peter Mandelson from office was a popular one. I was named Inquisitor of the Year by *The Spectator*, an award presented by David Blunkett, and Opposition Politician of the Year by Channel 4. I was of course pleased to receive these, though I suspected that snubbing Mandelson rather than rewarding me may have been the prime motivation of those who decided these things.

The written parliamentary question on the Hindujas generated a spectacular result, but in general the worth of this humble medium is underestimated.

There was, and is, a skill to the tabling of questions. The most effective are those that ask how many, on what date, in which location and so on: specific facts. The least effective are those that ask vague questions, and allow the government to answer, for example, that a number of comments have been received, both for and against a particular proposition, without giving any more detail.

At its best, an answer can shape a debate. One such question was when I asked for the relative change in the cost of different transport modes over a thirty-year period, a question I re-tabled at regular intervals. The 2010 answer showed that while the cost of travelling by bus had increased in real terms by 54 per cent since 1980, and travelling by rail had increased by 50 per cent, the cost of motoring had actually fallen substantially, by 17 per cent. Clearly, with around a quarter of our carbon emissions coming from the transport sector, this would have to be addressed.

Another useful question related to the school fruit scheme, whereby pieces of fruit were handed out to schoolchildren. This revealed that in 2003/04, fewer than half the apples were of UK origin, and just 10 per cent of pears: a question to the Department of Health, but actually good ammunition for the National Farmers' Union.

A third area related to the movement of radioactive material. A series of questions I submitted built up a useful – if, for me at least, somewhat concerning – picture.

I discovered that radioactive material could be moved through any port or airport, but no central record was kept of movements, and it was allowed on passenger ferries and through the Channel

Tunnel. The answers also showed that there had been twenty-three crashes on UK roads involving vehicles that had been carrying such material between 1985 and 1997, as well as two air crashes, in 1968 and 1987, and three rail crashes in 1998 alone. Reassuringly, no radioactivity escaped on any of these occasions.

Naturally the government was keen to avoid giving answers unhelpful to them. Early on, they picked up on the practice by some MPs of tabling identical questions to different departments and then producing league tables, a format the press generally warmed to. So it became standard practice for round-robin questions to be identified, and identical non-answers given.

To get one step ahead, I started to make invisible connections between questions and their answers, so creating a sort of media chemical reaction. For instance, by combining two answers from different departments, I was able to show that the government was spending almost as much on chauffeur-driven government cars as on monitoring air pollution. No computer system, no matter how sophisticated, was going to pick up this sort of thing.

Civil servants were told that they should answer the question asked, though sometimes that provided a misleading answer. Ask how much nuclear waste is transported and you get one answer. Ask the same question about spent nuclear fuel and you get a different one. To the layman, the dangers of carrying one are identical to the dangers of carrying the other. The distinction the civil service and ministers made was one of purpose, not consequence were anything untoward to happen.

An official once told me of a story in which an MP woke up dazed in a car in the middle of the desert, turned to the civil servant next to him or her, and asked: 'Where are we?'

To which the answer came: 'In a car.'

100 per cent accurate and totally unhelpful.

The Lib Dem peer Tom McNally, who by the way almost certainly holds the record for the longest gap between government posts, from 1979 to 2010, claims that Whitehall follows the bikini principle in answering parliamentary questions: to cover as little as possible while concealing the interesting bits.

To be fair to the Labour government, avoiding answering questions was nothing new. The Labour MP Mark Fisher once asked Prime Minister Margaret Thatcher how many written parliamentary questions addressed to her received the answer that the information could only be provided at disproportionate cost, that being a standard get-out-of-jail-free card. Her answer?

'This information is not held centrally and could be provided only at disproportionate cost.'

Another standard reply from the box of non-answers was that the matter in hand was commercially confidential. I had my office plot the number of times this response was given to a question, and produced a report setting out my findings.

These showed the use of this response had risen steadily under the Tories prior to the introduction of a code on open government, then dropped back. It dropped further under Labour in 1997 before rising sharply by 2001.

I had an interesting insight into the PQ process in early 1998 when I met up with an old college friend of mine, Mark Farrell, who was at the time a civil servant. He told me he was the main official working on the Confined Spaces Regulations. I did not, I hope, normally ask frivolous questions, but on this occasion, for a bit of fun, I put down a question on this topic.

About two days later he rang me.

'You bastard! I've spent the whole day answering your question,' he told me, relatively good-humouredly, I am relieved to say.

Interestingly, he told me his draft answer was about two

pages long. By the time it got to me, it had been reduced to about two lines.

The worst person by a long chalk in terms of not answering questions was the Prime Minister. Given that this description could be applied to both Tony Blair and Gordon Brown, I assume this was mostly an exhibition of the normal No. 10 arrogance that I would see more of when I was in government.

So bad was Blair, in fact, that I produced a dossier entitled 'Why won't the Prime Minister answer the question?' This covered the period May 2005 to May 2006, when I had received fifty-six replies to written parliamentary questions. I use the word reply rather than answer as, even by a generous interpretation, only a quarter were actually answered.

Of the rest, twelve referred back to previous, usually irrelevant answers, eight stated that the Prime Minister had 'nothing further to add', and eighteen can be classified as non-answers, where he answered the question he wanted rather than the one actually asked.

For example, as part of my efforts to get the government to wean themselves off ministerial cars, I asked each minister when they had last travelled by train on official business. While most gave a specific date, Tony Blair replied: 'I travel making the most efficient and cost-effective arrangements, and use trains as and when appropriate. My travel arrangements are in accordance with the arrangements set out in Chapter 10 of the Ministerial Code, and the accompanying guidance document, Travel by Ministers.'

Why did he not just say 22 March, or whatever day it was?

I repeated the exercise in 2009 for Gordon Brown, whose record proved to be even worse than that of his predecessor, with only 17 per cent of questions securing a meaningful answer.

Bringing the two together, I asked Gordon Brown on 18 October 2007 when he had last met Tony Blair. The reply given?

'My officials and I have meetings with a wide range of organisations and individuals on a range of subjects.'

Really? I would never have known.

The Freedom of Information Act 2000, which Tony Blair now so bitterly regrets, proved to be useful in levering out some information that he would have rather kept secret. For instance, my Lib Dem colleague Norman Lamb managed to extract a list of visitors Blair had invited to Chequers, which turned out to be peppered with B-list celebrities.

I was amused to see that at least one newspaper credited me big time with this story, rather than Norman Lamb. The media were always mixing us up, in fact, which I thought was rather sloppy.

The benefit of the parliamentary question is that it is much more immediate. A Freedom of Information request that is resisted can take literally years to resolve, as was seen in the case of Prince Charles's 'black spider' letters.

A third avenue to secure information was by personal letter, or occasionally by fax. This was the period when offices still had fax machines, but they were largely moribund, and thus a good way of getting an issue noticed was to fax a minister's office, so rarely would the machine start up.

One topic I pursued with Tony Blair was in relation to his unpaid strategy adviser John Birt. Birt had been Director-General of the BBC, and had introduced Producer Choice, which had the perverse effect of producers buying material from outside the BBC while its own resources sat idle because of the theoretical cost applied to using them. He was paid off to the tune of £370,000 of licence fee payers' money in 2000.

Lord Birt was frequently lampooned in *Private Eye* – or, it might be argued, simply accurately quoted – in their Birtspeak column, for his impenetrable jargon and love of employing expensive consultants.

The column was always accompanied by a drawing of him as a Dalek.

Greg Dyke joked that Birt was like a man who knew a hundred ways to make love, but did not know any women.

The same year Birt was paid off by the BBC, he was ennobled and made an unpaid strategy adviser to Tony Blair, supported by Downing Street's Forward Strategy Unit. He produced a number of studies, for example on transport and on crime, but they never seemed to lead anywhere. On transport, he is said to have recommended a new set of parallel motorways with tolls, apparently to ease congestion.

The narrow issue was that because he was unpaid, he was not therefore subject to the same rules as special advisers – the same problem that applied to Lord Levy. It was not clear, for example, how far his access to government papers went.

He was based for a while at No. 10, but then his ceiling fell in, which, as the Labour minister John Hutton remarked at the time, must have helped his blue-sky thinking.

I tried to pin down his location but the Prime Minister would not answer that question. I regarded that as a challenge to overcome. So my researcher rang up Downing Street, put on a cor-blimey accent, said he had a parcel for Lord Birt, and where should he deliver it? The receptionist helpfully gave the address out as 45 Old Bond Street.

I sent my researcher round. It was a rather exclusive area, as the address suggested. The Gucci shop was two doors along, and there was a Rolls-Royce parked opposite. At the entrance to his office was a large cardboard cut-out of Richard Branson, which might be thought to be partisan for someone advising the government on transport. Birt was also then chairman of Lynx New Media, an organisation in effect managed by Virgin Media Group.

Chapter 10

There cannot be many years when one event has such an enormous impact that everything else pales into insignificance by comparison, but 2003 was one of those. It was the year the US and the UK invaded Iraq, ostensibly to deal with weapons of mass destruction that in fact were not there at all.

The consequences were profound: for the direction of Middle East politics, for the rise of anti-western sentiment, for the political landscape in the UK, for the reputation of Tony Blair, and for the serious damage done to trust in politicians more generally. The invasion set the world on a dangerous course which does not look like being corrected any time soon.

As I write this, we are still, in the summer of 2015, waiting for the publication of the Chilcot Report on the Iraq War, a report commissioned by Gordon Brown back in June 2009, and the only certainty about it is that this book will be published before it finally emerges, if indeed it ever does.

I met Sir John soon after his appointment to make him aware of my interest and to discuss the boundaries he was setting himself and the approach he intended to take to his inquiry. He wanted to convince me that he intended to do a thorough job and revealingly added that perhaps sufficient time had elapsed for this to be possible. It should be even more possible now, by that yardstick.

We also discussed the earlier reports of relevance: the first, by Lord Hutton, ostensibly into the death of David Kelly, and the second, by Sir Robin Butler, into the intelligence available prior to invasion.

In terms of the first, it would be unfair to quote Sir John but suffice it to say I formed the impression that he regarded that work as inadequate, if not amateurish.

He was rather more complimentary about the second, and noted that it had been quite critical, but written in a somewhat Delphic, civil service manner that obscured that criticism. He volunteered that he would ensure his report was not written in that manner, but in unambiguous plain English.

I had met Sir Robin myself as part of my own detailed research into the events leading up to the war with Iraq, including the death of David Kelly. Sir Robin himself recognised that the way he had written his 2004 report had perhaps blunted its message and therefore its impact.

By February 2011, Sir John had concluded his public evidence sessions and announced that it would take 'some months' to complete his work and issue his final report.

On 16 November 2011, he announced that publication would not now occur until the summer of 2012 at the earliest.

On 16 July 2012, he said that the final report would not now appear until the summer of 2013, though it might be later.

In November 2013, he indicated that the inquiry could not proceed to its next stage because key documents had not yet been provided.

I wrote to Sir John in April 2014 to express concerns about the delay and to express the view that I thought it was important that publication was not delayed past the election. I also asked whether the delay centred around the release or otherwise of correspondence between Blair and Bush. He replied within a week, writing that he was 'able to confirm that the sensitive documents under discussion include Notes sent by Mr Blair to President Bush, and records of conversations between the UK Prime Minister and the President of the United States'.

The following month, the *Mail on Sunday* reported that a crucial letter from Blair to Bush had gone missing from the official presidential library. This letter, from July 2002, is said to have been a blank cheque to Bush, offering UK support for whatever he wanted to do.

On 21 January 2015, Sir John informed us that publication would be delayed until after the election in May. It is now thought that it will not appear in 2015 at all.

It is quite shocking that it took six years to set up an inquiry and even more so that a further six years on, there is no end in sight. The inquiry must have access to the papers it needs and, equally, the Maxwellisation process, whereby individuals who are to be criticised have an opportunity to comment, needs to be time-limited. This cannot be allowed to run into the sand. It is far too important for that.

Of course, we already know a great deal of what happened in 2002 and 2003. Military action against Iraq was launched on 19 March 2003 and lasted until 1 May that year, but had been anticipated for many months. Indeed, I had written a column for my local paper entitled 'Why We Should Not Attack Iraq' a year earlier, on 22 March 2002.

I wrote: 'I hope Tony Blair will accept that our foreign policy objectives are not necessarily met by slavishly following whatever lead comes out of Washington. Right now he should be using what little influence he has to do everything possible to stop Bush launching an attack on Iraq.'

We now know he was doing the exact opposite: slavishly following Bush and preparing to attack Iraq.

President Bush publicly said, on 8 July 2002, that he wanted regime change in Iraq. That objective of course is illegal under international law, so those rather more squeamish than Bush wanted to find a legal reason for invasion, hence the concentration on weapons of mass destruction. So the dishonesty that followed, all the dodgy dossiers and the rest, was down to Blair and his team. Bush was persuaded along this path but alone would have been quite happy with a Wild West approach, shooting first and asking questions later.

Exactly a year after, on 8 July 2003, in the wake of the war, Tony Blair was giving evidence to the House of Commons liaison committee and was asked when he had decided to go to war.

He replied: 'I decided that we could not avoid conflict in the few days before the vote on 18 March … Up until that point I was still working to avoid the conflict.'

Trying to avoid a conflict? He had spent months planning it, trying to make it happen. The whole purpose of the dodgy dossiers was to suggest that a serious and imminent threat faced us when no such threat existed.

In Chapters 8 to 10 of my book *The Strange Death of David Kelly*, I produced a detailed record and analysis of the incremental steps taken by Blair and his circle to heat up the ingredients for war, a vile stew of deception and innuendo, so cynical and wickedly immoral that even the spin curdled.

So let me here just highlight some key facts.

A meeting took place in Downing Street on 23 July 2002, just after Bush's public declaration in favour of regime change. At the meeting were Blair; Foreign Secretary Jack Straw; Defence Secretary Geoff Hoon; the Attorney General Lord Goldsmith; the head of MI6 Sir Richard Dearlove; John Scarlett, then chair of the Cabinet Office

Joint Intelligence Committee; and a handful of others including Alastair Campbell.

The minute of that meeting was to appear in the *Sunday Times* on the Sunday before the 2005 general election, which was probably a week too late to have a real impact.

The minute was taken by Matthew Rycroft, then the Prime Minister's private secretary, and now the British ambassador to the UN in New York.

It began: 'This record is extremely sensitive. No further copies should be made', and went on to report on the recent visit to Washington by Sir Richard, or 'C', as the head of MI6 is quaintly known:

> There was a perceptible shift in attitude. Military action was now seen as inevitable. Bush wanted to remove Saddam, through military action, justified by the conjunction of terrorism and WMD. But the intelligence and facts were being fixed around the policy. The NSC [National Security Council] had no patience with the UN route...

Geoff Hoon is recorded as saying: 'The most likely timing in US minds for military action to begin was January with the timeline beginning thirty days before the Congressional elections.'

Jack Straw appeared concerned not to stop an illegal war but to justify it:

> It seemed clear that Bush had made up his mind to take military action, even if the timing was not yet decided. But the case was thin. Saddam was not threatening his neighbours, and his WMD capability was less than that of Libya, North Korea or Iran. We should work up a plan for an ultimatum

for Saddam to allow back in the UN weapons inspectors. That would also help with the legal justification for war.

And so the drumbeats began to pound ever more loudly, spurred on by No. 10. In September 2002, the Blair government published a dossier which alleged, amongst other things, that Iraq was continuing to produce chemical and biological agents, had military plans for their use, and that some were deployable within 'forty-five minutes'.

This 45-minute claim would be blown up as the centrepiece of the government's evidence base for military action, but when you peeled away the surface there was nothing behind it. Sir Richard Dearlove later admitted it had come from but a single source. MI6 quietly withdrew the claim on 17 July 2003, the day David Kelly was found dead. The Butler Review would call it 'unsubstantiated', and criticised the impression given that this was more significant than it was.

The September dossier was a disgraceful document that was not an objective analysis of the position, as it purported to be, but a piece of crude propaganda designed to make the case for war.

Despite it being an intelligence document, Alastair Campbell was heavily involved in its editorial production, and chaired meetings on its progress. He suggested at least sixteen specific textual changes, virtually all strengthening the language. In respect of the 45-minute claim, he asked for 'may be' to be changed to 'are'.

Campbell later told the Hutton Inquiry: 'I had no input, output, influence upon them [the words in the dossier] whatsoever at any stage in the process.'

Robin Cook, in his resignation speech on 17 March, told the House: 'Iraq probably has no weapons of mass destruction in the commonly understood sense of the term.' He was right.

18 March, the date referred to by Blair in his evidence to the select committee, saw the key debate in the House of Commons when MPs had to decide whether or not to authorise military action.

We were warned about Saddam Hussein's weapons of mass destruction, quoted at from dodgy dossiers and asked to trust the Prime Minister. We had come a long way from the anthems of the 1960s. Now it was 'Give War a Chance'.

Most MPs went along with Blair, many against their better judgement, on the basis that no Prime Minister would mislead Parliament about something as grave as going to war, would they?

Blair won that vote by 412–149, that comfortable majority masking a huge revolt of eighty-five Labour MPs. I am proud that for that vote, every single Lib Dem was present, and every single one voted against.

He may have got over that hurdle, but the damage to his reputation, and to the confidence of the public in the political system, was very great.

For Blair, an astute politician, public opinion on this issue seemed to count for nothing. 15 February 2003 had seen a huge demonstration against the launching of a war, with between 750,000 and 2 million walking through central London, depending on whose figure you believe.

I came up with a contingent of Lib Dems from the constituency. Nobody had to be asked. We all knew that we wanted to go.

It was a good occasion, peaceful, even humorous, with plenty of 'Make Tea, Not War' placards. How very British, I thought. It moved Blair not a jot. The course was set, had been set a long time before.

It must be clear now to everyone except the most hardened Blairite that the House of Commons, and the public, was grievously misled over the threat posed by Saddam and his non-existent weapons of mass destruction. More than ten years on, nobody has been properly held to account for that. They need to be.

Tony Blair stood down as Prime Minister in 2007 and was then appointed as peace envoy to the Middle East, which is beyond the satirical skills of even Rory Bremner to deal with. And when he was not fostering peace, with such spectacular lack of success, he was traipsing round the world with a 'for sale' sign around his neck.

On one occasion Blair's actions were so rank that I issued a press line calling them shameless. In parallel, it turned out, Matthew Oakeshott had issued one calling them shameful. We had a brief discussion as to which one of us was right and decided we both were.

It is the blatancy of all this that leaves me standing.

Amongst all the high drama of 2003, one event stood out from the rest: the death of Dr David Kelly, the UK weapons inspector, whose body was found on the morning of 17 July on Harrowdown Hill, not far from his home in Oxfordshire.

I took a year out of the Lib Dem shadow Cabinet to investigate this, which culminated in the publication of my book, *The Strange Death of David Kelly*, in 2007.

Why would I do that? Why would I make that huge commitment? Why would I go against the grain and risk my reputation and my political career? Because the whole thing stank. And because virtually nobody else was doing anything about it.

As with the politics surrounding the decision to go to war with Iraq, I do not propose to replicate the exhaustive detail of my earlier book. But, put simply, I strongly believe, first, that Kelly's death was not properly investigated and, second, that the official explanation is unsustainable and frankly incredible.

Turning to the official investigation, an inquiry was set up under Lord Hutton and this was announced at 3.20 p.m. on the 17th, less than six hours after Dr Kelly's body was found at 9.30 a.m. and while Tony Blair was still in the air between Washington, which he had left at 1 a.m. UK time, and Japan.

The recommendation had come from the Lord Chancellor, Blair's old friend Charlie Falconer, who had consulted the senior law lord, Lord Bingham.

Lord Hutton had only ever chaired one inquiry before, into the diversion of a river in Northern Ireland. He did have other qualities, however, which might have appealed. He had a habit of coming down on the side of the establishment.

In 1973, he represented the Ministry of Defence at the inquests of those killed on Bloody Sunday and ripped into the coroner for 'venturing to suggest that the soldiers in question had no justification for their shooting of people on the streets of Londonderry'.

That was in fact typical of the position he took in many subsequent cases where soldiers or the army generally were involved.

In 1999, he successfully led the campaign to overturn the decision to extradite Augusto Pinochet to Chile.

In 2002, he was one of four law lords who stopped the former MI5 officer David Shayler from using a public interest defence in his trial for contravention of the Official Secrets Act.

I am not suggesting that Lord Hutton was anything other than fair in his own mind. I am, however, suggesting that his record indicates that he was predisposed to come down on the side of the establishment.

The speed with which the inquiry was set up showed that the government can certainly move quickly if it wants to – and it did want to. By setting up an inquiry the same day, the story could be controlled, directed down a particular avenue. That avenue was to be the political context. Alastair Campbell and his colleagues were effectively shouting, 'Hey, over here,' and the media duly turned away from Dr Kelly to follow the path laid out for them by Downing Street.

The circumstances surrounding David Kelly's death, which is what Lord Hutton was asked to look into, turned out to be largely a consideration of the interaction between the BBC and the government. Poor Dr Kelly did not get much of a look in.

I can do no better than quote Lord Hutton himself, writing subsequent to the conclusion of his inquiry in an obscure legal journal called *The Inner Temple Yearbook 2004/5*:

> At the outset of my inquiry … it appeared to me that a substantial number of the basic facts of the train of events which led to the tragic death of Dr Kelly were already apparent from reports in the press and other parts of the media. Therefore I thought that there would be little serious dispute as to the background facts … I thought that unnecessary time could be taken up by cross-examination on matters which were not directly relevant.

The most serious shortcoming, however, was that Lord Hutton's inquiry was a non-statutory one. That meant that the normal rules and safeguards that apply in court proceedings were simply absent here. Nobody could be compelled to attend and nobody was giving evidence under oath. Lord Hutton had sole control over who was or was not called as a witness, what documents were produced and, to a large extent, what questions were asked, or indeed not asked. And unlike in an inquest, where a verdict has to be 'beyond reasonable doubt', no such hurdle applied to Lord Hutton.

When I raised all this with Lord Hutton, he told me:

> I was not surprised to be asked to conduct the inquiry without formal powers. The reason was that it was very apparent from the outset that I would have to investigate very closely the actions of the government and the actions of the BBC

[and] thought it very unlikely that any witness from the government or the BBC or from any other organisation or body would decline to do so.

But Lord Hutton's inquiry replaced an inquest. The Oxfordshire coroner began to undertake an inquest, but was stopped from proceeding by written instruction from the Lord Chancellor, Charlie Falconer. The coroner wrote back to object: 'As you will know, a Coroner has power to compel the attendance of witnesses. There are no such powers attached to a public inquiry.'

It is standard practice in this country for any unexplained death to be subject to a proper inquest. Here was an unexplained death, a very high-profile one – even, in the context in which it occurred, a sensational one. Yet it alone was not to have an inquest, merely be handled by an informal inquiry without any of the normal rules and safeguards, and one where the man in charge wanted to concentrate on the government and the BBC and saw Dr Kelly's death in itself as a side issue, and thought 'unnecessary time could be taken up with cross-examination'.

This is a disgrace. How can established procedures just be swept aside in this way? Are our freedoms and protections in this country really so brittle? Twelve years on, still no inquest has taken place.

In the first instance, the issue is not what people think happened to David Kelly. The issue is that there is a well-established procedure for dealing with unexplained deaths and it has not been followed.

The man was entitled to an inquest. That – or, exceptionally, a statutory inquiry – is ultimately how the cause of death is established. Are we now going to tolerate situations in this country where someone somewhere can simply decide not to bother? Is nobody really concerned that an independent coroner has been bundled off a case by a politician?

So we have, uniquely, a case where an unexplained death is not dealt with by a statutory procedure, and where the man in charge of the informal alternative does not think it worth spending much time looking into it.

That would be bad enough if the case was an open-and-shut one, where all the key people have spoken, where all the evidence has been produced, where the explanation for the cause of death is unambiguous. None of that applies in this case.

It was suggested that Dr Kelly killed himself by using a knife to cut the ulnar artery in his wrist, coupled with an overdose of coproxamol.

Let me give you just a flavour, by no means exhaustive, of some of the many aspects that have not been resolved.

- Key witnesses were not called to give evidence at the Hutton Inquiry, including the police officer in charge of the investigation, Superintendent Alan Young, and Dr Kelly's close confidante Mai Pederson, with whom David Kelly shared three postal addresses.
- A number of expert doctors maintained it was impossible for Dr Kelly to have died in the way that Lord Hutton accepted, namely from blood loss due to a severing of the tiny ulnar artery in the wrist. Indeed, only one person in the country died from such a cause in 2003.
- The knife allegedly used to cut the artery bore no fingerprints and Dr Kelly was not wearing gloves.
- The evidence of empty blister packs at the scene of death suggested Dr Kelly had consumed twenty-nine coproxamol tablets, but only the equivalent of a fifth of a tablet was found in his stomach.
- Mai Pederson maintains that Dr Kelly had an aversion to swallowing tablets. She also said that shortly before his death he

had damaged the elbow of the arm he would have had to use to make the incision in his wrist.

- The paramedics who arrived at the scene said there was 'no obvious arterial bleeding' and no immediately visible wound. One of them, Vanessa Hunt, would tell *The Observer*: 'It is incredibly unlikely that he died from the wrist wound we saw.'

- The pathologist Nicholas Hunt testified that *livor mortis* was a clear *post mortem* feature, but that can only occur if the body retains a large quantity of blood.

- The closed police file on the incident, Operation Mason, was set up at 2.30 p.m. on 17 July, hours before Dr Kelly was reported missing.

- There were conflicting accounts of the position in which the body was found.

- There were multiple reports that he had left the house coatless, but was found at the scene wearing a Barbour jacket.

- The information given to Hutton regarding the flight path of helicopters sent to look for Dr Kelly was incorrect and it transpired that a helicopter with heat-seeking equipment had flown directly over where his body was found without it showing up.

- A death certificate was issued giving the alleged causes of death before the Hutton Inquiry, ostensibly established to look into the cause of death, had even started.

- Dr Kelly sent a friend an email on his last morning alive, telling her there were 'many dark actors playing games'.

- His dental records went missing the day after his death from a locked cabinet, were reported as such to the police, then reappeared in their proper place on the Sunday following.

This is just a smattering of the matters that have never been resolved. There is a great deal more that does not add up or has not been explained. It is perhaps typified by the answer given by the pathologist Nicholas Hunt, when asked by Lord Hutton if there were any signs of a third-party involvement in Dr Kelly's death. His reply was intriguing: 'The features are quite typical, I would say, of self-inflicted injury, if one ignores all the other features of the case.'

What did that mean? Lord Hutton does not ask and we do not find out. But the pathologist told Channel 4 in 2004 that he thought the abandoned inquest ought to be reconvened.

A coroner's court requires a verdict of suicide to be 'beyond reasonable doubt' before being returned. I challenge anyone to say that threshold has to date been met in this case.

In my book, I set out the evidence I had accrued, the unanswered questions and a possible explanation of what had happened. I was careful to distinguish between that which I had established as fact and that on which I was speculating. That nuance seemed to pass many of my detractors by.

The coverage that preceded the release of my book, and then the book itself, generated the biggest mailbag I have ever received, running into thousands of letters and emails, dwarfing even the volume I was to receive over my campaigning on MPs' expenses.

The response from the public was 99 per cent supportive. It included twenty or thirty contacts with specific extra and relevant information, some of which made it into the book, some of which came too late. They included serving police officers, civil servants and senior management at the BBC.

I had undertaken this project because I thought it was important and it was glaringly obvious that those who should have been investigating this properly had not done so.

Sad to say, I include in that category most of the media, with the notable exception of the Mail group and a few disparate journalists here and there on other papers. Quite a few MPs, too, including one former Tory Party leader, offered quiet support, but very few wanted to put their heads above the parapet.

I have observed that most people want to play safe, even where it is their job, in my view, as with journalists, expressly to do otherwise. They want to operate in the safe segment of the circle with everyone else, rather than open themselves to criticism or possible ridicule.

The consequence is that difficult issues are ignored. We are told that there were rumours flying around for years about Jimmy Savile. Hundreds of people must have known something, including journalists. Why did this story take so long to emerge? Was it because he was a household name and it was too risky for someone's personal reputation to open this can of worms in case they were shot down?

In the 1980s, there was knowledge in the US of Iran–Contra some time before it blew open, but the American press only ran with it after an article had appeared in a paper in the Middle East.

It is certainly easy enough to attack someone who dares challenge the collectively accepted truth rather than face the fact that that truth may be a lie. So the response from some quarters to the questions I have raised has been to ignore the awkward evidence and instead portray me as some sort of fantasist.

It was particularly wry to see David Aaronovitch, almost the last of the Blairites, write a scathing review of my book before it was even published. Perhaps a similar one will appear before this one is published as well.

Yet his own grasp of the events of 2003 was far from secure. He insisted that there were weapons of mass destruction in Iraq and that 'if nothing is eventually found, I, as a supporter of the war, will never believe another thing that I am told by our government, or that of the US, ever again'. One might have thought, therefore, that a bit more humility might have been in order.

The favourite term of abuse, of course, has been 'conspiracy theorist', a person who by definition must be wrong. It is a term that can be thrown without any knowledge of the subject at hand.

Jack Straw, for instance, told the House of Commons that any suggestions of UK involvement in extraordinary rendition were 'conspiracy theories' and should be disbelieved unless MPs thought he was lying. But in February 2008, the Foreign Secretary David Miliband told the House that the British territory of Diego Garcia had indeed been used for that purpose.

No doubt Galileo would have been called a conspiracy theorist if the term had existed in sixteenth-century Italy. Instead his theory that the earth revolved round the sun led to him being found 'vehemently suspect of heresy' and he was forced to recant.

To me, it is extraordinary that at a time when trust in politicians is at an all-time low, people – including journalists, who ought to know better – take as gospel what they are told on some subjects and ignore any evidence to the contrary.

I believe there is a strong case for the Attorney General to ask the High Court to reopen the inquest into David Kelly's death. Section 13 of the Coroners Act 1988 suggests this should occur where there has been 'irregularity of proceedings', 'insufficiency of inquiry' and 'discovery of new facts or evidence'.

I contend that all three tests are met in this case.

Chapter 11

On 12 July 2000, I sent in a request to MI5 under the Data Protection Act 1998 to ask what information they held on me. I was seeking to establish the principle that the blanket ban on the release of information was wrong, and that requests under the Act should be judged on their merits, even by MI5.

Shortly thereafter, two developments occurred. The first was on 22 July, when the Home Secretary Jack Straw issued a certificate under the Data Protection Act preventing any data from being released. This was the first such certificate under the Act.

The second was two days later, when I received an anonymous letter from someone who signed themselves 'The Mechanic', alleging that a file on me did indeed exist.

The letter included the following:

> I am writing to you as a serving MI5 officer.
>
> You may be interested to know that your recent request to the DG of the security service for data that it holds on you has caused a crisis amongst our managers. This is because there is information on your activities in the late 1980s. Not only would it be madness to admit that you have a file but the nature of the file and the reason for its creation would create a political issue that they could not contain.

So far, so lurid, but it then went on to make specific connections to my environmental and animal welfare activities, saying details had been forwarded to the security service by Special Branch officers in East Sussex in 1988.

The letter also suggested that with the reduction in other threats to the security of the country, attention within MI5 had been redirected towards the environmental movement, with the implication that this was more of a job protection scheme rather than because a real threat to security existed.

It added that a decision had been taken in mid-1989 not to monitor me further when I secured a job in the Lib Dem Whips' Office, as 'this was regarded as off-limits'.

The letter ended with this paragraph: 'If you do keep a copy of this letter then I would appreciate that you made a copy and destroyed the original: there are no limits to the lengths management will go to expose leaks.'

I did destroy the original and keep a copy as requested. I did not know whether the letter was genuine but the timing of it, immediately after the issuing of the certificate and before I actually received a formal reply from MI5, which was issued on 11 August, coupled with the detail provided, made me think it probably was.

I recalled that back in 1988, my partner had received a rather odd phone call at home in Beddingham when I was out. The caller purported to be from a named local paper, which, when subsequently checked, did not actually exist. He told my partner that he was a reporter collecting some background material on councillors and proceeded to ask a number of questions about my past which my partner answered and then rather felt she should not have done.

Naturally, the 11 August reply revealed nothing – MI5 would neither confirm nor deny they held any information – so, backed by Liberty, I decided to pursue the case. A special tribunal had to be set up, and the case was set down to be heard in the law courts in the Strand.

The missive from 'The Mechanic' may or may not have influenced those sitting in judgment. Be that as it may, we won the case, in that the tribunal quashed the ministerial certificate and ruled that a blanket refusal to consider each case on its merits was not justified, and that therefore MI5 should consider what information they could release about me, assuming some was held.

The timing of my request for access to information held about me coincided with general interest in files held by MI5 on politicians. This was given a particular spur by the renegade MI5 officer David Shayler, who told the world that files existed on both the Home Secretary, Jack Straw, from his time in the 1970s as president of the National Union of Students, when he was labelled a 'political subversive', and on Peter Mandelson, who had, difficult though it is to believe, been a Young Communist League activist.

By that point, the security service had largely abandoned its interest in such counter-subversion, with just half a person dedicated to the once substantial F branch, but there was a live issue as to what to do with the estimated 200,000 files that existed on allegedly subversive groups and individuals.

I took the view that the files should be kept or opened up, at least to the subjects of the files, rather than destroyed. Unfortunately, if predictably, the period before the passage of the Freedom of Information Act seems ironically to have speeded up the destruction process.

A couple of days after David Shayler broke cover, when it was unclear exactly what he was going to say, I went to Kensington to the offices of the *Mail on Sunday* to meet the journalist who was covering the story. As I came out of the building, itself situated down a quiet stump of a cul-de-sac, I noticed a man standing somewhat conspicuously in a doorway. I saw out of the corner of my eye that he moved off shortly after I did.

I turned the corner into Kensington High Street and stopped at a shop window. He stopped about ten yards behind me. I then went into the Tube station and quickly put myself out of sight close to the entrance. Sure enough, the man also entered the Tube station then stopped and frantically looked round, presumably because he had lost me. He then positioned himself at the top of the stairs to the platforms, looking out towards the street. I approached him and said hello. He looked crestfallen and dashed down to the Edgware Road platform. I took to the other, facing platform, to head back to Westminster. Both platforms were nearly empty, but he was nowhere to be seen.

I then telephoned my contact at the paper, but after about ten seconds, when I had begun to relay what had happened, the phone went dead. I later learnt that there had been a system fault in the newspaper's phone system which lasted about ten minutes.

I presumed this rather farcical cloak-and-dagger stuff, all so amateurish, was deliberately visible for my benefit.

About this time, I paid my first trip to the organisation to meet the then Director General, Stephen Lander. I had in my early years as an MP been asking a significant number of parliamentary questions about MI5, and one day I was approached by a Commons lobby journalist working for a tabloid paper, asking if I would like to meet the DG. A more unlikely connection with MI5 than this journalist I could not imagine. The journalist in question still works in the lobby.

I accepted, of course, and duly turned up at the appointed hour and day. I entered the imposing if somewhat anonymous building in Millbank and reported to the desk. Beyond the front door was a cavernous space, barren of people, furniture, decorations – everything, in fact. The only exception was a discreet plaque on the wall, commemorating the opening of the building by Margaret Thatcher. I marvelled at the waste of space in an expensive central London location.

I was accompanied on a relatively long trek upstairs, during which time I saw no one and heard nothing. It was as if I was in an empty building.

The DG's office was reassuringly comfortable, like a small room in a London club in Pall Mall, and the DG himself was very friendly. The same, however, could not be said for the two stony-faced officials from the Home Office who clearly thought I should not be there, and sat silent throughout the meeting. The initiative to meet had come from the DG, but the Home Secretary of the day, Jack Straw, had had to agree. It seemed clear he, or at least his officials, had done so reluctantly.

The object of the meeting, it became clear, was to try to dissuade me from asking so many parliamentary questions, though it was not put as crudely as that. However, in that regard it worked. I was able to discuss a wide range of concerns with the DG and came away largely reassured by what he told me. He was in fact rather impressive, or I was rather gullible.

The subject of my legal action did feature in the conversation, and he asked me how I thought this should be dealt with. I said that it should be treated on its merits, just like any other request, and the fact that the case had been initiated by an MP should not influence matters.

I felt that this was the correct thing to say, but in one sense I immediately regretted it when he said 'fair enough' or words to that effect and moved the conversation on. I realised at that point that the portcullis had been brought down, and so it proved.

173

After the tribunal had ruled in my favour, establishing the point of principle that each request for information should under data protection rules be considered on its merits, I received a letter from MI5 conceding that they did indeed hold some information on me, and enclosing copies of what they were prepared to release. I duly received copies of the letters I had written to them requesting the release of information, and copies of their replies to me refusing to do so. In other words, they provided me with that which I already had. It was a wonderfully British civil service answer: comply with a legal ruling but do so in a way that reveals nothing new. I had to laugh.

Another avenue I pursued did not even generate a pyrrhic victory. It related to the operation of what was known as the Wilson Doctrine, named after the Prime Minister who established it. This had been articulated to Tufton Beamish, my predecessor bar one as MP for Lewes, in the House on 17 November 1966.

In response to a question, Harold Wilson said, 'There is no tapping of the telephones of Hon. Members, nor has there been any since this government came into office.'

He went on to clarify, in response to a question from Tom Driberg, that he had given an instruction that there was to be no tapping of MPs' phones, 'but if there was any development of any kind which required a change in the general policy, I would, at such moment as seemed compatible with the security of the country, on my own initiative make a statement in the House about it'.

I had clarified through a written parliamentary question in December 2001 that the doctrine remained in place under Tony Blair, and that answer was referred to in April 2003 by the Labour MP Andrew MacKinlay. He challenged Blair that it was clear that two MPs at least had had their phones tapped: Mo Mowlam and Martin McGuinness. Blair, in the well-worn phrase, refused to confirm or deny the suggestion, merely repeating that the Wilson Doctrine remained in place.

We had not since 1966 been told of any occasion when an MP's phone had been tapped, but it seemed a reasonable assumption that this might well have occurred at some point, in the case of the Sinn Féin MPs, for example.

The wording of the doctrine allowed for the possibility that phones had been or were being tapped, but that no appropriate moment to tell the House had arisen. In other words, it was a robust-sounding statement of principle with a very big escape clause.

In January 2005, I submitted a request to the Cabinet Office under the new Freedom of Information Act, which had gone live that month. I asked whether any MPs had been subject to telephone tapping or other intrusive surveillance since 1966 of which the House had yet to be informed, and if so how many and in what years. I expressly indicated I was not asking for names or details.

This request was met with a rejection, citing the usual 'neither confirm nor deny' formula, so I appealed to the Information Commissioner. By December I had heard nothing bar an apology for the delay, but in that month Tony Blair told the Commons by means of a written statement that he had had advice from the Interception of Communications Commissioner, Sir Swinton Thomas, that the Wilson Doctrine should be scrapped, and he was considering that advice.

On 30 March, Blair issued another written statement, announcing that he intended to maintain the Wilson Doctrine despite the advice he had received.

In the meantime, the Information Commissioner's office had been helpful, as they generally were, in pushing the Cabinet Office, both to justify their original refusal and to explain their position more fully. A letter to me from the Cabinet Office duly followed on 5 May 2006.

It contained the following: 'If the Cabinet Office were to con-firm or deny holding the information which you have requested, a clear implication would be that either there had been a change in policy (if confirmed) or that there had not (if denied) thereby defeating the purpose of the exemption.'

The Information Commissioner backed the Cabinet Office in his formal decision, saying that to confirm that an MP, even an unspecified one, had been tapped would undermine the purpose of interception by alerting those involved to the risk, whereas to deny would be of assistance to anyone of interest to the security services.

I could see the logic but did not see why at the very least some generalised information relating to a period up to, say, 2001 could not be provided. After all, Harold Wilson in 1966 had gone so far as to say that no MPs had been tapped under his government, a current statement rather than the semi-historical one I would have settled for.

Moreover, back in 2001, Alastair Campbell had expressly denied that the Labour life peer Lord Ahmed's phone had been tapped. When I raised this with Blair at the time, he replied that 'it remains the normal policy' not to confirm or deny, normal being the extra word added.

I took the matter to appeal via the information tribunal, where the Treasury Solicitor's Office submitted a long justification for their position, including the novel argument that to release the infor-mation might be an offence under the Regulation of Investigatory Powers Act, an Act the Labour government itself had generated. My appeal was lost.

Subsequent to that, in 2008, an incident occurred that involved the bugging by counter-terrorism officers on two separate occasions of conversations between the Labour MP Sadiq Khan and a constit-uent, Babar Ahmed, whom he was visiting in Woodhill Prison in

Milton Keynes. The *Sunday Times*, which ran the story, said it had documents showing that the officers knew that Sadiq Khan, then a government whip, was an MP, but went ahead anyway.

Gordon Brown, by then Prime Minister, subtly altered the Wilson Doctrine to say it only applied to decisions taken by ministers to issue warrants, not to the police.

The Home Secretary at the time, Jacqui Smith, confirmed to the Commons that the bugging had occurred but said the Wilson Doctrine was 'not relevant' in this case.

In 2014, Justice Secretary Chris Grayling admitted to the Commons that confidential conversations between jailed constituents and their MPs had been taped and listened to by prison staff, and calls between prisoners and their lawyers could also have been 'accidentally' recorded.

Chapter 12

It was another Freedom of Information request that I submitted in the same month, January 2005, the first month of operation for the Act, that was to have rather more explosive consequences. I asked for details of MPs' expenses as they related to travel costs.

A common thread to my parliamentary activities was to challenge the cosy Westminster and Whitehall world, the abuse of privilege, the pomposity of power and the feathering of nests at taxpayer expense. I do not know why I was so attracted to this area of activity. Perhaps it was a throwback to my early, somewhat puritanical, Church of Scotland upbringing in Aberdeen.

I also felt strongly that I should not waste the opportunity I had been given, and should not hold back from making waves where there was an important issue at stake. The way I saw it, there had been countless Liberals up and down the years who had flown the flag for the party with as much chance of success as the man who stood in front of the tank in Tiananmen Square in the 1989 Beijing protests. I had to act for them too.

Be that as it may, my lines of enquiry were as popular with the press as they were unpopular with MPs. But I followed them because I thought it was the right thing to do.

For instance, I thought it hypocritical of John Prescott to champion green travel when he was driving around in a 4.2-litre government

Jaguar, not content with having one of his own, and I challenged him about this in the Commons, to the delight, it turned out, of the *Daily Mail*. Two Jags was born.

It was also hypocritical when, in the summer of 1998, John Prescott's department published a Transport White Paper which, amongst other initiatives, called for workplace charging for motorists, while at the same time MPs were allocated 521 free car parking spaces at the Commons. The value of this car parking was demonstrated by the charges at the public car park immediately opposite in Abingdon Street, which at the time were £4.50 for two hours and £19.50 for twelve hours. The costs are naturally considerably higher now. I calculated that if 400 spaces in the Commons car park were filled on a sitting day, that equated to an annual subsidy of £1.56 million.

Initiatives like this, and especially my campaigning from 2005 onwards on MPs' expenses, did not make me popular with my fellow MPs, or indeed some establishment journalists, but I accepted that that was part of the price to be paid.

Some commentators suggested I lacked self-awareness. On the contrary, I was only too aware of what I was doing, and of the disapproval, hostility even, that such campaigning generated amongst other MPs. I did not enjoy that, even wished it were otherwise, but that was not a reason to desist.

Of course, it was difficult for them to directly challenge the validity of the issues I was pursuing without looking self-serving, so people would criticise what I looked like, what I was wearing, how I spoke, how many questions I asked, the fact that I belonged to a minor party. They went for the player rather than the ball.

I did not help myself, I suppose, as I did not really make any efforts to be clubbable, and while there were MPs of all parties I enjoyed talking to, or sharing a coffee with, I could not be bothered to cultivate people I did not particularly want to spend time with merely because they might be useful to me.

When my day at Westminster was done, I wanted to escape the bubble and return to the real world outside. I could not understand, for example, the attraction of living cheek by jowl with other MPs in Dolphin Square and so, soon after becoming an MP, I found a flat in the West End. It was a rather seedy one-bedroom affair on the top floor of a building in Bateman Street, the sort where you would half-expect to find the word MODEL on a card pinned to the street entrance, as was common in that area. Had the word been at the entrance to this building, it would definitely not have been referring to the condition of the flat.

But it was in the heart of the West End, with cafés, cinemas, restaurants and music venues all within a stone's throw, and a welcome contrast to life in the bubble. I must have aged a bit while I was there, for initially it was quite common to be stopped and asked if I wanted to meet one of these aforementioned models. Later, I would get stopped and asked if I wanted a taxi.

In terms of pricking pomposity, the Lord Chancellor Derry Irvine presented a very attractive target. He was planning to spend £650,000 of public money on tarting up his Palace of Westminster apartment.

This included £60,000 for 200 rolls of wallpaper, £21,000 for carpets, £56,000 for brass light fittings and £8,500 for a handmade bed.

I commented at the time: 'This must be the first government to be involved with a scandal about a bed with no sex involved.'

It also transpired that the company supplying curtains and other fine silk upholstery had been required to sign the Official Secrets Act, at the same time as Freedom of Information legislation was being progressed.

Yet Derry Irvine's expenditure was dwarfed by what Tony Blair spent on Downing Street's refurbishment in 1999. That bill came to £971,000, not including the £50,000 he spent on improving the tennis courts at Chequers.

Even that, however, looked modest when compared to the £50 million spent on Parliament's estate the same year. It included an unbelievable £2.44 million to renovate the House of Lords car park, and the £422,000 spent on a short stretch of covered walkway in Star Chamber Court.

I never ceased to be amazed at the size of the bills that came in for works to the House. When the new Portcullis House was opened, we learnt that the twelve fig trees that adorned the atrium had been leased for five years at a cost of £150,000. They could probably have bought the same number of trees at a good garden centre for a fraction of the cost.

The problem was that the most competent MPs became ministers or shadow ministers, or chaired select committees and the like, leaving others to staff the committees that looked after the House, with money being no object. It might also help to explain why the flagship building logged more than 7,500 defects in its first year of operation.

The MPs' expenses saga began, then, in January 2005 with a request from me to the House authorities for details of MPs' travel expenses, broken down by mode. My primary motivation was actually an environmental one: I wanted to discover who was using the train, the plane and the car to get to London, and the subsequent cost to the taxpayer. I was also conscious, even at that stage, that misuse of allowances was occurring. For instance, I had been told that some Labour MPs from Scotland drove down to London together but each claimed separate mileage for the trip.

The Members' Estimate Committee considered my application

for information and rejected it. As required by the Act, I then asked for an internal review, which confirmed the original refusal.

I then wrote in April to the Information Commissioner, Richard Thomas, to appeal the decision, and received a holding reply in September. He overturned in my favour the decision of the Commons committee in February 2006, and gave the Commons thirty days to comply.

The MPs, however, were having none of this and appealed to the information tribunal, so dragging out the process. They argued that the existing arrangements meant that 'MPs are already subject to a high degree of scrutiny with regard to their expenses'. Except that there was precious little to scrutinise.

I formally asked the House which MPs had taken the decision to appeal and what the cost to the public purse would be as a result, but was told, without a hint of irony, that this was confidential. The following year I discovered that the cost was more than £17,000.

The tribunal ruled in my favour and at the end of January 2007, two years after I had first submitted my request, the House of Commons had run out of road in its attempts to block release of the information. It was given thirty days to appeal on a point of law, but even they stopped short of that. The details were finally released on 13 February.

The figures threw up some interesting comparisons in mileage claims from MPs in the same town or city, and revealed choice of mode of travel, the matter I had originally been keen to expose.

There were some very odd claims, such as that from the Labour MP for Rossendale and Darwen, Janet Anderson, who managed to claim £16,612 for mileage, £319 a week, equivalent to more than 60,000 miles a year.

The release of the figures made me few friends in the House, but quite a few amongst the public. To my astonishment, the *Daily*

Mail ran a full-page article about me by Peter Oborne, entitled 'Is This the Greatest Man in Politics?'

It was a generous piece, though I thought it exaggerated both my attributes and my deficiencies, but then, as H. G. Wells once remarked, a newspaper is a device incapable of distinguishing between a bicycle accident and the end of civilisation.

The Westminster machine was not going to give up without a fight, and my victory galvanised it. The Tory backbencher David Maclean connived with the Labour government to introduce a Freedom of Information (Amendment) Bill, with time and support for this being made available by Jack Straw, then Leader of the House. Jack had of course fought to limit the powers of the Freedom of Information Bill while it was being put together by David Clark at the turn of the century.

The Maclean Bill was breathtaking in its audacity and would have exempted MPs from the Freedom of Information Act entirely. The argument for the Bill was that somehow the details of constituents would be accessible, which of course was rubbish. They were protected by the Data Protection Act 1998, and in any case nothing of the sort had happened since FoI had come into force in 2005 to have raised concerns.

There was also a letter from the Speaker to the effect that if the Bill were passed and MPs exempted, then a voluntary scheme would continue to issue the same information. But if the intention were not to change anything, then why pass the Bill?

The Bill, with help from the Labour government, had got quite a long way through the system under cover of darkness before anyone hostile noticed it. Now it had to come back to the Commons for report stage, having been through committee.

Simon Hughes and I had decided to try to talk the Bill out and, with a handful of helpful Labour and Tory MPs, had tabled amendments accordingly. That, perhaps, had registered with MPs, who made their disapproval clear when we were each on the ballot paper to ask the Prime Minister a question on Wednesday 18 April, two days before the debate was due to take place.

Quentin Letts in the *Daily Mail* described the scene:

> The noise was astonishing. Even though Mr Baker had a microphone nearby his voice was lost in the clamour ... Given the noise Mr Baker was understandably taking it slowly. 'Too long,' yelled Labour voices. There must have been 100 MPs shouting at him, some of them going red in the face ... I suggest it must have been physically frightening for Mr Baker to stand there, separated only by a few feet from so many top-volume voices and so much flying spittle ... So why did Mr Martin [the Speaker] not call 'Order'? Why did he not stop the thugs? Was it not his duty to do so?
>
> A few minutes later Simon Hughes had the floor ... He, too, was heckled beyond any acceptable level. Labour MPs even hissed him. Hissed! He was asking a serious question about pensions ... Again, Mr Speaker let this happen. Worse, he sided actively with the hecklers when he told Mr Hughes (who had been struggling with the interruptions) that his question had gone on too long.

At 9.46 a.m. on Friday 20 April 2007, battle proper began. We had two groups of amendments and at least one had to still be in play by 2.30 if we were going to thwart the Bill.

Simon's contribution lasted just under an hour, and was followed by a short speech from the Labour MP David Winnick, who shared our concerns and so also made helpful interventions when it looked like we might be flagging.

We were not helped, though, by the Deputy Speaker, Sylvia Heal, who seemed to have been told to keep us rigidly within the tramlines of our amendments, with a view therefore to keeping our contributions as short as possible.

I took over at around 10.50, which I knew was a long way from 2.30, the point at which discussion on the Bill would be suspended. I kept going for just over an hour before another opponent of the Bill, the Tory MP Richard Shepherd, gave us a brief respite. Simon responded to the debate on the first group of amendments, and forced two successive votes, the maximum, which we lost 46–6, by which time it was 1.08.

The forty-six who voted to exempt MPs from public scrutiny included Labour ministers brought in specially, including Andy Burnham and Tessa Jowell, as well as the Tory front bench, MPs such as Patrick McLoughlin, and leading backbenchers Tom Watson and Stephen Pound. The list also included MPs whose own expenses would be subject to severe criticism in the future, such as Alan Keen, who, with his wife Ann, also an MP, claimed almost £40,000 on a central London flat although their family home was less than ten miles away.

There was only one more group of amendments between us and the Bill passing through to its next stage, and I rose to move them, conscious I had to drag this out to 2.30. Again I was helped by interventions from Simon Hughes and David Winnick, but by about 2.20, I was struggling to avoid hesitation, repetition and deviation.

The Deputy Speaker, Sir Alan Haselhurst, intervened, to tell me I was 'making the same point over and over again – it may have different clothing but it is essentially the same point ... to produce 100 or 200 examples of the same thing is not necessarily to advance it [the argument]'.

I was grateful for the thinking time this stricture gave me, allowing

'Buttering-up' voters claim

OLYMPIC STAR DAVID TURNS COACH

ABOVE: I thought my first front page might be my last

RIGHT: A 1991 vox pop in one of my local papers, undertaken shortly after I became council leader

BELOW: Paddy Ashdown joins me at Newhaven Port prior to the 1997 general election, where the future of the ferry was a major concern

WHO IS THIS MAN?

A cabinet minister? A comedian? A singer/song writer? We went on the streets of Lewes to see if people could identify him. He is actually Norman Baker, leader of Lewes District Council and Liberal Democrat candidate for the Lewes parliamentary constituency, currently held by Conservative Tim Rathbone.)

■ Graham Barnett from Laughton: He's a good looking chap and I know his face. Is he an accountant or a solicitor?

■ Wendy Gray of Lewes: I haven't a clue who he is. Has he something to do with transport...the Minister of Transport perhaps?

■ Miles Tucker from Lewes: He is Minister of Education. No, I'm not sure.

■ Lilian Knight from Lewes: He's MP for Lewes. Or is he a comedian?

■ John Whitcombe from Lewes: He's our local MP isn't he? Or is he a solicitor?

LEFT: Pictured at one of the distinctive fingerposts to be found in my constituency and across Sussex

POP GO THE POLITICIANS AS LIB DEM DUO RIP IT UP

ROCK AND POLL

MPs get in tune with the people

EXCLUSIVE

RUNNER-RIG: Donnie's on

EX-PUNK: Tory Stuart

ABOVE: The *News of the World*'s take on a gig by my band, The Reform Club

LEFT: With Charles Kennedy in Lewes for the 2001 general election

ABOVE: The rather wonderful Roy Martin amusing a constituent in Polegate

RIGHT: Cartoonist Andy Davey accurately captures the response of the Lib Dem leadership to my parliamentary question that forced Peter Mandelson to resign for a second time

BELOW: Promoting animal welfare produces some odd bedfellows: Jilly Cooper, Ann Widdecombe and a badger

...THE DISGRACEFUL AND SHAMELESS CONDUCT OF THE SECRETARY OF STATE FOR NORTHERN IRELAND AND WHAT IS MORE... **

I DON'T KNOW HIM →

Sport MANDELSON FOR HIGH JUMP Fabulous Baker Boy in pursuit

MANdy must diE

** continued ad nauseam

© daveycartoons@gmail.com

LEFT: As shadow Environment Secretary, trying to persuade Tony Blair and Gordon Brown to be rather greener than they were

BOTTOM LEFT: Outside my constituency office in Lewes, taking advantage of a rare fall of heavy snow

BOTTOM RIGHT: With Shirley Williams on the campaign trail in the constituency

Is this the greatest man in politics?

by Peter Oborne

DOUBTLESS there are innocent explanations in certain cases. But after this week's publication of the deeply embarrassing details about the MPs' expenses claims, it looks very much as if there is organised theft and corruption going on at Westminster.

Needless to say the House of Commons — led by the wretched Speaker Martin — fought a long campaign to keep these details secret. Expensive lawyers were hired — again at public expense — to make the case against publication.

The rearguard battle would have succeeded but for one man, Norman Baker, the Liberal Democrat MP for Lewes. He plugged away for two years for his colleagues' expenses to be made public, and eventually he won.

This morning Baker is the most unpopular man in the Commons. When MPs reassemble after their mid-term break next week, he will get the same treatment as a prison nark. And yet it is worth pondering the real reason why Baker is so unpopular. It is because he is a deeply honest man of utter integrity who is determined that British voters should know the truth about how we are governed.

Baker is neither flashy, smooth nor glamorous. He does not sit on the Front Benches. But he is, in his own way, the most admirable and heroic MP at Westminster.

In a decent world, all of Britain's 650 MPs would be like the indefatigable and incorruptible Norman Baker. Shamefully, there is only one of him.

THIS week marked only the latest of Baker's many victories over Britain's self-serving political establishment. His greatest achievement was forcing Peter Mandelson to admit to his links to the Indian tycoon Srichand Hinduja, a

From the Mandelson scandal to MPs' expenses, Norman Baker's ferreted out more shady secrets about our rulers than anyone...

that Baker was a loner. Yes, he may be on the plain side, visually. Yes, he may be an annoying, unclubbable — scruffy even — monk.

But Parliament needs such people. Baker's chosen seat on the Commons benches is right at the end of the Chamber, just below the sword-wearing Serjeant at Arms, away from the seats occupied by his party leadership.

When the Speaker calls his name he stands almost at a stoop, for there is little that is flamboyant or confident in his demeanour. His out-of-date trousers, which do not always match his jacket, flap around his shins.

He is sometimes to be found wearing sports jackets or yellow ties or suede shoes — the wardrobe of a prep school Classics master rather than a Blair-era politician. He never matches the Labour and Tory thrusters for their sleekness and shine.

Yet ministers have learned to listen closely to him. They have learned to beware giving him a loose answer. They have grown to respect, if not exactly to admire, the economy of his queries, the brevity of his often deadly interventions, and his remarkable persistence.

All this may, to the stranger, sound insignificant. But to stand outside the pack in politics takes guts. Baker persists with his campaigns despite often rancorous opposition.

SOMETIMES he will be heckled by Labour MPs sitting just 5ft or so in front of him — he stands just in front of Labour's 'awkward squad' bench — yet Baker sticks to his principles and to his arguments and keeps pinging in his Parliamentary written questions, demanding factual replies from a civil service machine which remains, despite Labour's worst efforts, the servant of the people.

Now he has won this victory over MPs, Baker's latest campaign concerns the death of government scientist Dr David Kelly at the height of the row between the present administration and the BBC in the summer of 2003.

Baker's forensic mind has already picked apart much of the evidence

ABOVE: I woke up to discover this in the *Daily Mail* one day

LEFT: Meeting the Dalai Lama in my capacity as President of the Tibet Society

RIGHT: With the mayor and mayoress of Lewes, John and Becca Stockdale, before I take to the footplate of a steam special leaving Lewes for Salisbury

MP hits high note

Lewes MP Norman Baker was out-selling Eric Clapton this week with the release of his debut album.

Always Tomorrow was officially launched at Octave on Monday – and the specialist music outlet had nearly sold out 48 hours later.

Proprietor Andy How said: "It has gone remarkably well – definitely our most popular item."

Mr Baker and his band The Reform Club performed their single from the album in Lewes High Street and secured widespread television exposure.

Piccadilly Circus achieved more than 10,000 hits on YouTube in the space of six days.

■ See page 5.

ABOVE: The release of my band's first album was enthusiastically received locally

RIGHT: The local brew, Harvey's Best, is so popular even the horses thirst after it

BELOW: Lewes is full of interesting types, here pictured at the ruins of Lewes Priory

Norman Baker: I resign – and it's Theresa May's fault

Liberal Democrat minister drives a stake through the Coalition with brutal attack on Home Secretary in resignation letter

EXCLUSIVE
NIGEL MORRIS
DEPUTY POLITICAL
EDITOR

A senior Liberal Democrat minister will launch a stinging attack on Theresa May, the Home Secretary, as he announces his resignation from the Government today.

Norman Baker, the crime prevention minister, is stepping down after a year of internal battles within the Home Office with his Conservative boss.

In a scathing verdict on Ms May's leadership, Mr Baker warned that support for "rational evidence-based policy" was in short supply at the top of her department.

The Lib Dem has publicly clashed with Ms May on issues including drugs policy and immigration.

He told *The Independent* yesterday that the experience of working at the Home Office had been like "walking through mud" as he found his plans thwarted by the Home Secretary and her advisers.

"They have looked upon it as a Conservative department in a Conservative government, whereas in my view it's a Coalition department in a Coalition government," he said.

"That mindset has framed things, which means I have had to work very much harder to get things done even where they are what the Home Secretary agrees with and where it has been helpful to the Government and the department.

"There comes a point when you don't want to carry on walking through mud and you want to release yourself from that."

His resignation is further

evidence that relations are rapidly deteriorating within the Coalition ahead of next year's general election.

It follows an acrimonious clash between Mr Baker and senior Conservatives over a three-month delay in publishing a Home Office report on drugs policies abroad. He accused them of holding it up because its findings could be politically embarrassing to the Tories.

In his resignation letter to the party leader Nick Clegg, Mr Baker said: "I regret that in the Home Office, the goodwill to work collegiately to take forward rational evidence-based policy has been in somewhat short supply."

Mr Clegg, who tried to persuade him to change his mind, paid tribute in reply to a "brilliant" minister who has always been "determined to deliver a more liberal agenda for Britain".

Mr Baker, the MP for Lewes, had been an unexpected appointment to the Coalition Government after the election in 2010.

His switch to the Home Office in September 2013, with instructions from Mr Clegg to raise the Lib Dems' profile in the department, caused even greater surprise. Yesterday he said he was proud of his part in tackling female genital mutilation, promoting alternatives to animal experiments, bringing in a new approach to combating anti-social behaviour and championing an "evidence-based" approach to drugs policy.

But he said Ms May had found it "hard to accept" that he had been given the role by Mr Clegg of ranging across Home Office policies. "To

Norman Baker says evidence-based policy is in short supply in Theresa May's department

Continued on P.5 →

MAY & BAKER, Ltd.,
BATTERSEA,
LONDON, S.W. 11.

Manufacturers since 1834 of Pharmaceutical and other Fine Chemicals.

All May & Baker's manufactures are carefully standardised and therefore invariably reliable. Buyers are specially recommended to insist always on having May & Baker's

CHLOROFORM — most carefully prepared for anæsthetic use, and perfectly free from all deleterious decomposition products.

ANÆSTHETIC ETHER — specially suitable for anæsthesia, and leaves no unpleasant odour on volatilisation.

BISMUTH SUBNITRATE — free from all traces of metallic impurities. Very light, and of uniform colour. Has by far the largest sale of any Bismuth salt manufactured in Great Britain.

CALOMEL. — The unpleasant results often attending the administration of Calomel are stated to be due to the presence of traces of Corrosive Sublimate. May & Baker's product is free from this impurity, and is generally acknowledged to be of a uniform high standard of quality.

STAND No. A. 35.

MAY & BAKER'S British-made **ARSENOBILLON** ("606"), **NOVARSENOBILLON** ("914") and **SILVER ARSENOBILLON** preparations are the most reliable of SALVARSAN preparations.

May and Baker – A Tale of Drugs and Crime at Bonfire Time

In olden days did May & Baker
help the needy sick to take a
draught to treat that desperate fear:
Bismuth Salt for diarrhoea!

Chloroform & Anaesthetic,
Calomel (a diuretic),
drugs for all by M & B,
made in perfect harmony.

But now - a sorry tale to tell-
'twixt M & B all is not well.
Drugs became the source of friction
as Baker tried to cure addiction.

While all the time Theresa May
was locking troubled folk away.
But Baker said "the Portuguese
have come across this triffic wheeze:

Prison sentences are found
to cycle users round and round".
Baker said "by doing time
they learn about a life of crime."

With splutt'ring May now turning red
our Norman raised his voice and said
"Addiction can be cured the best
by going through the NHS (t)*

* *the t is silent as in cup.*

He said "the scientific proof
is irrefutable, you goof."
"We don't want reason here" said May
"We'd rather throw the keys away"

"What Nonsense" Norman B replied
"You have to see the other side.
The way to rid men of this vice
is through Restorative Justice."

In Whitehall May ranked over Norm
and sticking to her previous form
she wouldn't budge, so Norman B
waved his farewell to Ministry.

A perfect pair these two are not.
Theresa doesn't know how hot
revenge will be. –The Final Story?
Norm's a match for any Tory.

Moral

The moral of the story's clear
don't give Theresa May your ear
before you go to meet your maker
Get out the vote for Norman Baker.

Presented to Norman Baker at the Liberal Democrats Annual Dinner November 2014 by the members of the Executive Committee of Lewes Constituency Liberal Democrats. May and Baker print from 1908 Cartoon by Adams. Poem, if such it is, by Harvey Linehan and Peter Gardiner.

© Rob Stothard / Stringer / Getty Images

ABOVE: With Nick Clegg on the campaign trail in Newhaven in 2015

LEFT: Representing my old college on *University Challenge*, December 2014

BELOW: The Reform Club 2015, with my 1971 Triumph Herald

me to work out what to say next to fill the remaining minutes. I began with a fulsome apology to the Chair, which ticked by a few more vital seconds. Then I returned to the amendments, but the Deputy Speaker was now intervening again. David Winnick rose to help, and in return was admonished by the Deputy Speaker for asking if I would agree with a sentiment which I had in fact just explained at great length and in great detail. But it wasted a bit more time.

Running on empty, I then began reading out Amendment 14 in full, but did not get very far before the Deputy Speaker interrupted again to tell me that there was no need to do so, that everyone had the amendment in front of them. Effecting a hurt air, I protested that I was merely trying to be helpful to the House. A bit more desperate batting followed, like the last man in trying to get to stumps without losing his wicket, and then Big Ben sounded half past two. We had made it.

Quentin Letts again:

> Mr Baker made two immensely circular, yarny speeches, each
> of them more than an hour. While speaking he paced up and
> down, perhaps to prevent himself getting deep-vein throm-
> bosis. His faintly burred voice kept going, becoming slightly
> dry but never losing its bloody-minded determination. On and
> on he went, as tireless as an Ethiopian runner...

We all thought that we had won, that the rules governing the allocation of slots for Private Members' Bills meant that the Bill was lost, that it had returned to the bottom of the pile, but no, with government help it was scheduled to reappear the following month, allegedly because the six Bills above it in the queue were 'not yet ready'.

The reintroduction forced more into the open the support for the Bill from the Labour and Tory front benches. David Winnick revealed that Labour backbenchers had been sent an email urging them to turn up on the Friday to support the Bill. So Labour MPs were being asked to support a former Tory Chief Whip in undermining their own Freedom of Information legislation.

Under pressure, on Wednesday 16 May, the Speaker said that 'I am here to defend backbenchers, and on Friday everyone will get a voice in this Chamber'.

I read that quote into the record when battle resumed on 18 May. This time, the opponents were better organised and we had tabled numerous new amendments, but so, crucially, were the supporters of the Bill, both in tactics and in numbers.

Those of us opposed to the Bill, predominantly Lib Dems, it has to be said, began by introducing a large number of petitions on myriad subjects, albeit each with very few signatures. Unfortunately, because this tactic had been used many years earlier to talk out a Friday, we were limited to half an hour on these.

Then there followed some ingenious Points of Order, including one from David Heath about an alleged trip hazard arising from a bucket on the floor of the No lobby.

Meanwhile, the Deputy Speaker, Sylvia Heal again, in noting that I would begin proceedings by continuing my long speech from a month before, told me that she expected me to bring my remarks to a conclusion before long. This generated a further Point of Order from the Labour MP Mark Fisher, a long-time supporter of open government, who challenged the Deputy Speaker to identify the Standing Order under which speeches could be time-limited. She could not.

I finally got under way at 10.06, with thirty-six minutes having been whiled away. This time I was helped by interventions from those both for and against the Bill. But at 10.25 David Maclean stood up to propose a vote to bring discussions on this group of amendments to an end, and despite a large number of MPs wishing to exercise their right to contribute, and the Speaker's words of only two days earlier, the Deputy Speaker immediately accepted the call, and a vote was held.

The supporters were out in force, and won the vote 113–27. Amongst those supporting it were numerous Labour and Tory frontbenchers, as well as Janet Anderson, who I imagine had driven down for the occasion as part of her annual 60,000 miles, Elliot Morley, who would subsequently be jailed for expenses fraud, and Jacqui Smith, who was to claim that the single room she rented in her sister's London house was her main home, rather than the West Midlands home she shared with her husband and against which she had by 2009 claimed £116,000 in second-home allowance. She also employed her husband as a 'parliamentary adviser' on a salary of £40,000 a year.

Not a single Lib Dem joined this unsavoury lot in the voting lobby, I am proud to say.

We then had a debate on a further group of amendments, when again, after just an hour, David Maclean moved that a vote be taken, despite the fact that no Labour MP had been called, and in apparent contradiction of the Speaker's assurances just two days earlier. The Deputy Speaker readily agreed again. This time we lost 100–33. Sylvia Heal also limited the number of divisions to just two, so amendments not discussed could not even be voted on, and cut short MPs, including me, who tried to raise Points of Order. It was, in the description spat out by Mark Fisher, 'outrageous'. The final vote, for third reading, was 96–25.

The response from the press and the public to these blatant shenanigans was overwhelmingly negative, so much so that David Maclean could not find a single member of the House of Lords to sponsor his odious Bill for its next stage, or indeed to touch it with a bargepole. The Bill was dead, but the Commons had been exposed as self-serving and hypocritical in the process. It was to be a prelude to something much worse.

Stories continued to drip-feed through, like the 2008 reports of the Tory MP Derek Conway allegedly employing on the public payroll his son Freddie, who was a full-time student in Newcastle. A further accusation would follow about another son, Henry.

But 2009 would be the year MPs' expenses really hit the headlines. Once again MPs were fighting a rearguard action to stop details of their expenses being revealed, and once again with the support of the Labour government. A committee chaired by the Speaker, Michael Martin, had argued that it would be 'excessively burdensome' for MPs to have to supply receipts for purchases made, an argument shamefully accepted by Harriet Harman, who announced that the government was pulling the plug on the imminent publication of a huge number of receipts.

But the *Daily Telegraph* was leaked full details of the expenses of every MP, and sensational reading it made too. There was the duck house, the moat to be cleared, and, in David Cameron's case, the removal of wisteria from a chimney, a claim he subsequently repaid.

I urged the House authorities on day one of the *Telegraph* coverage to publish everything immediately, but they still held out, allowing the paper to control the issue and drag it out over a period of six weeks.

While some of the claims revealed were unedifying, to my mind the worst practice by some distance was that of claiming one property to be your main residence and another to be your second, the one therefore that expenses could be secured for, when all the evidence suggested the designations were the wrong way round.

Or perhaps even worse was 'flipping', when the designations were switched between first and second residences. While this may have represented a genuine change of priority on some occasions, all too often it looked like an excuse to pay the mortgage or do up a property at taxpayers' expense after the other house had had the same treatment.

Matthew Oakeshott, from the Lib Dem Treasury team, publicly accused George Osborne of avoiding £55,000 capital gains tax by flipping his second-home allowance.

Yet by and large those MPs who made the big money from property machinations got away with it.

I am sure there are elements of my claims over the years that people can find to criticise, and indeed one or two have. The *Daily Telegraph* went to town on the fact that my office had included in a big stationery order a pencil sharpener. But on the big picture, I have always felt it wrong that an MP could use publicly provided expenses towards a mortgage and then pocket the capital gain at the end. That is why, in my eighteen years as an MP, I only ever rented a one-bedroom flat in London, which I duly gave up when I lost my seat in 2015.

One of the reasons the problem had been allowed to fester was undoubtedly the attitude of the Speaker, Michael Martin, who appeared to see his role as that of a shop steward for MPs.

By May 2009, pressure was mounting on him, with one MP telling the *Sunday Times*: 'We handed him the bottle of whisky and the revolver, but he appears to have thrown away the gun and drunk the whisky.'

Matters came to a head on the 11th, when he used the first full day's sitting since the *Daily Telegraph* had begun publishing its revelations to turn on Kate Hoey, the Labour MP, and me. In doing so, he crossed a line.

He interrupted Kate, who was complaining about the expense being incurred as a result of the Speaker calling in the police to investigate the leak to the *Daily Telegraph*, sneeringly referring to her 'pearls of wisdom' on TV.

I asked him a straight question about the publication date for expenses, to which he replied, accusing me of being 'another individual member who is keen to say to the press whatever the press wants to hear and say that the House of Commons Commission has done nothing'.

By the 20th he had resigned and within a month he was gone. The expenses scandal had not, however, and would be a towering backdrop to the 2010 elections. Its reverberations continue to this day, with big movements of voters away from the established parties. More than ever, politician is a dirty word.

Chapter 13

The 2005 general election came and went without a great deal of fanfare or excitement. Notwithstanding the fallout from the Iraq War, there was never very much doubt that Labour would be returned to government, only perhaps the extent to which the Lib Dems would benefit from this.

The Tories were still regarded as unelectable, and the disastrous interregnum of Iain Duncan Smith had done nothing to help. In Lewes we literally got out the champagne on the day IDS beat Ken Clarke for the leadership, as we knew that the major threat to our holding the seat in 2005 had been lifted.

The switch in November 2003 to Michael Howard, clearly an interim leader but at least a competent one, had helped stabilise things. But the Tories were still fantasising that if only they were a bit truer to themselves, a bit more right wing, then the public would respond positively. They had to wait for David Cameron before they could unlearn that, though by 2015 they were showing clear signs of reverting to type.

In Lewes, we did indeed hold the seat comfortably, with a slightly reduced majority against a Tory Party led by someone called Rory Love, who used the slogan 'Lewes Needs Love', which it turned out it did not.

There was an attempt at dirty tricks at the start of the election campaign, though. One day the doorbell rang at my home and my daughter, then five, answered the door and a man asked to see my wife.

'Mummy, your friend's here to see you,' she shouted, running back to the kitchen.

The 'friend' turned out to be a reporter from *The Sun* who looked suitably embarrassed by the introduction he had been given. He asked my wife if it was true that I had moved out and was living in a flat in Brighton with a man. It was not. I had not moved out. There was no man in Brighton, and no flat.

The reporter apologised and said he had to check these things out. My wife asked if the allegation had come from the Tories and he half-nodded before escaping. My wife was left comparing the innocence of a child with the machinations of the media.

I received the news with equanimity. My view was that even if the story had been true, it would have been nobody's business anyway, but that, I suppose, would have been a forlorn argument to put.

One major local issue bubbling away for that election related to the battle over a new football stadium proposed for Falmer, on a site literally inches outside both my constituency and the Lewes District Council area.

This was controversial for a number of reasons. Firstly, the reason Brighton and Hove Albion were in need of a stadium was because their previous home, the Goldstone ground, had been sold in 1997 to deal with the financial challenge the club then faced, a decision which was blamed, fairly or otherwise, on the Lib Dem David Bellotti, then chief executive of the club.

Secondly, the planning application, submitted in 2001, was for a site officially designated as being in an Area of Outstanding Natural Beauty (AONB), even if right on the edge of it.

Thirdly, there were concerns about the impact on nearby Falmer village, and the implications for transport movements.

I never disputed the need for the club to find a place for a new ground locally, and indeed supported this, but felt that Falmer was the wrong site and that the huge expanse of land then available near Brighton Station would have been much preferable. I was also lobbied heavily, naturally enough, by my constituents in Falmer village.

The real opposition, however, came from Lib Dem-controlled Lewes District Council, which felt strongly as a matter of principle that the AONB should not be violated. They were also concerned about the impact on Falmer village.

The matter went to public inquiry in 2003, and in December the planning inspector, a Mr J. Collyer, recommended the four connected applications for the development all be rejected, saying the case for refusal was 'overwhelming'.

The Deputy Prime Minister John Prescott, to whom the report had been sent, did not want to accept this, and reopened the inquiry in February 2005, to consider whether a better alternative site existed. In October, John Prescott announced that he was granting permission for a stadium at Falmer.

Lewes District Council responded by launching a bid for judicial review to derail this, alleging errors of fact. Their complaint was upheld and though it did not ultimately stop permission being granted, it did mean that the Lewes taxpayer had most of the council's costs met by central government.

I was dragged into all this in the 2005 election in particular. I agreed with the council's general view that this was the wrong site for a stadium, but I was worried by the potential political and indeed economic consequences of the council's actions.

I did, however, feel the need to get involved in one aspect, namely the behaviour of John Prescott. I had harboured a suspicion that the fact that there were three marginal Labour seats in Brighton and Hove had been a factor in his decision to reject his own inspector's unambiguous recommendation for refusal, not far ahead of the 2005 election, though of course he would maintain that that was not taken into account.

But in December 2005, shortly after judicial review proceedings had been issued by Lewes District Council, the Deputy Prime Minister visited Withdean Stadium, then the temporary home of Brighton and Hove Albion, and received hospitality from the club. Brighton's newspaper, the *Argus*, printed a photo of the DPM next to the club chairman, Dick Knight.

I wrote to the Prime Minister the following month, saying this was indefensible and if a local councillor had behaved in this way, he or she could be barred from office under rules brought in by, yes, John Prescott, in 2001. I asked that he be removed from determination of the case.

Instead of a reply from Blair, I received one from Prescott himself, so I wrote back to Blair on 1 March: 'Can I ask if it is now government policy that ministers investigate themselves when allegations of breaches of the Ministerial Code are levelled?'

The PM did reply this time, saying he was satisfied that Prescott's attendance at the stadium, his meeting with the applicant and his acceptance of hospitality were in order.

Prescott grumbled afterwards to anyone who would listen that 'it was only a bloody pasty', but that was hardly the point.

In 2006, Greene King made a big mistake. They decided to remove the much-loved Lewes brew, Harveys Best, from one of the real landmark pubs in the town, the Lewes Arms.

When I learnt they had decided to do this, I contacted them and advised them strongly against it. There will be significant opposition, I warned.

The Suffolk brewery was rather dismissive, and no doubt thought I was being a touch melodramatic. They had taken local beers out elsewhere and replaced them with their own. Why should Lewes be different?

It is, and it was.

Not only was a massive petition generated, but a picket was begun outside the pub, which reduced trade by up to 90 per cent. In addition, Lewes being full of media types, the move won Greene King a drayload of bad publicity, from the *Today* programme on Radio 4 to the local paper on home turf in Bury St Edmunds.

Eventually Greene King had to give in, and I received the welcome news by pager on 20 April while I was in the Commons. Not only was Harveys Best reinstated, but the pub ended up being sold on.

The affection in Lewes was not just for the local brew but for the whole ethos of the brewery. Harveys is a family-run business that supports a great deal of local activity in the town. Moreover, the brewery itself is as it would have been decades ago, full of wood rather than the miles of steel that you can now find in other breweries.

While I was vice-chair of the county council's Public Protection Committee in the mid-1990s, I was woken early one morning to be told there was a fire at the brewery and could I come down. I duly arrived, bleary-eyed, at about half past six, and was ushered into a small cherry-picker by the local firefighters and shot up into the air so I could see the fire from above. I presume this was not in any way necessary, but an amusing diversion for the firefighters.

Rising parallel to the building was a touch scary but as soon as I was above the fire with nothing to relate to, the feeling went.

The fire had wreaked enormous damage, and the inside of the old wooden building was just a shell. It is a huge testament to Harveys that they painstakingly put the building back to how it had been, so that today you would never know that there had been a huge fire.

There was in fact another occasion, this time as MP, when I was raised up in a cherrypicker. It was to 'open' the solar panels on the roof of Ringmer School in my constituency. A ribbon had been stretched across the roof for me to cut.

That, however, was not as challenging as another opening I was asked to perform, of the new climbing wall at Seaford Head School. Again, the ribbon had been placed high up, but, this time, I had to use the new climbing wall to get there.

You cannot really refuse this sort of request, with lots of people present, so I gamely climbed and cut the ribbon, to wild cheers.

I went even higher one day in 1999 when I was invited to take to the air in a glider at Ringmer by the local club. I was offered the choice of a tow across the field to get started or being pinged up by a giant elastic band. I chose the former but as I bumped across the field at high speed I concluded that I might have made the wrong choice. However, being up in the air in silence was a wonderful experience, which I recommend.

Unlike many MPs, I enjoyed the constituency end of my work. People were more, well, normal, and genuinely pleased when I was able to help them out with a problem.

I was aided over the years by a super team of staff, from caseworkers like David Orr-Ewing to diary secretaries to office managers, and lots of volunteers too. Often these were young men and women, perhaps just out of university, who wanted to work for an MP for a year or two to get that line on their CV. It was certainly not for the money, which frankly was not great.

Sometimes the age differences showed up in unpredictable ways.

Noticing we had rather a lot of milk in the fridge, I asked Ben, my friendly office manager, who was about twenty-five, to cancel the delivery for the next day. Both in the constituency office and at home, I had milk delivered in the old-fashioned way, in glass bottles by a milkman.

I do not think I registered Ben's blank look when I asked him to do this but fifteen minutes later when I came out to ask him to do something else, he was frantically typing and looking worried.

'I can't find who supplies our milk,' he told me. 'I've searched all the websites I can think of.'

I laughed and told him to put a note in an empty bottle and leave it outside the door. People under thirty sometimes do not think anything can be done that does not involve being online.

I always took the view that if someone had taken the trouble to write a letter to you, stick a stamp on it, then walk down to the postbox, then it was something they cared about enough to write to their MP and I should respond accordingly.

The theory wore a bit thin as email became more prevalent. It became too easy to come back from the pub and take a matter of seconds to send me a one-line email that might nevertheless require much more than a one-line reply.

This became much worse with the advent of 38 Degrees, the internet-based campaigning organisation, which became prominent during the coalition government. In theory, they empowered people and improved the engagement between the public and their representatives, and at its best, that was how it worked.

One flaw was that the people behind 38 Degrees decided the subjects upon which campaigns should take place, although they sought views from their followers as best they could, no doubt. More serious was that the information they put out was sometimes wrong, or at least open to other interpretations than the ones they ascribed. At worst, I would receive emails asking me why I was planning to kill every tenth child, and would have to write back to say I had no such intention. I exaggerate, but not by much.

It did not help that a good many constituents appeared not to have read the emails they received from 38 Degrees, but simply pressed the forward button on their computers. I regularly received emails that began: 'Dear (insert name of MP)'.

I would also receive emails asking me to sign an Early Day Motion, despite having told that same constituent many times that, as a minister, I was not able to sign any.

I even received emails exhorting me to 'back Norman Baker' in some campaign or other I was running, or to sign an amendment I had myself tabled.

I would reply to each and every piece of correspondence I received from a constituent, and the volume multiplied exponentially over my time as an MP. This was partly down to the wider use of email, partly down to campaigning organisations like 38 Degrees, but I like to think also because I took my responsibilities to my constituents seriously.

One of the most satisfying parts of my job was to be able to make a difference for someone locally, often by breaking through some inflexible bureaucracy. People were generally very appreciative when I got a result for them, and my office regularly received thank-you letters, cards and emails. This also made my excellent team of caseworkers feel good about their job.

Naturally, all dealings with constituents were confidential, so the wider public never knew about all the cases I took up, only ones which they themselves had raised with me. I was subject to the Data Protection Act 1998 just like any other public office.

Occasionally, however, a constituent would want to make his or her situation public. I generally advised against this, on the basis it would probably not help them get the right result, and might generate other problems in the meantime. Yet, sometimes, that was the only card left to play.

One such time was the case of Adrian Patrick, thirty-one, a constituent living in Newhaven and a chef by profession. Mr Patrick had a rare eye condition that meant he could suddenly go blind, as his retina might at any time detach, something that had already happened in one eye.

There was a drug, infliximab, which Professor Susan Lightman, his consultant at Moorfields, recommended, to protect the jelly between the eyeball and the retina, yet nobody seemed able or willing to authorise it.

The essential problem lay with the management at Moorfields, who would not pay for the drug their own consultant was recommending, and the local Primary Care Trust in Newhaven was unwilling to receive a representation direct from the consultant as opposed to from the hospital as an entity.

I took the matter up with the then chief executive of Moorfields, Ian Balmer, who to my consternation seemed completely uninterested, and had to be repeatedly chased to get any sort of a reply. When he did reply, some two months later and only after I threatened to raise the matter in the House, it was to say he could not help. In other words, Mr Patrick was going to be left to go blind.

This made me very angry. How could the chief executive of Moorfields, of all people, show what seemed to me to be callous disinterest?

With Mr Patrick's agreement, I raised a debate on the matter in the House on 8 December 2004. The minister who responded, Stephen Ladyman, was sympathetic and shared my unhappiness with the poor response from Moorfields, if in slightly more diplomatic language than I had used.

The upshot of all the activity was that Mr Patrick got access to infliximab, it worked, and his eye was saved.

When he told me it had worked, I felt brilliant. This was what being an MP was about. I celebrated that evening.

I had also begun to enjoy canvassing, and had got rather better at it since that first 'butter' election. I now understood that the purpose was to identify voting intentions rather than try to convert, though I was not able to resist the temptation sometimes.

It probably helped that very few people were unpleasant or antagonistic towards me or the Lib Dems in general, even if they did not intend to vote for us. Indeed, the reception became friendlier over the years.

In the 1980s, there had been a general assumption in the constituency, at least outside Lewes, that everyone voted Tory. When my wife-to-be moved into Ditchling, a nice lady came round to welcome her to the village and tell her what went on. After she had listed all the activities, she added: 'And for politics, there is the Conservative Party.'

Equally, when I first canvassed Seaford, it was not uncommon to be met with almost incredulity on the doorstep when I said I was from a party other than the Conservatives. I recall one terribly smartly dressed woman of about sixty opening her door. She smiled a sort of absent smile, then caught sight of my yellow rosette, and her face began to melt like some sort of Salvador Dali clock, and she gently moved to shut the door, intoning 'no, thank you' repeatedly until this incantation was replaced by the click that brought this little interaction to an end.

My Seaford colleagues, who had had years of this, were not unnaturally pessimistic, and would point out doors at which there was no point in calling. I protested that, as we had not won last time, by definition we had to persuade some Tories to vote for us, so we could not just ignore all these people.

Over the years, I noticed that certain features of house and garden were a good guide to how the inhabitants might vote. Some were obvious: big houses with sweeping drives would tend to contain Conservatives, especially those with 'No Turning' signs. But some signals were less overt.

Gardens where the grass appeared to have been manicured with nail scissors tended to belong to Tories. Gardens where the grass had given way to concrete tended to be Labour, especially if there was a car jacked up in the driveway with a wheel off. Gardens where people had made an attempt of sorts to maintain the garden but nature had won through tended to be Lib Dems. Wild flowers were definitely a good sign for us.

Houses with cartwheels or lions outside, no matter how small the property, tended to be Tory, as did houses with lead black lattice patterns on the windows. One house I once canvassed in my county division in East Saltdean had all these features and, as a bonus, a set of Shakespeare's works with the spines facing out so that any visitor could read them through the window by the door. In poker terms, it was a full house and, true to form, the inhabitant was an arch-Tory.

It was also useful to spot any tell-tale signs before ringing the doorbell, for example window stickers supporting a particular charity or campaigning group.

I also learnt that you could not necessarily believe what people told you, and that body language was a much better guide, especially eye contact or the lack of it. It was not unusual for people to tell you they intended to vote for you when they had no intention of doing so, either because they were embarrassed to say otherwise or simply because they wanted you off the doorstep as soon as possible.

In the early part of the 2005 parliament, I continued in Westminster with the environment as my main focus, as it had been since my election in 1997, barring a short period when I shadowed the Home Office. I had even won out as Best Newcomer in the 1998 Green Ribbon awards, where I was described as 'arguably the greenest MP in the House'.

I served for some time as the party's shadow Environment Secretary. The Lib Dem membership has always been sound on green issues, though the leadership has not always given the area the prominence I would have liked. Paddy Ashdown did, but none of his three successors, Charles Kennedy, Ming Campbell and Nick Clegg, seemed particularly interested, though Nick at least did understand the political value of campaigning on green issues.

Before the 2005 election I had released a report, 'How Green Is Your Supermarket?', which was, I believe, the first definitive report to compare the environmental footprint of the big supermarket chains. They all provided information to me to allow the report to be compiled in the end, but only after a certain amount of blagging. About half did not want to co-operate, so I told each of them that theirs was the only chain that would not play ball and that would not look good when the report came out.

The report covered the nine biggest chains, and revealed, amongst other things, that six supermarkets were between them handing out an unbelievable 15 billion – yes, billion – plastic bags each year, that their customers spent up to £15 billion a year on packaging alone, and that supermarket lorries travelled 408 million miles each year.

Buoyed by the positive reception this initiative received, I followed this up in 2005 with a report entitled 'How Green Is Your Parliament?' The answer was 'Not very'.

Compared with the 1997 baseline, water consumption was up

58 per cent, electricity use up 45 per cent, and gas up 34 per cent. Purchases of bottled water had risen 85 per cent since 2001, one in three beers on sale had been imported and one in three fish used came from threatened fish stocks.

Apart from the carbon footprint, it was also clear that the House was spending a great deal more public money on running itself than it needed to. Overall, I made fifty-six recommendations for changes to existing practice and passed these on, with a copy of my report, to the House of Commons Commission. This did spur the House authorities into some sort of action, including accepting my idea of annual environmental reporting of energy and water use.

I was particularly exercised by the use of bottled water, which I calculated to be 25,000 times more expensive per glass than tap water. And environmentally, the idea of transporting a heavy commodity hundreds of miles by lorry when it could be accessed from a tap within about twenty yards or less seemed to me absurd.

However, trying to wean the House off bottled water proved to be monumentally difficult, and my efforts threw up the same kind of nonsensical objections I would meet later when I tried as a minister to deal with the windows at the Department for Transport.

Bottled water was 'highly valued' by MPs, there was concern about the quality of tap water (which is actually regulated to a higher standard than bottled water) and there could be health and safety implications in filling up jugs and taking them round to committee rooms.

My Lib Dem colleague in the Lords, Sue Miller, met similar resistance when she pushed for tap water to replace bottles at her end of the building. Rejecting her call, Lord Brazabon told her: 'The House began to use bottled water following a number of breakages of carafes and glasses, which caused minor cuts and injuries to staff.'

How do people cope at home? Plastic cups anyone?

My report and work on the environmental footprint of the House would anticipate the work I would do several years later as a minister, co-chairing the Greening Government Committee, undertaking a similar exercise for the government estate – so the various departmental offices, Downing Street and the like. Parliament is run by the MPs rather than the government.

In big-picture terms, I decided that we needed to establish some cross-party consensus on tackling climate change, and thought it was worth a try, given the sentiments the Tories and Labour had been expressing, and the general public mood for action.

Oliver Letwin was up for this, even if the Tory response was a touch marred by David Cameron claiming subsequently that it was all his idea. In the end, we managed to put together a joint statement, which was also endorsed by the SNP and Plaid Cymru.

The statement called for a new independent body to set annual binding targets for reducing greenhouse gases to achieve a cut of at least 60 per cent by 2050, and for an annual report to be presented to Parliament on progress.

The Labour government cautiously refused to sign up, but did then produce the Climate Change Act a couple of years later, so I like to think this may have helped spur them into action.

In 2006, I visited Tasmania at the invitation of the green movement over there, specifically the Wilderness Society, to help draw attention to the shocking forestry practices in the state. Tasmania has one of the world's greatest temperate rainforests and the world's tallest hardwood trees, and I was smitten with the imposing beauty of the natural environment when I visited the Styx and Upper Florentine areas.

But I was also horrified by the wanton destruction being wreaked by the forestry company Gunns, which seemed to have the state government in its pocket. It was following a scorched earth policy, literally, with forests being firebombed from the air, to be replaced by monoculture plantations with all the diversity of a car park.

Gunns was also using a mammalian pesticide called 1080 (sodium fluoroacetate) to remove wildlife. In 2005, up to 200,000 of the native Bennett's wallabies were deliberately exterminated on King Island. While I was in the state, I saw a TV clip in which a leading state politician defended the use of 1080 against the charge that endangered species were being killed by saying that there were too many of them.

My visit followed two Early Day Motions I had tabled in Parliament, the latter of which had attracted the support of more than 100 MPs of all parties. It was widely covered in the Australian media, with opinion splitting along predictable lines. I thought it was interesting that those who wished to defend the status quo chose to attack me as being 'an interfering Pom' rather than address the issue at hand. Another case of going for the player rather than the ball.

My response was to say that the environment belonged to us all, and they had a unique asset which belonged to the world, not just Tasmania. I added that I was well known for criticising my own government's environmental performance and they would probably be glad I was out of the country for a week.

My visit, where I was also able to meet the federal forestry minister Senator Eric Abetz, certainly helped to raise the issue, and I hope helped secure the protection designations subsequently agreed. However, the landmark agreement between the timber industry and the environmentalists came under threat in 2014, with Tony Abbott, the Australian premier, saying he wanted to strip Tasmania's forests of their World Heritage special protection.

I was sensitive to the accusation that my journey to Tasmania would make me responsible for lots of carbon emissions so I asked my office in advance to calculate what the figure would be and how many trees I would have to plant to compensate.

Alarmingly, I would have to plant seventeen trees to make up for that one return journey, so I arranged in advance that I would do so when I arrived in Tasmania. Planting trees also made a nice contrast for the media to the shots of burnt-out stumps all too easily accessible.

The calculation made by my office had also suggested that half my personal carbon emissions for the year could be ascribed to that one flight, which really brought home the impact of aviation on climate change, and helped firm up my determination that the Lib Dem 2010 manifesto should take a hard line on new aviation capacity.

Given the impact of aviation on climate change, I found it perplexing that it was not a greater focus than it was for the environmental lobby. In 2007, for example, David Cameron, who was then going through his phase of pretending to care about the environment, clocked up 36,345 air miles, mostly on private jets supplied by wealthy donors to the Conservative Party. The mileage included a trip of thirteen miles by helicopter between Sunderland and Newcastle, where an excellent train service operates, and another of twenty miles from Birmingham to Warwick. I called him at the time 'a one-man climate change hazard'.

Just two years earlier, in 2005, I had received an email from David Cameron entitled 'Liberal Conservatism', in which he invited me to join the 'modern, compassionate Conservative Party'.

He went on: 'My Conservative Party believes passionately in green politics ... Improving the environment and our quality of life by turning green words into action.'

I did not find this at all convincing, even in 2005, but then the email also maintained that his Conservative Party 'wants Britain to be a positive participant in the EU'.

The same year Cameron was jetting round the world, William Hague flew almost 20,000 miles by private jet to talk to South American leaders about climate change, taking in detours to Iceland, Belize and the Falkland Islands. In two days, the jet produced the same carbon emissions as an average household would produce in a year.

Even Prince Charles, who has over the years shown a genuine interest in tackling climate change, has seemed oblivious to his own carbon footprint. So the royal train, he once told me proudly, is powered by used cooking oil, which is great. But the carbon savings here have been outweighed many times over by his flying proclivities.

In 2007, he was to be given the Harvard Club's Global Environmental Citizen Award at a ceremony in Philadelphia. Yet the opportunity to take the climate change agenda forward was undermined when it was revealed that he was taking twenty people with him.

On another occasion, he chartered a luxury private jet for a five-day tour of Europe to promote the government's climate change policies. Using a chartered plane rather than scheduled flights multiplied the trip's carbon emissions thirteen times over.

But at least Prince Charles has been trying to do the right thing. No such excuse can be found for Prince Andrew, dubbed Air Miles Andy by the press, who was not averse to unnecessarily using helicopters at public expense. In 2009, for instance, a helicopter was hired for £2,000 to take him from his home in Windsor Great Park to a golf club in Deal. The previous week, according to the press, he had run up a £60,000 bill for a private jet for a four-day visit to Azerbaijan.

MPs' expenses may finally and painfully have been sorted out, but those for the royal family most certainly have not. Indeed, an exemption from the Freedom of Information Act and changes to publication details mean we now know less of the detail than we did before.

I have always taken the view that the royal family is part of the structure of government of this country, it spends public money, and so it should be properly accountable for that money. Yet it is extraordinarily difficult to achieve this.

For one thing, MPs are strongly discouraged from being critical of the royal family. Indeed, the oath we are all obliged to take upon arriving in Parliament requires us to pledge blind allegiance.

I did manage, on one occasion back in 2002, to introduce a debate on royal finances, but only through the prismatic device of linking it back to an obscure Treasury document, the 1993 Memorandum of Understanding on Royal Taxation. I queried, amongst other points, why it was that there was an exemption from inheritance tax. It was estimated that the Treasury was between £20 million and £25 million out of pocket after the Queen Mother died.

As with MPs' expenses, the way forward is to have openness and accountability when it comes to public expenditure incurred by the royal family. We are some distance from that at the moment.

Chapter 14

In 2006, I got pulled into an issue relating to a 1990 British Airways flight to Kuala Lumpur via Kuwait when I was contacted by people who had been on board.

The flight, BA149, has been exhaustively researched by an investigative journalist, Stephen Davis, who has written a book on the subject. It also featured in a BBC documentary, which was broadcast at such a late hour that I doubt more than a handful of people saw it.

Mr Davis maintains that the flight was deliberately landed in Kuwait, despite the dangers, in order to allow UK Special Forces personnel into Kuwait.

As a consequence of the decision to land, the crew and passengers were captured by Iraqi troops. They were held for weeks in pretty awful conditions. Although when I was first approached my memory of the event was hazy, I did recall the disturbing picture that filled the media of a traumatised five-year-old lad, Stuart Lockwood, being patted on the head by Saddam Hussein.

The official version of events is that the situation could not have been foreseen, that it was unhelpful and unfortunate for those involved and that the plane landed before the invasion of Kuwait had taken place. The Prime Minister at the time, Margaret Thatcher, said: 'The British Airways flight landed, its passengers disembarked, and the crew handed over to a successor crew and went to their hotels. All that took place before the invasion: the invasion was later.'

Yet the crew and passengers said that when the plane touched down they heard the sound of tanks and gunfire, clearly indicating that the invasion was well under way by that point. I had been contacted by passengers on BA149, angry that the facts surrounding the flight had been stifled – indeed, misrepresented.

I met some of those who were held in Kuwait and subsequently in Iraq by Saddam Hussein. They came from the normality of Britain and were catapulted into that situation for months on end. They had to live in terrible conditions, often with no running water, and it is not surprising that the scars from this episode have remained with them for many years.

Some of them experienced physical abuse and more witnessed horrendous examples of brutality by the Iraqis on Kuwaiti civilians. They could see them from where they were staying. There are eye-witness accounts of murder, mock executions, serious assaults, rape and other sexual assaults. A dossier of the full horrors was compiled. Some 1,868 people were interviewed at the instigation of the then Defence Secretary Tom King, but the dossier has never been released. Geoff Hoon was asked, when he was Defence Secretary, to release that document by the Labour MP Ann Clwyd, but refused to do so.

One of the major demands of the crew and passengers I spoke to was that the dossier compiled in Operation Sandcastle, as I believe it was called, should be put in the public domain. If it contained sensitive security details, such as the names of individuals, they could obviously be redacted before publication.

Those to whom I spoke were not, I believe, motivated by a desire to obtain compensation. However, they were angry that French passengers won more than £3 million from British Airways in compensation, and that US passengers were paid off when BA settled in secret rather than have the matter exposed in a Texas court, but they had received nothing. Even BA got a huge insurance pay-out for its plane, subsequently destroyed on the runway where it had touched down.

I was also contacted by two individuals who said they were connected to UK Special Forces. They handed me copies of signed affidavits, from October 2006, to the effect that they were on that plane and were put there to carry out a mission at the request of the British government. They also provided a separate sheet, naming the six individuals who formed the unit undertaking the operation, listing their pseudonyms, and providing their SAS and SBS numbers.

The first affidavit included the following:

> I submit this affidavit/statement of truth as my final correspondence on the matter regarding my involvement with Flight BA149. That details ... are true and accurate accounts of events as recalled by me to the very best of my memory and ability as per my direct involvement in the covert operation flown into Kuwait on flight BA149, and the subsequent gathering of intelligence material of Iraqi troop strengths, positions and unit identification in 1990. That Operation Iscariot was an INC organised and executed operation. That I was on flight BA149, as a member of INC and the subsequent mission/operation as outlined.

The second included this:

> That entire operation ... was ... authorised by Prime Minister Margaret Thatcher ... That 'Iscariot' was an INC operation, INC standing for 'Increment'. INC was formed shortly after

the Iranian embassy siege of 1980 when Margaret Thatcher
authorised the set-up and operation of INC due to increased
media attention being focused upon the Special Air Service
after 'Operation Nimrod' was screened live worldwide that
ended the siege. Members are/were drawn mainly from ex
forces and even serving forces personnel.

When challenged in 1992 by John Prescott, then shadow Transport
Secretary, Prime Minister John Major told him: 'I can confirm,
however, that there were no British military personnel on board
the flight.'

The soldiers who spoke to me said that the use of INC was
intended to provide ministers at the time with perfect deniability,
that members of INC were paid from secret overseas bank accounts
and, crucially, promised immunity from prosecution for any alleged
crimes committed while overseas.

According to the soldiers, there were indeed no serving British
personnel on board, but only because serving British personnel
were not used. Instead, others who had resigned were used in an
arm's-length capacity.

There was also some external support for this version of events.
Corroboration came from Nate Howell, United States ambassador in
Kuwait at the time, who confirmed publicly on the record that such
an operation took place, and from one Ed Ciriello, who declared
himself as a CIA agent working alongside MI6 in Saudi Arabia
at the time of the invasion. It also came from Captain Lawrence
Eddingfield, captain of the USS *Antietam*, who rescued two of
the mission team. Richard Tomlinson, the former MI6 agent, also
emailed me to confirm that he was aware of the operation and that
it did take place. He gave me details consistent with the affidavits
that I have referred to.

John Major, in reply to John Prescott, had said that 'no firm evidence' was available to suggest that an invasion was to take place. We know from public records now open that the head of the CIA told President Bush a week before the invasion that the Iraqis would invade, and that this warning was passed to both Washington and London.

John Major also said this in his reply to John Prescott: 'The British government did not attempt to influence BA's decision to operate flight BA149 on 1–2 August.'

Given that we know that the invasion started when the plane was four hours' flying time from Kuwait, the decision not to inform the captain clearly suggests that a decision was taken to allow the plane to land. BA had also sought advice from the Foreign Office shortly before take-off and had been told it was perfectly safe for the flight to proceed.

It is also clear from evidence in sworn affidavits submitted to the US courts that the government of the day advised British Airways that it was safe to fly. In particular, BA had been briefed by the person described to me as the MI6 head in Kuwait, whose name I was also given, that there would be no invasion, so BA appears also to have been misled.

With 200,000 troops and tanks gathered on the border very close to Kuwait, and given the general background noise from Iraq at the time, even the most junior Foreign Office official must have concluded that an invasion was likely and that it would not be sensible to send a passenger airline into Kuwait at that point, even if there had been no detailed intelligence to confirm that.

The plane touched down, moreover, at a deserted airport. Every other flight from every other airline had been cancelled for hours, there were no staff, and the one or two individuals who were hanging around were considerably surprised when a plane touched down.

We are asked to believe that Britain, with all our expertise and intelligence, and with people on the ground, was the only country in the world not to realise what was going on, and to be unable to cancel our flight into the country. That stretches credulity.

There is a further source to support the proposition that the time of invasion was known, even if an unlikely one. Margaret Thatcher's memoirs, *The Downing Street Years*, gives a timeline significantly different from the one that she gave to Parliament, and one which corresponds to the timeline that others have insisted was accurate. However, no correction of the comments made at the time has ever been given to the House.

I wrote to Prime Minister Tony Blair on 16 October 2006 to ask him to do three things. First, if he would meet a small delegation of passengers and crew to hear their concerns, which had not happened since their return from Iraq. Second, if he would arrange for the release, subject to the removal of operationally sensitive material, of the internal review papers relating to Operation Sandcastle. Third, if he would instigate an inquiry to consider all aspects of the episode and what might be learnt from it.

The Prime Minister did not reply, so I sent him a reminder on 20 November. In December, I received a reply not from the Prime Minister but from a minister at the Foreign Office, whose substantive comment was: 'Regarding BA flight 149, the government of the day made its position clear and I have nothing further to add.'

I decided to pursue the matter further, not least because of the evidence that had been presented to me, and secured a debate in the House, again in the graveyard slot of last business on a Friday.

The minister responding was Geoff Hoon, a key figure, of course, from the Iraq-related events of 2003 and the minister who had refused to release the report on the episode to Ann Clwyd. In his reply to me, he held the line that had been set by Margaret Thatcher all those years ago, oblivious, it seemed, to the mass of evidence that pointed elsewhere.

He added this comment:

> I am going to read out some words very carefully, which go beyond what has been said before, and should not be capable of misinterpretation. I want to make it clear that I have been told that the government at the time did not attempt in any way to exploit the flight by any means whatsoever.

His main thrust, however, was to press me for the names of the two soldiers who had contacted me, saying he would look further into matters if given that information, and indeed interrupted me very early in the debate to make that point and repeated it later. I did not have the authority to pass those names on and doubted whether a willingness to help investigate matters was the motivation behind the request.

At the end of the debate, when the mace was being removed, he came across to me in a very friendly style and engaged me like an old friend in a conversation about The Beatles, he and I both being serious fans. While I am always happy to talk music, this did all seem a little forced.

Notwithstanding the graveyard slot allocated for the debate, I was surprised by the complete absence of any coverage of the issue in the next day's media. After all, the fact that something is said in Parliament gives the media extra protection not otherwise available. It seems there are some issues the media decides to put in the 'too difficult' box.

Chapter 15

Early in 2010, about four months before the general election, I asked to see Nick Clegg. I wanted to talk about where we would be post-election. The two of us duly met in his office in the House of Commons, and I set out my stall.

Labour under Brown were going backwards and were clearly not going to have a majority, but neither were the Tories. At that point they had 198 seats and to secure another 128 to be able to govern alone was, in my view, too tall an order. There would therefore be a hung parliament.

I told Nick that, given the situation, we should take the opportunity to form a coalition and go into government. And even if it might arithmetically be possible to get over the line with either other party, I thought we would have to deal with the Tories, if we had the choice. Coalition was an alien enough concept for the British public to accept without complicating it by being seen to prop up the party that had 'lost'.

A full coalition would be better than any other arrangement, as it would give us the opportunity to enact Lib Dem policies, and would give us credibility as a party. Oh, and by the way, could I be Transport Minister, please?

I think Nick was a little taken aback by my willingness to do a deal with the Tories, given that I am generally regarded, accurately, as being on the left of the party. But I was merely looking at matters pragmatically. I thought we should take advantage of the hung parliament I saw coming, and it would have been suicide to prop up Brown, especially if Labour had gone a long way backwards.

I should add, for the avoidance of doubt, that my wish to be Transport Minister fell out of my logic rather than preceding it, but in my experience it was wise to plant these seeds early.

I had actually been mulling over whether to stand again or not. Having done thirteen years in opposition, I did not wish to carry on doing the same thing indefinitely. Before I became an MP, I had had a number of varied jobs and tended to move reasonably often. In the end, as I weighed up what the 2010 election might bring, I concluded I had in any case left it too late to leave my constituency party looking for a new candidate.

The election campaign nationally brought few surprises. It was clear to everyone that Gordon Brown had blown it, and really, he had no one to blame but himself. It is difficult to credit now, but the country had largely welcomed him into No. 10. Yes, there was an issue in the public's mind about his legitimacy, as he had not won an election as party leader to be Prime Minister, but then neither had John Major in 1990.

The great asset he had was that he was not Tony Blair, and most people said hooray to that. He also started well, and someone in his team captured the moment with the slogan 'Not Flash, Just Gordon', which I thought very smart. If he had gone to the country in 2007 to ask for his own mandate, I believe he would have got it, with an overall majority. But instead he bottled it, holding on against all advice, put off by a temporary blip in Tory fortunes over inheritance tax. In doing so, he signed his own political death warrant.

The 2010 election produced the hung parliament I had expected, though as Lib Dems we were all disappointed to have actually lost a handful of seats overall, especially after the way Nick Clegg had performed so well in the televised debates, even if as a party we had become unprepared to follow through the enthusiasm from the public that immediately followed those.

In addition, our vote only edged up one point, to 23 per cent. In my own seat, my majority was down from 8,474 to 7,647, although my vote was up almost 2,000 and my share of the vote stayed at 52 per cent.

Nevertheless, looking at the percentage of votes we had secured against the number of seats, and comparing that to previous elections in the 1980s and 1990s, it was indisputable that we had not been attracting ever more of the electorate to vote for us. Rather, we had simply got much better at making first past the post work for us.

Of course, that also meant that while we were winning seats in some places, black holes were opening up in others, exacerbated by exhortations to members and supporters in those seats to go to work in target seats.

The results of this were particularly clear in Scotland, where we won eleven seats, but of the other sixty-one, we only managed seven second places, and a couple of those were what might be called technical seconds, where we were a very long way behind Labour, as in Glasgow North West.

The targeting strategy, therefore, was bringing us short-term gains while simultaneously storing up trouble for the future.

Immediately after the election, a fevered period followed when negotiations took place between the Lib Dems and the Tories, and also with Labour, even though a deal with Labour would have left such a coalition well short of an overall majority. The negotiations have been well described in David Laws's book *22 Days In May*.

The Conservative negotiating team comprised George Osborne, Oliver Letwin, William Hague and Ed Llewellyn, the latter of whom was appointed as Downing Street Chief of Staff. Ours officially was David Laws, along with MPs Chris Huhne, Danny Alexander and Andrew Stunell, but the process, for our side at least, was quite inclusive, particularly for those of us who had been shadow Cabinet members.

My contribution to the final agreement was to ensure the environment was given proper weight, particularly in respect of the need to tackle climate change, and to add in matters I cared about and which might well have been left out otherwise, including a ban on private sector wheel clamping and moves to promote alternatives to animal testing, both of which I would help to deliver in government.

During this interim period I received in my constituency office quite a few emails from constituents, urging me to do a deal or, more usually, not do a deal with the Tories or with Labour, depending on their point of view. It was obvious, if it had not been before, that doing a deal with either was going to annoy a lot of people whose sympathies were in the opposite direction, including many who might have been persuaded to vote for us.

The negotiations with the Conservatives were concluded in a matter of just a few days. Our sister liberal parties in Europe were amazed at the speed with which this had occurred. Their negotiations took weeks, months, even years in the case of Belgium, who went 589 days without a functioning elected government from 2010.

Of course, in Britain we almost take it for granted that one removal van will move out from Downing Street almost immediately after an election, and pass another coming in the same day. But in May 2010, it was not clear to the public, nor indeed the money markets, what was going to happen, and in the meantime Gordon Brown stayed in Downing Street, as he was not only perfectly entitled to do but almost obliged to do. Government ministers, including the Prime Minister, remain in office until they are replaced. There cannot be a vacuum. It was unfair, therefore, for the papers to portray him as clinging on.

But there was a need to reach an early agreement, as both sides recognised. David Cameron had made what he publicly called a very good offer to the Lib Dems and was, not unreasonably, pressing for an answer.

Within the Lib Dems, there was restrained excitement that the electorate had at last delivered a hung parliament and that we would have a chance to be back in government for the first time since 1945. There was also a cold realisation that the cards we had been dealt were difficult ones to play.

Forming a coalition with the Tories was going to be difficult to sell to our grass roots, who are broadly left of centre, and also risked losing the support from the left that we had picked up over the years, particularly over the Iraq War.

On the other hand, allowing the Tories to form a minority government would rob us of influence, and most likely lead to another election in a few months, called on Tory terms, and produce a Tory majority government – the precedent here was Harold Wilson and Labour in 1974.

Apart from the not inconsequential fact that we would have no money to fight a second election, people would scorn us for having campaigned for a hung parliament for so long and then thrown away the chance to do anything with it.

The good news was that we were better prepared for coalition negotiations than the Tories, and the fact that the wider party was given the opportunity to comment on the negotiations and indeed validate the outcome meant that the party as a whole was tied into the coalition, in sharp contrast to the undemocratic way David Cameron handled matters within his own party.

The bad news, it was to transpire, was that the Tories knew a lot more about government than we did, and were much better at using the system to get what they wanted, especially in the first year, before we understood better how the system worked.

Shortly after the coalition agreement had been finalised, I received a phone call on my mobile while I was sitting in my back garden in Lewes. It was the Downing Street switchboard, asking if I could take a call. It seemed a rhetorical question – has anyone ever said no to such a request in this situation?

Nick Clegg came on the line, and he was upbeat and friendly, but also business-like and no doubt keen to complete the rest of a long list of calls to Lib Dem colleagues and others. He had remembered our discussion from a few months back, and duly offered me a position as Transport Minister. He told me the Prime Minister would at some point ring for a chat and to formally confirm the offer.

I had barely spoken to David Cameron before, except on one occasion when I was hosting a visit to Parliament for the Dalai Lama in my capacity as chair of the all-party Tibet group, when one of his meetings was with the Leader of the Opposition.

That is not to say, of course, that I had not taken an interest in the Conservatives while I was in opposition. Quite the opposite.

In December 2006, I lodged a formal complaint about the then Leader of the Opposition, following the production of a leaflet by the Tories that was distributed at a meeting of the City Circle, a group of financiers helping to bankroll them. The leaflet promised those who joined the 'Leader's Group' immediate access to David Cameron after Prime Minister's Questions. The joining fee was £50,000.

It read: 'The most senior club, its aim is to support David Cameron, providing sustainable and renewable income for the party.'

The rub was that at least some of these meetings were to take place in David Cameron's parliamentary office.

In my complaint I wrote: 'In essence, it appears to me that Mr Cameron is charging for access for himself in order to boost Conservative Party funds, and using a House of Commons facility, provided to him at public expense to facilitate parliamentary duties, to do so.'

The Parliamentary Commissioner for Standards, Sir Philip Mawer, recommended that my complaint be upheld, and the House of Commons Committee on Standards and Privileges, chaired by the Tory grandee Sir George Young, agreed, saying: 'Mr Cameron was in our view ill-advised to link directly, in promoting the Leader's Group, the issues of access to his office and party fundraising. We agree with the Commissioner that Mr Baker's complaint should be upheld.'

David Cameron, who had held a further lunch in his parliamentary office some time after my complaint had been lodged, namely on 17 January 2007, accepted the Commissioner's judgement and made the committee aware of this by letter on 22 March before it deliberated. He apologised 'unreservedly for inadvertently contravening the Code [of Conduct and Guide to Rules for Members] in respect of my parliamentary offices' and promised no recurrence.

Between that event and the general election in 2010, David Cameron had one day made a party visit to Brighton, and mingled with the crowds. A constituent of mine gleefully told me afterwards that he had spoken to the Tory leader and asked: 'My MP's Norman Baker in Lewes. What do you think of him?'

To which David Cameron had replied, with feeling: 'He's the most annoying man in Parliament.'

I regarded this as a badge of honour.

His opinion of me seemed not to change with me in government. He told a press gallery lunch early in 2014 that one of his wishes in the new year was to see less of me on television. I thought this a rather inappropriate thing for a Prime Minister to say about one of his ministers.

So the Prime Minister finally spoke to me on the Sunday afternoon following the election after a couple of cancelled calls. It was a slightly stilted conversation, but we were both on our best behaviour, trying to make it work.

I mentioned to him that he did of course have a Lewes connection, in that Tim Rathbone had been his godfather. The PM informed me that he had also worked for him during university holidays, which I had not known, and observed drily that Tim would think it rather rum that he was phoning up to appoint me to his government.

The PM confirmed my appointment and told me who my colleagues would be at the DfT. He asked me to be friendly to his Conservative colleagues and to try to make the coalition work. I do not know if this was a plea just for me, or a general one to Lib Dems, but I was pleased that he had taken that line and promised that I would indeed be a collegiate member of the government.

I meant this. I had spent my life fighting Conservatives. My political views had not changed and I intended working to give effect to them in government; but the electorate had in its own way thrust us together and I thought we had a duty to work together for the benefit of the country, and to be honest about our differences and handle them in a mature way. After all, before the election the public had regularly said it wanted to see less of the yah-boo stuff and more of parties working together, so that was what we were now doing.

Later that evening, at about a quarter to ten, I received a phone call from the Department for Transport. The caller introduced himself as James, congratulated me in a friendly but rather mechanical way and told me he was my private secretary. I arranged to come into the office.

Chapter 16

As I arrived at the Department for Transport on my first day, officials were scurrying around.

It turned out that Theresa Villiers, the new Minister of State, had arrived before me and erupted when she saw an EU flag on the flagpole that protruded from the building at a 45-degree angle, demanding that it be removed immediately.

Unfortunately, the flag had become tangled on the pole and would have to be removed from outside. This was arranged for the Saturday, as it would necessitate closing Horseferry Road for half a day and the use of scaffolding, no doubt at some little cost.

It was an early indication, if I needed one, of the violent reaction the EU generates in many Conservatives who otherwise behave calmly and rationally. It is as if they turn into political werewolves when the Europe moon comes out.

The Permanent Secretary at the DfT was Robert Devereux, whom I had met in June the previous year. It is standard practice for the opposition to have confidential access to the civil service shortly before an election, to test the practicality of ideas and to let the civil service know what might be coming. For the first time, and with a hung parliament looking likely, that facility had been made available to the Lib Dems.

The meeting was guiding us as to the legal obstacles to particular proposals we were interested in, such as road pricing. It was also useful to learn of the thought that had already been given at that time, at least in the DfT, to preparing for a coalition government.

In my three and a half years at the DfT, I would see four different permanent secretaries. They seemed to me to be not very permanent.

Nor in fact were the officials in my own private office. Of the four civil servants I was allowed, James, the head of office, told me on day one that he had secured a move elsewhere in the department, and within a week he was gone. Nick, my diary secretary, followed shortly afterwards. I learnt that this merry-go-round was quite normal.

Fortunately, that meant I was able to recruit new staff and secured the really good Jo Guthrie, who was everything a minister could want in a competent head of office. Having her, and then eventually her replacement Alex Philpott, helping me made a huge difference to what I was able to achieve.

Despite having been an active opposition MP, I realised I knew very little about how a department actually works. Indeed, one of my main points of reference was the 1980s BBC comedy *Yes Minister*, which in many ways turned out to be a useful guide, but not always.

In one episode, the fictional Sir Humphrey observes that ministers come and go while civil servants stay put. The fictional minister, Jim Hacker, then speculates, to Humphrey's horror, that it might be fun if ministers stayed put and civil servants were reshuffled.

That turned out to be my experience. After three and a half years in the department, virtually nobody, civil servant or minister, was in the same job except me.

The Conservative team was headed by Philip Hammond as Transport Secretary. Philip did not know very much about transport, and did not really have a huge interest in it. He had been preparing for the job of Chief Secretary to the Treasury, which doubtless he would have got in a Conservative-only government. Indeed, the industry wondered, only half in jest, whether the Prime Minister had not appointed the wrong Hammond by mistake, as no place had been found for Stephen Hammond, who had been quite an effective shadow Transport Minister before the election.

Just about the last edition of *Transport Times* before the election had had a front page featuring Stephen, Andrew Adonis as Labour's Transport Secretary, and me.

'I bet you wouldn't have put money on me being the only one of the three to make it to the DfT following the election,' I observed shortly afterwards to David Begg, the well-connected transport expert who had been responsible for the cover. David had to agree.

Supporting Philip as Minister of State was Theresa Villiers, who had been shadow Transport Secretary before the election and was of course disappointed not to have got the top job. I liked Theresa, who was always quite open and friendly and whose views on transport were in most respects not dissimilar to my own.

The team was completed by Mike Penning, who I hope will not mind if I describe him as a rough diamond. Mike had been a fireman and brought to the department a down-to-earth realism that was valuable. He had his own mind and was not afraid to express it, which I welcomed. He also appeared to be well connected within the Tory hierarchy, which would do his ministerial career no harm.

Theresa was given responsibility for rail and aviation, Mike for trunk roads, road safety and shipping, and I took local transport in all its forms, including buses, trams and local authority roads. I had wanted some rail responsibilities but was not initially successful. I did, however, succeed in incrementally adding bits to my portfolio over my time in the department, including much of rail, electric vehicles and corporate matters.

Philip was rather suspicious of me, as became apparent when we sat down together for the first time. I did not take this personally, as I think he would have been suspicious of any Lib Dem. I told him that both the PM and the DPM had told me to be a good departmental minister and to help make the coalition work, which was true. This seemed to assuage his concerns to a degree.

The four ministers would meet together once a week, normally when Philip returned from Cabinet, of which he would relay the highlights. I was surprised in my first week to receive in my red box a copy of the Cabinet minutes of that week, as I would subsequently every week. I always skimmed them, though they were written in a way that revealed little and will disappoint historians in thirty years' time. The exception was when foreign affairs had been discussed, where the minutes were often quite revealing.

Aside from the Cabinet rundown, we would discuss parliamentary business for the week, and flag up any other burning issues. Naturally policy positions had to be discussed, and it was often the case that Theresa and I would be on one side, with Philip and Mike on the other. I suspect Philip found slightly irksome the axis between Theresa and me.

The first major challenge was to deal with the spending review and the cuts that this would entail. Philip, still in Chief Secretary mindset, launched himself into the exercise with enthusiasm, papers and figures spread out over his table. To my mind, and I think Theresa's as well, he was in danger of looking at the problem through the wrong end of the telescope.

About a week or two into the exercise, a story appeared in one of the nationals that suggested a leak from the department, or perhaps just some clever detective work from a journalist, picking up pieces of the jigsaw from here, there and everywhere to make a picture. For all I know, it may have come at least partly from comments Philip himself might have inadvertently made.

Either way, the story was broadly accurate and Philip unilaterally decided to exclude Theresa, Mike and me from further detailed consideration of the options, which was pretty outrageous in my book.

I do not know what my Tory departmental colleagues did, but I insisted on seeing the papers I felt I was entitled to, on behalf of the Lib Dems. If I could not access something in the department I simply rang up Danny Alexander's office and got feedback from the Treasury.

Philip was to my mind too ready to make cuts that might be regretted down the line. While I accepted that savings had to be made in line with the agreed coalition position, there were some cuts I was determined to fight.

One of these was support for buses, and not just because I was by now buses minister. I knew from my time in opposition that, although they may be regarded as unglamorous by MPs and journalists alike, buses are the backbone of the public transport system and most heavily used by those on lower incomes, often to get to work.

There was a proposal for a cut to the main support mechanism, Bus Service Operators' Grant (BSOG), of up to 40 per cent. Philip, who I doubted was a regular or even occasional bus user, seemed relaxed about this. He seemed to think any budget line could take what he called 'a haircut', implying that what was lost was unnecessary and indeed the service in question would be tidied up, better without it.

In the end, and quite late in the process, I leant on Danny Alexander and he found some extra money to limit the cut to 20 per cent. When the news reached Philip, I half-expected him to be annoyed but in fact he seemed both surprised and a touch impressed that I had secured more money for the department.

The other area of great concern to me was rail fares. Since 2003, under Labour, regulated fares, accounting for about half the journeys made, had risen 1 per cent above inflation each year and in opposition I had campaigned for that to end and indeed be reversed.

To my horror, and also that of Theresa Villiers, the rail minister, Philip was attracted to the idea of a one-off increase of RPI+3, which he said would provide a step increase in the base income stream into the future. On 28 June, he received an unhelpful paper – or submission, as they are called – from an official, suggesting all sorts of damaging ways in which money could be saved from the rail budget.

The paper suggested extending the delivery timescale for already agreed enhancements; deferring completion of the Thameslink programme to 2020; delaying electrification to south Wales; deferring the planned new inter-city rolling stock for ten years and instead extending the life of existing diesel stock; and reducing preparatory spending on HS2 by 25 per cent.

This was all deeply unimaginative and self-defeating, but the worst to my mind was the idea of raising fares by RPI+3. This would generate £450 million in the spending review period: £1.6 billion over four years.

Again, I had to weigh in with the Lib Dems at the centre to ensure this idea would be blocked. In the end, regulated fares continued to rise at 1 per cent above inflation until, after three years, the Lib Dems were able to force through a policy of RPI+0, our argument being that as the Chancellor had continued freezing fuel duty for cars, it was unfair not to take a similar approach to rail fares.

In the department, I was, with Mike Penning, on the third tier of responsibility as Under-Secretary, below Theresa as Minister of

State and Philip as Transport Secretary, but I soon learnt I could have more influence on specific issues than either Theresa or Mike.

This was not a reflection on them, but came about because they answered direct to Philip, who liked to keep a firm grip and was not very keen on delegating, whereas I had a certain status as the representative of the other coalition party. I also had links to the Lib Dems in No. 10 and the Treasury that could bypass the department.

This, of course, was true for all Lib Dem ministers, though some were to take advantage of the position rather more than others.

One good thing about Philip was that, because he did not have a transport background, he was generally prepared to listen to any argument I put and judge it on its merits. It could be hard work, but once he was persuaded of a case, it nearly always happened, even if it required Cabinet clearance.

He was generally content to let me get on with bus policy, in which he thankfully had little interest. About a fortnight into the new government, a round table took place with the great and the good from the bus industry. Philip made a few short introductory remarks and then handed the meeting over to me to take forward.

We had not discussed this and I was taken completely by surprise. Unprepared, I reiterated the Lib Dem policy on which we had fought the election, which was not what the industry wanted to hear, as they politely made plain. Philip said little more during the meeting.

I gather the industry, already concerned before the meeting that I was now the bus minister, was, on the evidence before them, even more concerned that I was to be given something close to free rein.

It was a difficult start, but I am pleased to say that I built up a very good relationship with the industry over my time as minister. I came to the conclusion that they were a good bunch, and I think they came to respect me as a minister who was actually interested in buses and able to deliver money and helpful interventions for the industry.

In early July, Brian Souter came along to meet Philip and me. Brian is a very colourful figure and an extremely successful businessman. He started as a bus conductor in Perth and by the time we met he was running Stagecoach and was a multi-millionaire.

He arrived at the DfT looking very scruffy, in dirty trainers and carrying a supermarket carrier bag. I assume it was on purpose. He was certainly a contrast with Philip in his sharp tailored suit and immaculate shirt and tie.

Brian's unconventional approach appealed to me, as did his sense of humour. He once told me that in Perth, protected sex was when you did it in a bus shelter.

Despite his limited background knowledge of transport, Philip did have one or two ingrained prejudices, as I suppose we all did. I found out about one of these after he returned from holiday at the end of August.

The coalition agreement had committed the government to 'tackle rogue private sector wheel clampers'. I interpreted this, as did virtually everybody else, as a complete ban on private sector wheel clamping, and goodness it was needed, as I had seen from my own constituency. Indeed, it had been that experience that had led me to push for the insertion of the commitment into the coalition agreement.

In far too many places, such as in the car parking area outside Laura Ashley in Lewes (an area not controlled by the shop), what looked like public parking bays were in fact cash cows for shady private companies. In this particular spot, people would park at around 8 a.m. on a Sunday morning to visit the nearby boot sale, only to find on their return that their car had been clamped. A payment in excess of £100 was demanded before the clamp would be released. Any appeal would therefore have to be made after the money was paid, and in any case was made to the company itself. In many cases around the country, the clamping operatives were working on a commission basis.

In Scotland, the courts had ruled in 1994 that this practice was extortion and it had ceased virtually overnight. I agreed with that judgment. After all, in what other sphere could a private company or individual take over your property and demand an eye-watering fee for it to be returned?

During August, therefore, when I was working in the department and Philip was on holiday, I progressed the normal write-round to other departments including No. 10 to clear the decks before proceeding with the ban. No objections were received and I was given the green light to proceed.

When Philip came back and found out, he went ballistic, accusing me of exceeding my authority. He called in the officials, who would in fact confirm that I had acted in line with their advice. His interpretation of the coalition commitment was that 'rogue' operators should be banned, but others should be allowed to continue clamping.

I could not understand why he was so upset. After all, one of the first statements he had made upon taking up post was to declare 'an end of the war on the motorist'. Personally, I did not agree that there had been any such war on the motorist, though I recognised it was a good sound bite for a Tory audience.

But if helping the motorist was what Philip wanted to do, then surely banning private sector wheel clamping was a good expression of that.

He told me he was worried that a complete ban would leave private sector landowners effectively defenceless against intrusive parking on their land. He referred in particular to Royal Holloway College in his constituency in Egham. I deduced he might have been contacted by the college and been caught wrong-footed. As it happens, Royal Holloway was where I studied for my university degree so I knew it well.

Naturally, I had considered the position of private sector land-owners in working up the detailed proposals and was able to tell him that no such problems had arisen in Scotland following the ban. I even had officials contact ScotRail, legally a large private sector car park landowner running 345 stations, to ask them specifically about their experience. They told me that they had had virtually no problems and on the very rare occasions that an issue had materialised, British Transport Police had helped.

Philip would not let the matter go, nagging away at it for the rest of the year. I tried to engage constructively on the aspect he said concerned him, namely the position of private sector landowners, though I began to suspect he was motivated more by pique that I had got one over on him, as I think he saw it, than by the issue itself.

Finally, he set out the criteria he wanted to see met for the scheme to be acceptable to him. These were:

a) that what we do is compatible with what has been said publicly;
b) that the replacement arrangements are effective;
c) that there should be no financial burden on landowners;
d) that the outcome is consistent with the government's approach to reducing regulations.

In response, and keen to put the matter to bed once and for all, I produced my own paper, which I submitted to him. This was, unusually, written by me rather than by civil servants, though I did pass them a copy, which they subsequently complimented me on. They seemed surprised that a minister could write a cohesive policy paper.

My paper set out four options and indicated for each which of the criteria he had set were met.

My suggested way forward was for the ticketing regime on private land to be strengthened by making the keeper of the vehicle liable rather than the driver, and to encourage the private sector to contract the local council to run their parking scheme for them on a cost-neutral basis for the council. I also envisaged that there would have to be backstop powers for the police, for example to deal with foreign vehicles where the keeper could not be identified.

Bob Neill, the local government minister, had confirmed to me that councils had powers to undertake this role under a 1984 Act, which he was happy with, but would oppose anything that required councils to undertake this function, even on a zero-cost basis. I had favoured this latter option, which I thought could have been bolted onto the Protection of Freedoms Bill then going through Parliament.

In the end, I was satisfied that we had acted to eliminate a number of bad practices and put the whole industry in a better place. The ban on wheel clamping finally took effect from 1 October 2012.

One change Philip was particularly keen to make was to increase the speed limit on motorways from 70 to 80 mph. It was a change I was keen to resist.

Politically, it seemed to me that at a time when the department was facing criticism for allegedly cutting back on road safety, this was a gift to the opposition. But my objection was not primarily on safety grounds, although I did think that raising the limit was likely to marginally increase the numbers of people killed or injured on motorways, but rather on climate change grounds.

In response to my query, officials had calculated for me that raising the speed limit from 70 to 80 might increase total surface transport emissions by up to 5 per cent, and 1.4 per cent at a minimum. The Department for Environment, Food and Rural Affairs

(DEFRA) was also concerned about the impact on air pollution levels.

The department also confirmed to me that in 2010, 49 per cent of cars were already exceeding 70 mph on motorways, and 14 per cent travelling faster than 80. An increase in the speed limit was likely to push these speeds up further, particularly if the police continued to apply a tolerance above the limit before they took action.

Philip was not happy with my objection. I had simultaneously been pushing for steps to make it easier for local councils to introduce 20 mph limits in urban areas, and Philip saw his acquiescence to this as a sort of coalition trade-off, though I had never made that connection and did not do so now.

We had already had a run-in over 20 mph limits back in July when I wanted to refer to these in a press notice I was planning to issue about cycling. Philip was against, and various drafts went back and forth between our offices. I was adamant that a reference should be included. He was equally adamant it should not. In the end, I threatened to put out a parallel release via the Lib Dem press office, and he finally gave way. It may help to explain, though, why he was so determined about the motorway limit.

He eventually took it to Cabinet and secured approval for the increase to 80, rather to my annoyance, as I had not known the item was being raised so had had no chance to brief my Lib Dem Cabinet colleagues. In the event, he was moved to Defence before he had the opportunity to enact the change.

The push for 20 mph limits was to be contained in a White Paper I wanted to bring forward on local transport and about which I had informed Philip in July.

This followed one of the most effective interventions I was to make in my time as a minister. It happened very early, in the first week, when, with serendipitous timing, I spoke to Danny Alexander about securing a large sum to allocate to local sustainable transport – serendipitous because he was at that very point looking at the DfT allocations.

As a result, I secured £560 million for a new budget head, provisionally called a Carbon Reduction Fund. This was subsequently renamed the Local Sustainable Transport Fund (LSTF) and proved to be a great success.

The overarching requirement for any scheme to be funded under the LSTF was that it would both cut carbon and help the local economy.

The way the fund was to operate was that local councils would put forward schemes for their area and they would be scored against the two overarching objectives by an independent expert panel including representatives from business, the environmental sector and local government. Their recommendations would then come to me for approval, with Philip overseeing the process, normally in a light-touch way.

Because the objectives were broad in nature, councils were able to come up with what was best for their area, rather than having to fit into a policy straitjacket. In other words, the way to cut carbon and help the economy in Brighton would be very different from what worked in Manchester.

The range of approved projects included new train stations and improved bus or train services, bus priority measures, improved road junctions and traffic flows, new cycle hubs and new cycling and walking routes, often between concentrated housing areas and places of concentrated employment.

The LSTF has made a real difference across England and even changed the mindset of councils, who until that point had paid little attention to sustainable transport interventions. With the introduction of the LSTF, they began to realise that doing the right thing for the environment could also be beneficial to the local economy.

I was keen to create behaviour change, not only in terms of how councils acted but also in terms of how the public thought. I wanted to change mindsets.

I had been appalled when, in 1986, Margaret Thatcher had said that 'a man who, beyond the age of twenty-six, finds himself on a bus can count himself as a failure'. Nor did I like cyclists being seen as Lycra-clad fitness enthusiasts or slightly eccentric environmentalists. I wanted to change the view that we should all aspire to use a car and that anything else was second best.

Some of these attitudes ran deep, not least with ministers themselves, too many of whom seemed to regard a ministerial car as a status symbol. In opposition I had criticised ministers for this and was determined not to succumb to the same easy option.

On my first day as a minister, I walked from the House of Commons to the Department for Transport and timed it as taking ten minutes. This was significant because as an MP you have eight minutes to reach the voting lobbies in the Commons when the division bell sounds, and many votes of course come suddenly, at unpredictable points.

I asked my private office how ministers in the previous Labour government had solved this. Very simple, I was told. They had a car constantly waiting downstairs with a driver in the event that a division was called.

This struck me as an appalling waste of public money and I said that I was not going to follow that practice and indeed did not want a ministerial car at all.

There was a barely audible intake of breath and then a slight pause. How was I going to get to the Commons in time for a vote? I said they could get me a bike.

I was to discover that the DfT civil servants were a good lot:

committed, friendly, helpful and professional. I would enjoy my time there.

The next day, a bike duly appeared: a fold-away green Brompton that had, it seems, been languishing somewhere in the bowels of the department. I would use it to cycle to the Commons and occasionally to Downing Street when I had meetings there.

When I first turned up at Downing Street on my bike and showed my ministerial pass, the police officer on duty looked at me askance and said he had had no notice that I would be arriving by bike. Here was someone who needed a mindset change. I pointed out that ministers arriving by car did not give notice of their vehicle.

He then suggested there was nowhere to put the bike. I pointed to a large expanse adjacent to the end of the terrace. He then suggested it might get stolen. From Downing Street? Behind a secure set of high railings with police officers everywhere?

He eventually let me through but I remembered this irritating exchange some time later when I heard reports of the cycling Andrew Mitchell and his famous altercation with the Downing Street police.

Apart from the practicality of using a bike, I wanted to set an example as cycling minister. I had long taken part in the annual all-party cycling group bike ride, and thought we could encourage this at ministerial level too.

Theresa Villiers was also a cyclist, sometimes arriving at the department on her bike, so in good coalition mode, I suggested that, as a stunt, Theresa and I might cycle to the Commons on a tandem.

I mentioned this in passing to Philip, who immediately asked who would be at the front and who behind. I confess I had not considered this, but he seemed to think it important. I was the cycling minister, but Theresa was a minister of state, and I an under-secretary. In addition, she was, of course, from the larger coalition party.

In the event, we could not source a tandem and in the cold light of the next day, it no longer seemed such a good idea anyway.

The Local Sustainable Transport Fund was also an expression of how the coalition parties could come together to produce a good outcome. I began by being more interested in carbon reduction, and Philip by being keen to help economic regeneration, but the cross-fertilisation that came from this actually produced a more balanced policy than either of us would have constructed on our own.

Politically, it was helpful too, because the fund enabled a large number of relatively cheap but effective interventions to be delivered across the country, and indeed to be delivered within the lifetime of the parliament. Very often, transport projects take much longer, and ministers end up conducting opening ceremonies for schemes a long-forgotten predecessor had agreed. The quick-turn-around nature of many LSTF projects, coupled with the fact that I was to stay in the DfT for three and a half years, meant that, almost uniquely, I was able to inaugurate schemes which I had myself approved earlier in the parliament, which was personally very satisfying.

The White Paper itself finally appeared on 19 January 2011, when I presented it to the Commons through an oral statement. As well as the LSTF, it contained measures to provide more support for cycling, to promote the concept of the door-to-door journey, to review road signage and to simplify funding streams.

Philip and I had a conversation as to the title. I had suggested 'Cutting carbon, creating growth', as to my mind the second followed the first. He was unsurprisingly in favour of 'Creating growth, cutting carbon', which I accepted, firstly because I thought the Secretary of State had come a long way and it would have been churlish of me to have dug my heels in over such a point, and secondly because I was keen to keep the funding stream flowing, and thought that Philip's title would resonate more with the Treasury.

The LSTF had seen central government set high-level objectives but give wide freedom to local councils to determine how to deliver those objectives. This seemed to me to be how devolution, to which both parties were committed, should work.

That the Lib Dems should want to pursue devolution cannot have been a surprise. It had been a mantra in the party for a very long time. That some Tories also shared this enthusiasm was more surprising. They, after all, had never been particularly keen on the concept when in government before.

The problem was that while both parties embraced the idea of devolution right at the outset, it was never clearly defined as to what should be devolved and to whom. For me, the LSTF model made intellectual sense but, all too often, devolution appeared to be much more haphazard, granted to anyone who wanted it or who happened to be in the right place at the right time.

Perhaps for the Conservatives the motivation was about a smaller central government full stop, echoing the philosophy of the Republican Party in the United States, whereas for the Lib Dems it was about having decisions taken at the lowest appropriate level, but still largely within the public sector.

I was particularly unhappy about the handing over of large amounts of decision-making to the new Local Economic Partnerships (LEPs), often drawn from a narrow and unelected section of society – the 'big business' community – and whose quality varied wildly across the country.

In my own area in Sussex, for example, we had a sharp contrast between the South-East LEP, covering Essex, Kent and East Sussex, and the Coast to Capital LEP, roughly following the A23 corridor north from Brighton to the outskirts of London.

East Sussex County Council, under its rather self-satisfied leader Peter Jones, had thought it could create an LEP mirroring the area covered by the council, despite clear indications that this would not get past the government. Accordingly, when the all too predictable refusal arrived, the council had to go cap in hand to Essex and Kent to ask to join. Of course, by that time the early spending priorities had been set and they did not include East Sussex. Another triumph for the county council.

Peter Jones and I had never got on, so I was interested one day to see a matey-matey letter he had written to the Transport Secretary, Philip Hammond, with some ideas he had come up with. Philip was not interested and passed it to me to reply to, which of course I was more than pleased to do.

If the South-East LEP was useless for my patch, Coast to Capital, led by Ron Crank, was a well-organised, far-sighted organisation. They understood that Newhaven had an important economic relationship with Brighton, and also recognised that the port town needed help in its own right. Despite the fact that the Lewes district was not technically in their LEP area, only adjacent to it, they engaged constructively and helpfully, unlike the South-East LEP, which showed no interest at all.

I did actually negotiate with ministers the right for Lewes District to move into the Coast to Capital area, but at the last minute the council backed off, under pressure from the county council.

So it was to this patchwork of unelected bodies that it was proposed to delegate money and authority. This included a new role on selecting local transport schemes for investment.

In the coalition agreement, at my suggestion, there was a commitment to reform the way transport schemes were evaluated 'so that the benefits of low-carbon proposals (including light rail schemes) are fully recognised'. I had long been concerned that, on paper, it was 'cheaper', and so produced a better cost–benefit ratio, for a road to go through a pristine and protected area of beautiful countryside than for it to go virtually anywhere else. This was because no economic value was attached to natural beauty.

I had an ally in Oliver Letwin, with whom I had occasionally worked in opposition on environmental matters when we were both shadowing the portfolio. Oliver, like me, shared an interest in how the economy and the environment dovetailed, and was to raise this issue at one of the regular breakfast meetings that took place monthly to discuss environmental matters.

These breakfasts had been initiated by Caroline Spelman when Secretary of State at DEFRA, and brought together what might be termed 'green ministers' from different departments.

Oliver was always worth listening to and, not untypically, on this occasion posed the question of how we should value Stonehenge. It was possible to quantify a tourist income stream, but what about the value of the stones themselves? How could that be captured?

I found the breakfasts useful occasions to cut across departmental boundaries and ensure environmental considerations were not forgotten. Unfortunately, they ended as soon as Owen Paterson took over from Caroline Spelman at DEFRA.

Philip and I had actually between us produced a better metric to measure schemes. He wanted to call this 'the business case', which is not what I would have called it, but I saw no reason to object.

It had taken some time and put the department's assessment process, already probably the best in Whitehall, on an even stronger footing. So it was with dismay that I learnt that we would have to devolve decisions about significant local schemes, called 'LA majors' by the department, not to local councils but to unelected LEPs and with the minimum of strings attached.

I thought an LSTF-type arrangement should be applied whereby councils, having consulted LEPs, would put forward schemes that would have to meet certain basic criteria. In this instance, that would have been an assessment of each scheme based on the new 'business case' we had introduced. The DfT, in my view, should have the right to veto schemes that had met the minimum criteria, or where the cost–benefit ratio that emerged was poor.

There were, it transpired, people up and down the country who saw this shift in decision-making as an opportunity to reheat old schemes.

'We've been campaigning for a bypass here since 1938,' one of them told me. The reason they had not had one provided, of course, was because it made no economic sense, even under the old pre-business case rules, and had continually been rejected by successive governments as bad value for money.

Now some of these hopeless schemes were to benefit from scarce public money. I also worried about what would happen when someone called in the National Audit Office, which I thought was inevitable. I suspected the department would be held responsible for the scheme, no matter how barking, as we had handed over the money.

The position was made worse by the lack of accountability. I wrote a note to Philip making all these points, and adding: 'I fail to understand how passing decision-making to unelected LEPs in any way improves the democratic accountability of decision-making.'

He was not unsympathetic when we discussed the matter, even if he did observe, accurately, that my position was closer to where the Tories would have been expected to be, whereas his colleagues who were pushing this devolution at the Communities and Local Government (CLG) department and at the Treasury were closer to the classic Lib Dem position.

However, the direction of travel was set, and not by us, so all we could do was set very clear guidance for the LEPs, working alone or in a local transport consortium, and hope for the best.

In fact, the Treasury – and by that I mean the Chancellor – was very happy to make very political decisions whatever the assessment for a particular scheme showed. In 2012, he clocked that the DfT was funding lots of rail schemes and wanted to redress the modal balance in the Budget that autumn.

The DfT had a list of road schemes, some much better value than others, and a handful quite controversial in environmental terms. No matter, the Chancellor rang up to see what schemes were potentially available to announce, then said he would take the lot and pay for them. We had twenty-three in the pipeline. I was happy with eighteen of these, offered qualified support for two others, and opposed three.

The three schemes I was unhappy about were the Norwich Northern Distributor Road, the South Devon link road and the Hastings–Bexhill link road in East Sussex.

The first of these I could live with, especially as I was able to insert a requirement that Norfolk County Council invest in some sustainable transport in Norwich as part of the deal. It was confirmed in these terms in December 2011.

The South Devon link road, designed to bypass Kingskerswell, I thought was not justified and had a worrying environmental impact. However, it was championed rather effectively by my Lib Dem colleague Adrian Sanders, the MP for Torbay, who, sensibly from his point of view, lobbied Danny Alexander for the green light. Danny was much keener on new roads than I was and was not known for his green credentials.

But the most offensive of the schemes was the Hastings–Bexhill link road. This was a pet project of Peter Jones, the Tory leader on East Sussex County Council, who was always more interested in the east of the county than the west. He himself represented Rye, right on the Kent border.

It had a very low cost–benefit ratio, in fact the lowest of any of the forty-five or so local authority schemes we had assessed. It was also highly destructive to a pristine bit of landscape and would threaten rare species and disrupt Bronze Age and Iron Age remains.

The scheme had been due to be approved in November 2011 but I objected very strongly, and a decision was put off while other transport options for the area were looked at. This was the compromise I had come up with.

Peter Jones asked for a meeting with the Transport Secretary to lobby for the road, which took place in March 2012. His face was a picture when he arrived and saw me there as well, in my capacity as Local Transport Minister. Back in June 2010 he had already written to the Tory Chief Whip to complain about a press release I had issued in my capacity as a local MP when I suggested the county council might follow the government's lead on ministerial pay and cut councillors' allowances, rather than increasing them as they were doing. The Chief Whip at the time was of course Patrick McLoughlin, later to become Transport Secretary.

The department's civil servants shared my view that the road was not a good investment and made that view plain to ministers. It might well have died a death had it not been for the Chancellor scooping up whatever road schemes he could find for his Budget announcement. Credit, if that is the word, should also go to the Hastings MP Amber Rudd, who was strongly in favour of the road. It was finally given the go-ahead in April 2013.

Other problems also came about as a result of actions by other departments, especially from CLG under Eric Pickles, who was more willing than most to brazenly interfere in DfT responsibilities.

His first foray was to demand that councils embark on a programme to remove 'street clutter', by which he meant unnecessary signs. As it happened, I shared his view on this and had tried unsuccessfully to get something similar going in East Sussex a while before, but it was clearly a DfT matter, not one for CLG.

For my part, I embarked on a street signs review to identify ways to improve signage, including reducing the number of pointless signs, as well as making other changes to help cyclists, for example. One such change was to allow councils to add the plate 'Except Cyclists' to a No Entry sign, rather than relying on what I called the Evel Knievel sign, namely the one where a motorbike appears to be jumping over a car.

Pickles was not sympathetic to the need for investment in rail freight facilities, necessary to help shift freight from road to rail, and something Theresa Villiers was keen on. Good schemes near Maidstone and Radlett were lost, the latter when an inspector's recommendation for approval was overturned.

Pickles's next foray was even less to my liking. Indeed, it cut across what the department was trying to do through the LSTF, and this time I was annoyed to find he had squared Philip but I had been kept out of the loop, although the issue fell within my portfolio.

It related to a joint DfT/CLG announcement on parking spaces policy for new homes, and I only learnt of it when I saw the press statement.

I sent an uncharacteristically sharp note to Philip on 5 January 2011:

> Last week you made a joint announcement with Eric Pickles on parking space limits for new homes and the scrappage of higher parking charges guidance. Despite parking issues being within my ministerial portfolio, I am concerned to report that I was not made aware of this latest development, or invited to offer my input.

There had been a submission to the Transport Secretary, copied to me, on 16 September but my office had been sent nothing beyond that.

Then, somewhat bad-temperedly, I added, referring to the wording of the press statement: 'Running on from that, in my view the "ending the war on the motorist" rhetoric is not agreed coalition policy but Conservative policy.'

Of course, the horse had bolted, and I doubt if my note had much effect, but I felt better for sending it.

More generally, I could not understand how Eric Pickles, who was by all accounts genuinely committed to devolution, could at the same time try to micro-manage councils on how often they emptied their bins and other such minutiae.

That all said, I did have a degree of reluctant admiration for him. He was undoubtedly a good political operator, and was not afraid to speak his mind.

Later, when I was a Home Office minister, I recall one ad hoc committee meeting in Downing Street, chaired by the Prime Minister, looking at steps to tighten the immigration system. The PM did not believe enough progress was being made quickly enough to close loopholes, and wanted stringent checks to be carried out by landlords.

Pickles thought, and my Lib Dem colleagues and I agreed, that this would place a huge burden on landlords, and he said so clearly. The PM tried to ignore this and to sum up the item as he had wanted. Eric then cut across him, slapping his hand on the table: 'Prime Minister, you're not listening!'

Cameron was taken aback, and shortly afterwards the meeting fumbled through to a close. That particular group was not asked to meet again.

Pickles was, along with Justine Greening, one of the few

Conservative ministers prepared to really stand up to Cameron and Osborne. He was keen to stress that there needed to be a proper planning regime, even if it was less restrictive than I might have liked, and was not afraid to make the point to the Chancellor, who regarded planning controls as an obstacle to growth.

He was the only Tory Cabinet minister to be sacked when the new government was formed in 2015 and was given a knighthood as a consolation prize. Shortly afterwards, the Chancellor used his first Budget of the new parliament to sweep away a plethora of planning protections.

Amongst my portfolio responsibilities was corporate issues – in other words, the internal matters of the department. These provided some real *Yes Minister* moments.

In January 2011, I felt obliged to write to the Permanent Secretary to ask for action on two connected fronts: the building's air conditioning system and staff access to window keys. They were connected because the air conditioning did not work efficiently, creating a temperature that was either chilled or stifling, and the ability to open windows was the only real way to affect this.

The position was most acute after 5.30, when the air conditioning promptly cut out, despite the fact that there were often large numbers of officials and ministers still working.

In response, I was given an assurance that the air conditioning was working in optimum fashion, which it clearly was not, but that it would be looked at afresh at some unspecified point in the future.

I decided to concentrate on the windows, and get some keys so that those in the building had at least some control over their environment.

After weeks of prevarication and inaction, exasperated, I demanded a note as to why keys could not be distributed. It is worth quoting at some length the reply I received from the unfortunate civil servant deputed to deal with this. They were determined not to give me a key and piled reason upon reason:

> As a result of low window sills, staff could fall out of the open window if someone was to trip over an obstacle or absent-mindedly leant against what they thought was a closed window … the more windows are open, the bigger the risk.
>
> A significant number of staff use the window sills for storage, and such items could be knocked out of an open window and fall onto passers-by below with possibly serious consequences.
>
> There have been some instances in the last two years of people firing air guns from the flats behind GMH … open windows could allow staff to be targets.
>
> Continually opening and closing windows can weaken the locks on the windows which are fifteen years old and could allow the window to open unexpectedly (this has already happened at least once). At the moment the windows can only be opened and closed by security staff.
>
> Providing staff with keys could lead to a security breach. [On the sixth floor?]
>
> There can sometimes be strong draughts through the windows especially on the higher floors which can blow papers around.
>
> To agree to open a window for one person immediately sets a precedent for others who may not find the air conditioning to their liking so we could end up with windows being opened across the building.

Presumably because the air conditioning was not working properly.

Faced with this barrage of guff, I took a practical and pragmatic approach. Jo Guthrie, the excellent private secretary who ran my office, went out to a buy a window key from a hardware shop in Strutton Ground. We then had to keep it hidden, as, if it became known we had one, it might have been confiscated. Besides, the Secretary of State's office wanted to keep borrowing it to open their windows.

My private office team and I hit upon another stratagem to get some air into our office. We would keep the doors to the corridor open. Because of the way the doors were hung, this required a couple of door wedges. However, we were told we could not have any, as the doors in question were fire doors so had to stay shut. More business for the hardware shop.

I was finding it easier to squeeze millions out of the Treasury than to get simple changes enacted within the department itself.

Incidentally, Jo Guthrie's direct contact with Philip's office went beyond window keys one day, when she set the fire alarms off while she was using the toaster in the small kitchen on our floor. The building was evacuated, which including turfing Philip out of a board meeting with all the department's non-executive directors. Needless to say he was furious and had the toaster removed immediately. Mike Penning was very sweet about the whole thing and gave Jo a box of chocolates.

Chapter 17

The abiding image of the coalition government has to be the famous – or it is infamous? – joint press briefing in the rose garden of 10 Downing Street, when David Cameron and Nick Clegg strode out together to address the assembled media. It was a good setting and I wondered why previous prime ministers had not sought to exploit it further.

Before the election, the public had seemed favourable to coalition. As politicians, we were told that the public did not like the Punch-and-Judy politics they saw at Prime Minister's Questions, which for many represented what politics was. We were encouraged to work together more in the national interest. Now the election was out of the way, the public did not seem so sure.

The general view was that a coalition could not be formed, and when it was, that it could not last. Yes, it was the normal state of affairs across the Channel, but this was Britain. It was different. Even by 2012, with the coalition firmly established, only one voter in six thought it would survive through to 2015.

As Lib Dems, we regarded it as important to show that coalition could not only survive, but deliver good government too. If the public concluded that coalition was a bad idea, that could herald a return to two-party politics. We therefore set great store by making it work, and sacrificed a good deal in the beginning to do so.

Like many, I watched the rose garden event on television, and with some bemusement. The two leaders were just so friendly.

It is easy to be wise after the event, but looking back, something more formal, perfectly polite but business-like, would have been better for us, such as the two men sitting behind a desk in a sober room, signing an accord. The rose garden event looked like a love-in rather than a business arrangement, and suggested to some, wrongly, that we had just joined the enemy, or been annexed.

Well, we did prove that coalition could work, and work well, and a lot better than the previous unofficial coalition between the Blairites and the Brownites had. The country would not have had the stability it badly needed in 2010 without it, though doubtless exam questions in years to come will ask to what extent we saved the country and destroyed ourselves in the process. We have, I think, won the public over to the concept that coalition can work, but ironically we are no longer in a position to take advantage of that success.

We were all incredibly naive about how government actually worked when we took office. It might have been sensible to have tapped into the knowledge base that we did have – people like Shirley Williams and David Steel – more than we in fact did.

Nick was told by the Cabinet Secretary, Gus O'Donnell, that the civil service was all geared up for coalition. It was not.

Nick himself was allocated next to nobody to help him and for the first few weeks was up until 2 a.m. quite often, trying to wade through the boxes of government papers that relentlessly turned up, until he worked out he could have some more help.

There was an absence of comprehensive protocols, and much was left to individual ministers to sort out for themselves, which helps to explain the vast differences in approach I experienced in the two departments where I served.

Even where the coalition arrangements broadly settled down all right, as at the DfT, there was only a hazy understanding of how the politics was working, and almost none at all of the Lib Dem mindset. My civil servants found the internal democracy of the party bizarre, particularly the fact that I would have to share information and consult with party members, including other MPs, to come to a party view. This contrasted with the Tories, who felt no such obligations. On one occasion, Simon Burns, who replaced Theresa Villiers as rail minister, simply refused to meet the Tory leader of Buckinghamshire County Council because he, Simon, did not want to talk about HS2. I would never have got away with such an approach.

When the House was sitting, we as Lib Dem ministers would meet once a week on a Monday for an hour to take stock and plan future activity. This followed directly from a short meeting of Lib Dem Cabinet members to which other ministers were sometimes invited, depending on the agenda. We would also have a meeting of the whole Commons parliamentary party every Wednesday, scheduled for two hours though it sometimes ran longer.

In addition, there was a team led by an MP and a peer which shadowed each department and met weekly. It also had the task of producing forward policy. I did not want to cramp their activity but nor did I want to send a message that they were unimportant, so I would tend to appear about once a month.

Then there were the non-parliamentary structures, the most important of which was the federal executive, comprising ordinary members of the party elected to this body, and of course our twice-yearly conference. Unlike the other two parties, our conference was sovereign, and whatever it decided, that was then party policy.

This was no abstract issue. Conference decided before the 2010 general election that we were to go into that election with a pledge to end tuition fees. The saga that followed was mishandled at every step and did the party immense damage.

Somehow the other two parties managed to escape the opprobrium heaped on our heads. Labour had promised not to introduce fees, and then done so, and then it had promised not to introduce top-up fees and had broken that promise.

For the Tories, David Cameron pledged in 2003: 'A Conservative government would scrap Labour's plans for tuition fees for university students.'

After the 2010 general election, both Labour and the Tories made it clear that fees were here to stay and that this principle was non-negotiable.

Our 2010 manifesto intention to scrap fees was well meant, and there was no attempt to deceive. Conference had been accustomed over decades to passing motions that MPs could then articulate in Parliament. The idea that we might have to implement something was a novel concept, whatever we had been told about going back to our constituencies to prepare for government.

However, there were some who knew even before the election that this was a hostage to fortune, including our universities spokesman Stephen Williams and indeed Nick Clegg himself. The two of them tried to ditch the policy but could not get the party to agree. It is ironic that Nick took the hit for a policy he had tried and failed to get rid of.

If the first mistake was to adopt the policy, and the second to refuse to change it, the third was not to give it sufficient weight in the coalition negotiations. We needed to negotiate a right to vote against, given that we had all publicly signed up to a pledge. We did not. Instead, there was an agreement for us to collectively abstain, so that the net result of Lib Dem votes was plus or minus zero.

The fourth was then to fall apart over the issue in the parliamentary party, with a good number determined to vote against, meaning that those of us on the payroll were told to vote for, in order to achieve the plus or minus zero. We split three ways, so looked a shambles, and I and others were left trying to explain our vote for. It was a futile exercise.

The tuition fees vote was the only one in my time as a minister that I actively considered resigning over. Naturally, I did not relish this. The vote had come early in the parliament and I had only just got my feet under the table and was already getting things done at the DfT.

Some of the commentators, knowing my independent spirit, had predicted when the government was formed that I would be the first to resign over something, and I had no wish to prove them right.

Our Chief Whip Alistair Carmichael knew I was very troubled and I was twice called to see Nick Clegg in his spacious room in the Cabinet Office. Nick leant on me heavily not to resign. All other ministers were going to vote for, he told me. How would it reflect on them if I were to vote against? In the end, I promised to do as he had asked.

As I went up the stairs to the voting lobby, I did so with a heavy heart and the Nina Simone song 'Either Way I Lose' in my head. I felt dirty as I went through the lobby and gave my name to the desk clerk. I had lost my political virginity.

I must have looked terrible, for Alistair saw me and invited me in for a drink.

'Have a glass of whisky,' he said.

'Have you got the revolver as well?' I returned.

The fifth mistake was to allow the phrase 'tuition fees' to stick when actually Vince had succeeded in turning the thing into more of a graduate tax.

The sixth was to take ownership of the policy rather than explaining that we did not like it but it was a coalition trade-off.

This, in fact, was a recurring fault with our presentation throughout the parliament. Coalitions meant trade-offs in both directions, so why not be open and say so? And while we often told voters what we had stopped the Tories doing, we did not tell them what they had stopped us doing, which might have given the public more of an idea of what we actually stood for.

I was dismayed time and again to realise that even those members of the public in my constituency who took an active interest in politics did not seem to understand what the ramifications of a coalition were. Many thought, for example, that Lib Dems could regularly vote against the Tories, seemingly mixing up a coalition with a minority government, except that somehow there were Lib Dem ministers taking decisions too. That we did not do so reinforced the inaccurate view that we had become Tory patsies.

Others complained that we had not enacted all our general election promises. It was in vain that I would point out that we only had fifty-seven out of 650 MPs. How were we supposed to force things through from that position?

Yet more people thought I personally should vote according to my conscience on every issue, thereby sweeping away in one go the entire party system, not to mention collective ministerial responsibility. They seemed astonished when I told them that the first time I voted against the government I would have to resign as a minister.

Locally, and especially in Lewes, people were used from my opposition days to me being bolshie and loudly declaring exactly what I thought. They seemed to think I could continue to do so as a minister. Others, who recognised that this was not possible, wanted me, and indeed the Lib Dems generally, to leave the government. But what sense was there in arguing that those they broadly agreed with should leave the government to those whom they detested? Was government in their eyes only for the bad guys?

The tuition fees episode could not have gone more wrong. And of course it played to the toxic view of politicians as people who cannot be trusted. I knew just how powerful that sentiment was from my work on MPs' expenses. We had come out of that as the cleanest of the three parties, and now that crucial advantage had been lost. For many of the public, 'Nick broke his promise' and that was that.

And that was that for many of our activists too, who were deeply uncomfortable anyway at being yoked together with the Conservatives. The internal opposition was muted, however, first by the fact that we had made it into government, and second because we had actually gone through a democratic process, even if it had to be a rushed one, to validate the decision.

If our side were uneasy, so were the Tories, not least because the whole thing had been bounced on them without any sort of consultation. They particularly objected to the notion that Nick Clegg had been made Deputy Prime Minister, and that the Lib Dems had all these ministerial positions.

Some, like the Wellingborough MP Peter Bone, would not let go. He was always trying to establish what would happen if David Cameron disappeared under a bus, perhaps thinking of the Scottish precedent when Jim Wallace had stepped up when there was no Labour First Minister for a time. Nick told him he had an unhealthy fascination with the demise of his leader.

The Prime Minister himself was very open to coalition. For him, it made more sense than trying to run a minority government, and the combined total of the two parties was such that damage from renegade elements in his own party was unlikely to result in lost votes.

Perhaps this was linked to his personal style. During my time in government, I formed the impression that the Prime Minister was often acting as chairman of the board rather than chief executive. He did not seem to bother much about detail, unless it was a topic he had seized on, in which case he could become quite petulant.

The Chancellor, on the other hand, was much more on top of the detail. He was also, in a sense, much more political. Everything was a battle to be won, whereas the Prime Minister was more prepared to give and take, and so much better suited to coalition than his Chancellor. Had the 2015 election left the Conservatives short of an overall majority and the Lib Dems in greater numbers, I am in little doubt Cameron would have sought to continue the coalition.

Chapter 18

I cannot say I was sorry to see Philip Hammond moved to the position of Defence Secretary. He had become increasingly hard work, from my point of view, and I actually thought he was an excellent choice to go to the Ministry of Defence. That department was legendary for its financial overruns and sloppy accounting, and Philip, known for his forensic attention to figures, was just the man to sort it out.

Some time after his appointment, when we were in the chamber together, I drew to his attention a fact I had discovered that morning, namely that service personnel reporting for duty were given a rail warrant that entitled them to an open ticket, the cost of which is normally way in excess of that for an advance ticket. As the day and time they were due to report was known in advance, here was a way to save a tidy sum. He lapped up the information, though whether he acted upon it I do not know.

Philip, who had been one of the least coalition-friendly Tories while at the Department for Transport, became noticeably worse when he moved to Defence. I was told that this was because I had got too much past him and he was determined not to let it happen again. That is rather satisfying if it is true.

Certainly, later on when Nick Clegg had swapped around our ministerial allocation and left us without a minister at the MoD, Philip neatly locked the door and made access to information and meetings virtually impossible for the Lib Dem special adviser, Monica Allen, whose job it was to represent us in the department.

Philip's replacement at the Department for Transport was Justine Greening, who was altogether much more to my liking. She was open and friendly, for a start, even to the extent that she regularly called me Normski, for reasons she never explained. I doubt if it was linked to the British rapper who uses that handle. Moreover, her transport instincts were much more akin to mine. No 80 mph limits with Justine.

I did think, though, that her appointment was a somewhat peculiar one in one key aspect. She was violently against a third runway at Heathrow, and indeed had come to my attention in opposition when she made an impressively well-researched case against it from the Tory backbenches.

The general view was that her position on Heathrow had not been factored in. Reshuffles tended to be more haphazard than they publicly appeared.

The coalition spent the parliament putting off a decision about runway capacity in the south-east and deliberately fudging the various options. The Tories had been against Heathrow prior to the election, largely for local environmental reasons, for which read 'votes in marginal seats'.

That factor was not without significance for Lib Dems either, but we also took a wider environmental view that aviation was a major problem in climate change terms, and that it could not simply be allowed to grow without a solution, or at least without substantial mitigation to this being found. It had become very clear that the industry's promises not to use capacity had been broken time and again, as Justine herself had set out. Our position therefore was against any new runway in the south-east.

Earlier in 2011, Philip had asked me for the Lib Dem view on aviation and I set this out in a note:

> Just as I have suggested that the enemy is not the car, it's the carbon, so it is the problems associated with aviation that need to be addressed rather than the concept itself ... the government should aim to do what it can to 'clean up' flying to get it in a better place for the future.

I then drew his attention to proposals from the Lib Dem manifesto:

a) no more capacity increase in the south-east;
b) the use of fiscal measures including the replacement of Air Passenger Duty with a carbon-based per-plane duty;
c) the inclusion of aviation in the EU Emissions Trading Scheme;
d) measures to reduce stacking over London;
e) more use of biofuels.

There was actually a commitment in the coalition agreement to introduce a per-plane duty, but that ran into trouble, notably with the Americans, who argued that it breached international agreements. The point was never tested but the fact that these agreements had been entered into long before anyone had ever heard of climate change, and were international, made them particularly difficult to change.

An aviation scoping document followed in March, with a helpful commentary from Theresa Villiers. I wrote a note to say I agreed with her comments on climate change, biofuels (which she correctly identified as potentially helpful on the edges but incapable of existing in sufficient quantity to be a silver bullet) and the need for a section on alternatives to travel.

I also made the point that the document needed to look beyond the big three airports serving London. 'A restriction on runway capacity here without restrictions at, say Luton or Southend, could lead to an unplanned and uncoordinated leakage of flights to smaller airports in a way that could thwart moves to control carbon emissions,' I wrote.

The coalition duly established an Airports Commission under Sir Howard Davies in September 2012, after much anguish about who should chair it and what the terms of reference might be. I was content in the end that Sir Howard was a good choice, and the leeway given to him was sufficiently great not to be a problem in terms of what our manifesto had said. Conveniently, the Commission would not produce its final report until after the general election.

Philip had been pragmatic over aviation, recognising the position set out in the coalition agreement. He and I independently came to see merit in the idea of 'Heathwick', creating a better hub airport by linking Heathrow and Gatwick. This could be achieved by extending HS2, then planned with a spur to Heathrow, onward to Gatwick. The plan was also favoured by Oliver Letwin, and I tried to interest Sir Howard in the concept when we met.

Philip even went as far as getting Andrew McNaughton, then the chief engineer at Network Rail, to sketch out a route, which hugged the M25 and disappeared beneath Staines. Journey time would be just fourteen minutes. Naturally, the aviation industry hated it, as it ruled out an extra runway, and they did their best to rubbish it.

In the end, not only did we not get the extension to Gatwick, but the spur to Heathrow was lost as well, as was the link between HS1 and HS2. On the latter, it is certainly true that the link proposed, a clunky arrangement using part of the north London line, would have done immense damage to Camden, but there is a tunnelled route available that could have been used instead. Isolating HS2 from HS1, and not connecting it into Heathrow, is a false economy and must adversely affect the cost–benefit ratio of the scheme.

With Justine replacing Philip and Theresa Villiers and I remaining in post, we now had the Transport Secretary, the aviation minister and the Lib Dem in the department all on record as being strongly against a third runway.

Justine had been appointed Economic Secretary at the Treasury in 2010 and promoted to Transport Secretary in October 2011 when Philip Hammond had moved to Defence to replace Liam Fox. Hers was a big promotion, and one which suggested that Osborne rather than Cameron had determined the posting. If she was the Chancellor's choice then I suspect he may have been disappointed, for she frequently adopted positions that I cannot think the Chancellor would have wanted. She would be moved again, sideways if not downward, at the next reshuffle.

My route to achieving what I wanted changed with the replacement of Philip with Justine. Philip tended to be much warier of any idea emanating from me or the Lib Dems generally, but was ultimately open-minded and if he could be persuaded of a course of action then it would happen. Justine needed much less persuasion but then seemed unable on too many occasions to get a move past her Cabinet colleagues, to the extent that I would use my contacts at the centre, not to block as I had sometimes sought to do with Philip, but to support Justine.

She never said so to me, but I was told by officials that she resented the fact that I often seemed to have more clout in the centre than she did.

Justine was a good supporter of public transport and when a departmental under-spend was identified in late 2011, she was very open to using much of this for buses. Perhaps, being a London MP, she was more appreciative of the role the bus can play. Bus use in London had been rising for years, and generally falling elsewhere.

Justine did, however, almost derail the long-awaited tram–train pilot. This was a novel idea that trams might switch between tram and train lines and would mean, for example, that where you had a station with limited through capacity, like Manchester Piccadilly, you could have a tram approach on normal rail lines, but then divert onto tram lines on the street, before rejoining the rail lines further on.

The Labour government had progressed this over a long time and concluded that Sheffield–Rotherham was the corridor for a trial. Philip had wanted me to re-examine this, and I did at some length, looking at alternatives. But because you need an electrified section – there are no diesel trams – I concluded that Labour's choice had been right. I also told Philip I had knocked a large amount off the estimated cost, which caused a particular expression of restrained delight to flit across his face as if he had just eaten a surprisingly tasty liqueur chocolate.

So far, so good, except that Justine, having been a Rotherham girl, wanted to look at the matter again in detail and was concerned that the trial might affect the regular train operation. Her intervention, in October 2011, risked causing a problem with agreed investment in new trams for Sheffield, the case for which partly rested on this project.

I wrote to her on 7 November:

> In summary, the pilot has been properly cleared and has been announced publicly … it has been well received … for these reasons and because there is synergy with the extra vehicles bid for the Sheffield Supertram, due to be announced in the December Development Pool, I would now like to progress this without further delay.

Then the Treasury started raising questions, wanting to go over old ground yet again. Finally, on 15 May, I got hold of Danny Alexander who, when faced with a prolonged phone call from me, instead decided to sign the project off. I would announce the decision at the Annual Light Rail conference, having tabled a ministerial statement earlier that day.

The project went ahead, though by the 2015 election we were still waiting to see the results.

Justine also had to deal with Sheffield matters when she spoke to the Deputy Prime Minister, whose constituency was Sheffield Hallam.

Her dealings with Nick Clegg were friendlier than Philip's had been. Normally, Philip had only rung Nick when he wanted to complain about me, particularly about any media coverage I had secured which expressed views he disliked. He would never tell me he had done this, and nor would Nick, who regarded his whinging as a pain and never acted on the calls. I would only find out through Nick's staff.

Sometimes Nick and Justine seemed almost too friendly. One late evening, the two spoke on the phone when Justine was by all accounts more than a little tired and emotional. She mentioned to Nick that she had had a good day out courtesy of Pete Waterman, the steam train fanatic, and Nick then said he would look out for the song titles in this conversation.

It was a throwaway line and not a terribly funny one. In any case, Nick's knowledge of '80s pop is not extensive so when Justine began dropping song titles into the conversation, they were passing him by.

Nick wanted to talk about HS2, particularly as it might affect Sheffield, and in response to one point he made, Justine replied: 'I should be so lucky.'

This did not seem to make sense. Nick ploughed on about the

political difficulties he might face from Labour in Sheffield if the route was wrong.

'Never gonna give you up,' replied Justine, which to Nick must have sounded unnaturally effusive.

At the end of the conversation, Nick wondered whether she was all right and if he should take any action. Those who had been listening to the conversation, as civil servants and special advisers often would in such circumstances, had to gently explain to Nick why she had been acting as she had.

I got involved in this because both the line options being seriously considered for the city were highly destructive. One would have to go through the major shopping complex at Meadowhall, while another would effectively shut down Firth Rixson, a hugely important local employer. Nick was naturally worried about the impact of either option, including politically.

I got hold of a detailed map and studied it. It seemed to me there was an obvious third way, if I can use that phrase, pulling the line slightly to the east. I pointed this out to the HS2 people, who looked taken aback, and then agreed that, yes, this would work although it would lengthen journey times by perhaps a minute. Just do it, I said. That is the route that was then progressed.

I was pleased to be able to come up with a solution, as was Nick, though I do not believe it required a great feat of imagination and I did wonder why those to whom we were paying vast sums could not have come up with it themselves.

A good deal of my time at the DfT was spent on buses, which I regarded as the backbone of public transport, and which I felt had been neglected. It helped that two of the secretaries of state I served under, Justine and Patrick, were broadly supportive and the third, Philip, was not really interested so was generally content to let me handle bus matters myself.

I became rather good at securing regular sums for various funding streams beyond those in the Local Sustainable Transport Fund, such as successive iterations of the Green Bus Fund, which the industry naturally welcomed.

In March 2012, I was able to launch a major package of measures to help the bus industry, set out in a paper, 'Green Light for Better Buses'. This included a new concept, the Better Bus Area, which was a construct of mine to try to get the industry and local councils to work better together. Where they did work well together, as in Brighton or Oxford, bus patronage was on the increase.

Essentially, we would make money available to local councils who had plans to improve bus services in their area – but, crucially, they had to get a sign-off from the major operators in that area.

The idea was welcomed both by local councils, who controlled the bids and could win extra money, and by the industry, who had an effective veto. It was a neat way forward.

While the concept was mine, the name came from one of the bright civil servants in my private office, Adam McIntee. I had originally intended to call them Bus Improvement Zones, but Adam pointed out, rightly, that this might create a stigma, might be read as implying areas where there was a problem that needed to be rectified.

As well as the new Better Bus Area, there was more money for a third round of the Green Bus Fund. This was something I was keen on. It cut carbon emissions from buses, and a great many of the new buses tended to be British-built, so it also helped our own industry. Community transport got a handout too.

There was also the government's response to a recent competition inquiry into buses, which recommended more multi-operator ticketing and other passenger improvements, and a policy announcement of the future of BSOG.

I thought this merited an oral statement to the Commons, and Justine agreed that I could deliver this. To my frustration, we were blocked by Sir George Young, then leader of the Commons, who did not think buses were an appropriate topic for an oral statement.

One innovation I narrowly failed to get adopted as government policy was a proposal for discounted bus travel for young people. The scheme I worked up would have given either a 50 per cent or a 67 per cent discount on full fares for all 16–19-year-olds, twenty-four hours a day.

I thought this would go some way to repairing the damage caused by tuition fees; help offset the problems caused by the removal of education maintenance allowance early in the coalition; and provide more foot-fall for the bus operators.

The scheme was worked up by officials, based on my steer, and was essentially ready to go by September 2013. We needed a Lib Dem idea to match the Tory wish for the reintroduction of married couple's tax allowance, and my scheme was one of two front runners. In the end, Nick plumped for the other front runner instead: free school meals.

Chapter 19

The nature of my portfolio was such that I would often visit somewhere different in England each week. I found such visits useful in getting feedback on what we were doing, and in picking up ideas.

When I first became a minister, I was shocked to be accompanied by four civil servants on a visit. I told them this was a waste of money and henceforth I would have two at most: one from my private office and one from the relevant policy section, or a departmental press person.

The visits were co-ordinated between my private office and the relevant policy section, though occasionally that meant some bits fell in the gap between. On one visit to Derby in 2011 to open a new road, nobody seemed to have noticed that a contingent from the local Mercian regiment was due to be in attendance.

So, when I arrived, I was greeted by a long line of soldiers that I was apparently expected to inspect. I knew nothing about the regiment. It occurred to me that I ought to know if they had been on active service recently in Iraq or Afghanistan but there was really nobody I could ask. Those with me from the DfT to whom I had mumbled some urgent questions knew as much, or as little, as I did.

To add to that, I had never inspected soldiers before, and anyway it seemed a weird thing for a transport minister to be doing.

But I walked along the line, making comments and asking questions that I hoped were not too facile.

At the end of the line was a ram. A real one. I tried to look matter-of-fact. Of course. What else would you expect to meet but a ram when you had come to unveil a plaque on a new road?

This, I was told, was the regiment's mascot.

'What is his name?' I asked, not knowing what else to say.

'Lance Corporal Derby XXIX, sir,' I was told. I did not ask what he had done to progress through the ranks.

I understand the ram died on 6 December 2013. His replacement is the humbler Private Derby XXX.

It would be unfair to imply that this surprise element was typical. The contents of visits were normally well planned by my office, though they could not always anticipate events.

In April 2012, I went to Blackpool to launch the town's new state-of-the-art trams, and was able to see Britain's newest and oldest trams side by side. Even though the weather was not great, the trip up the line was jolly, enlivened by some rather good musicians at one of the stops. It turned out, though, that I left just in time. Shortly afterwards, the first passenger journey saw one of the new trams derailed by sand in the tracks, which I suppose made a change from leaves on the line.

Normally, coalition issues did not arise in these visits. Councils of whatever persuasion were just glad to see a minister and a department taking an interest in them. One exception was the invitation the department received to open the new Buckshaw Parkway rail station, which fell to me. This was scheduled for 16 November 2011, but the Tory council took exception to the idea that a Lib Dem was to open it. In the end, the friendly Tory spads had a quiet word with them and the opening eventually proceeded instead on 5 December.

If the visits on the ground were generally well organised, the same cannot always be said of the transport arrangements to get there.

I made it plain at the outset that I wanted to use the train on all occasions, not least because it let me get on with some work on the way to and from engagements, and in any case I disliked the concept of ministerial cars. In opposition, I had established through parliamentary questions that ministers were clocking up over a million miles a year.

I do not know whether rail travel had been something of a rarity, but on the first trip on which Adam McIntee was to accompany me, he managed to miss the train at King's Cross and I was left travelling alone and ticketless to Newcastle, he having the train tickets for both of us.

I did not fancy the headlines about a transport minister being caught fare-dodging, and neither did Adam, who had to frantically blag his way past four levels of Network Rail management to get them to call the train and ensure the conductor was aware of the situation.

Nor did the department seem to understand how to buy cheap rail tickets, and in particular to understand that advance tickets were much cheaper than open ones. How was it that the department responsible for rail did not seem to know this?

When I had to go abroad on one occasion, I indicated that I wanted to go by train. The advice came back that it would cost several hundred pounds more by train than by air. I did not believe this and within a few minutes on the internet had found a rail option in line with the air price.

In Berlin I attended the international rail exhibition called InnoTrans. It was a useful trip, but I came away thinking Britain was missing a trick. While other countries like France and Germany were offering comprehensive rail packages off the shelf, we had no

such co-ordinated offer to help some of the great small companies who were out there. On my return, I wrote to Stephen Green
at United Kingdom Trade and Investment (UKTI) to suggest we
create a 'UK Rail' to offer comprehensive packages for overseas pur-
chasers. He replied saying my letter was 'timely', adding, 'There is
strong merit in exploring "UK Rail" as a "virtual" marketing brand
to help support the UK rail sector, especially SMEs.'

I also insisted, when I represented the government at the
International Transport Forum in Leipzig, that we would use the
train. The cost was about the same, and the journey very pleasant, not least because Deutsche Bahn offered me a ride in the cab
of one of their super-fast high-speed trains. The sensation of speed
you get when looking forwards is much greater than I was used
to when looking out of the window of a high-speed train. Distant
objects are overtaken in seconds and, to the amateur eye, the train
looks more vulnerable.

Others who had come from London to Leipzig were travelling
back by air. They had quietly scorned my decision to go by train,
but they encountered delays and I was back in London before
many of them.

It occurred to me that if even the DfT was missing a trick with
prices, the chances of other departments getting best value was
remote.

As part of my wider role within government, I co-chaired
with Oliver Letwin something called the Greening Government
Committee. This had been set up in the heady days of 2010 when
the Tories were still interested in the environment, or at least pretending to be.

To be fair to Oliver, he still was, not least because he realised,
as I did, that reducing the environmental footprint was likely to
reduce bills as well.

The committee had a list of areas it was monitoring across government, such as energy and water consumption, with targets to reduce use. One target was to reduce UK air travel by 20 per cent by 2015. Some departments, like the MoD, seemed to take an enormous number of internal flights, and that was discounting all operational flights, which were outside scope.

As part of the work, I established that the government was, on average, paying 43p per mile for rail travel, whereas the private sector was paying only 36p. If we could adopt the approach of the private sector, we would save the taxpayer £6.5 million each year. Oliver and I wrote round to all departments to cajole them into getting smarter, though I doubt it did much good.

One of Justine's initiatives was to invite female civil servants to come up with 'small acts of love'. These were small interventions that might resonate with the public, and especially women.

I thought this was an interesting idea and a good way to tap into the knowledge base of the department, including those further down the chain whose views would not normally be sought.

Accordingly, I consulted with women in my policy areas and had nearly a hundred ideas put forward. These included:

- An open day where women could have a go at driving a bus (Arriva had initiated this)
- Train and bus companies to advertise jobs in women's magazines
- Loyalty cards, whereby public transport operators work with retailers to give public transport discounts in return for purchases
- Rail carriages where mobile phone signals are jammed
- Female-driven taxis on request
- Reduced-rate carnets for rail

- Plug sockets and Wi-Fi on all trains
- More controversially, means-testing pensioners for eligibility for free bus passes

Some of the recommendations were impractical, and others for bodies other than government, but it was a useful exercise, not just generating interesting ideas but making everyone feel part of the team.

Another initiative that Justine and I were keen on was what she called Project Light Bulb. This was the work we were undertaking to promote the uptake of electric vehicles. This hit all the policy buttons, particularly reducing carbon and helping manufacturing. The government's efforts to date had given a clear and consistent message to industry, and they had responded well. Investment was occurring and, for the first time for about forty years, as a nation we were exporting more cars than we were importing. By 2014, the UK sales of electric cars were the highest in Europe.

Justine was keen to see what further incentives we could apply, and whether some equivalent of the Green Deal could be worked up. Of course, it was important to ensure that the infrastructure was there to enable vehicles to be recharged, and this too was going well, through a combination of the government's Plugged-In Places scheme and private sector initiatives.

The one frustration came at the hands of Eric Pickles, as it so often did. Philip and I had argued for building regulations to be amended to require charge points to be fitted as standard in new homes. The cost would probably have been less than £50 per home, as opposed to maybe £1,000 to retrofit subsequently, but Pickles would have none of it.

Unfortunately, the good position we had established by the 2015 general election has been put in jeopardy by vehicle excise duty changes in George Osborne's post-election Budget, where he seemed to want to gratuitously undermine any green policies he could, irrespective of their merits and, in this case, the negative effect on British manufacturing.

I was spending more and more time on rail. At the start of the coalition, all rail had fallen under Theresa Villiers, but to my surprise, one day she told me that she was finding her portfolio too onerous and did I want to take some of rail? Naturally, I had said yes.

Theresa used to spend hours preparing for transport questions in the Commons and got noticeably stressed about it. Mike Penning and I would typically spend less than an hour each and busk it.

I would get irritated by the briefings I was given at both the DfT and later the Home Office for oral questions. They would come in the form of a huge pack, filled with irrelevant material, such as policy I knew anyway and had probably helped to create. Vainly, month after month I told them that all I wanted were key statistics, constituency information about the MP asking the question, and anything topical I needed to know. In the end, I pointed out that ministers had about five seconds max before they had to start answering the question, and how likely was it I would find the statistic I needed, probably hidden away on page ninety-four? Gradually, they got better.

Following Theresa's decision to hand some rail to me, the rough division was between future rail, which she kept, including HS2, where much of her work was, and present rail, which I took. This included performance monitoring and the like. The division worked well, not least because we kept in close contact with each other and got on well on a personal basis. She even came down one year to see Lewes Bonfire – the only time I have had a Tory minister in my home.

There was a perception that the railway was not working properly, that it was too expensive, and that it compared badly with other European railways.

Actually, this was not fair. Frankly, we have a good railway service in this country that delivers people safely and reasonably efficiently despite huge constraints on the network.

In terms of fares, the media always reach for the open single, the walk-on fare, as the one to quote. It is tempting to do so, and to be honest, I used to do the same thing in opposition. Yet most commuters buy season tickets and most long-distance travellers buy much cheaper advance tickets.

In essence, every airline ticket is an advance ticket, so the media should compare advance tickets across the modes for a fairer comparison.

Other European countries may have cheaper walk-on fares, but they have far fewer bargains, and the price of travelling by rail in the UK actually compares favourably with other EU countries. But there was, and is, a PR job for the industry to do and they have not done it successfully.

One story that got headlines was the first fare over £1,000, which turned out to be a walk-on first-class ticket between somewhere in Cornwall and some remote spot in the far-flung Highlands of Scotland. The papers lapped it up, and it generated bad publicity for the industry. But the truth was that nobody at all, except possibly the journalist who wrote the story, had ever bought this unlikely ticket.

I suggested to the industry that they should cap the maximum fare at £500, on the basis that the PR advantage was significant, and the loss of income minimal, something they agreed to do.

In fact, the main issue with the railways was a problem of success. Over the previous twenty years, passenger numbers had doubled, with more people being carried than at any time since 1929, and on a railway about half the size it was then.

The relatively easy steps had been taken. Trains and platforms had been lengthened, more trains added, improvements to passenger flow introduced.

All this meant that the network was very heavily used, on some lines with all trains at maximum length and no train paths left at all in peak hours. If just one train is delayed, it can have a knock-on effect on many more behind it.

Even though I recognised the constraints, I was exercised by the deteriorating punctuality across the network and felt the industry could do better.

Once a month I would hold a formal meeting in my office with senior representatives from Network Rail, the train operating companies and the Office of Rail Regulation (ORR) to discuss performance. Not all of the loss of punctuality could be explained by congestion. In particular, there were too many failed signals and broken rails, squarely in Network Rail's area of responsibility.

These were often challenging meetings. For one thing, I did not rate the senior civil servant who led on this area. For another, Network Rail tended to be represented by Robin Gisby, who would smoothly explain at length why the latest terrible figures caused by infrastructure failure presaged an improvement, and then take umbrage when you questioned his logic.

I decided that opening up information was part of the answer. I had tried to get Network Rail made subject to the Freedom of Information Act, on the basis that it was delivering in effect a monopoly public service. This looked like it might fly until the Treasury took to its heels, fearful that this would make it more likely that the organisation would be reclassified by the Office of National Statistics as being on the public books.

Eventually, of course, this did happen, and Network Rail was in effect renationalised in September 2014, though you will of course never hear a Conservative describing it as such.

Another innovation I wanted to bring forward was the publication of what the industry calls 'right-time' information. Unknown to most people, the official figures for punctuality (PPM) classify a train as being 'on time' if it is up to four minutes fifty-nine seconds late at its destination, or nine minutes fifty-nine seconds for longer journeys. Right-time information says a train is late if it is more than fifty-nine seconds late.

Most of the industry hated the idea and did their best to put obstacles in my way. I had first suggested it to Justine and Theresa in early January 2012 as part of my input into the Rail Reform paper, in which I had also pushed for Network Rail to be subject to Freedom of Information.

I agreed with Theresa that the official yardsticks should continue to be 4:59 and 9:59, since to change these would have all sorts of legal ramifications, and in return she cautiously supported what I wanted to do via publication.

Publication would help drive up performance, I argued, and was necessary to give the public a true picture of what was happening. For instance, recent figures showed the following:

- Arriva Trains Wales 94.0 per cent PPM and 87.1 per cent right time
- Merseyrail 95.1 per cent PPM and 71.3 per cent right time

On the basis of publicly available information at the time, it appeared that Merseyrail was performing better than Arriva Trains Wales, when in fact the opposite was true.

Maria Eagle, the Labour shadow Transport Secretary, asked a

parliamentary question requesting right-time data for train service punctuality for each train operating company over the last ten years. But we were not in a position to release the information and in any case I had no wish to give Labour the credit for something I had been battling to achieve.

I did not think Maria was very good, and she never seemed very interested in transport, though that might have just been her normal manner. At one session of transport questions in the Commons, she asked me a question about buses that laid her wide open to a scathing reply, which I duly gave her, finishing with the observation that 'the Eagle has crash-landed'.

Nevertheless, her question on rail performance was helpful to me and I reiterated my view that we should release the information ourselves now to control the process, but without success.

We were making little progress, so I decided to take an unconventional approach. I knew that right-time information could be obtained from the ORR in any case through Freedom of Information, although nobody at that point had sought to do so. I therefore arranged for a friend to submit a request, allegedly from a journalist on a national paper, and the data was then released within a week, which must be some sort of record.

Faced with this imminent release, I won agreement that we should give out the information ourselves, and it was published amid much grumpiness from the train companies. I issued a ministerial statement putting the information in a fair context, and am glad to say that the world did not fall in, as they had gloomily predicted it would.

I also thought we should tidy up some of the anomalies in the system while we were at it. For example, London–Birmingham Chiltern services had a 4:59 leeway, whereas Virgin services between the same two cities were allowed 9:59.

Moreover, it seemed wrong to me that we should penalise train companies when their lateness arose because they had decided to hold connections to help passengers, and suggested the department should develop a schedule of 'Notified Connections'.

I also thought we should deal with the padding out of the time-table to avoid lateness. For instance, the Southern timetable allows nine minutes for a train to get from Clapham Junction to London Victoria, whereas the reverse journey is allowed just six minutes. There is not a noticeably large gradient for trains travelling into London on this route.

Part of the answer is to measure punctuality at intermediate stations, not just at the terminus. Trains from London Victoria to Ore will have discharged most passengers by the time the train has reached Eastbourne. The arrival time at Ore, many miles on, is largely irrelevant. Very few people have even heard of Ore or could find it on a map, let alone get off there.

To my disappointment, I was not able to do much about these matters before I was moved from the department. Nor was I able to tackle my other *bête noire*, the excessive use of rail replacement buses.

I felt that the rail industry was far too comfortable with what they call 'possessions', where Network Rail takes the track out of use for maintenance and enhancement. Now, of course this has to be done, and done more often given the growth in rail use. But I did not accept that this was being done in the most efficient manner to minimise the effects on passengers.

The evidence suggested that Network Rail was taking possessions for longer than they might need so as not to over-run, with the result that track was often available but no trains were running.

Similarly, the train companies received compensation from Network Rail for the occupation of the track, so did not really mind having to run buses instead, especially when those buses were owned by the same company.

It was all a bit too cosy. I had taken steps to stop rail replacement buses from being eligible for fuel subsidy through the BSOG mechanism and was also pushing the ORR to address the whole problem through the levers they had over Network Rail, but I wanted to do more.

I suggested to Justine and Theresa that we should introduce an incentive regime for railway possessions, to push for maximum access to the track for train companies, and to penalise them if they did not use it. Sometimes for their own operational convenience, and never mind the passengers, train companies would run buses when they could run trains.

The incentive scheme would have required fares to be reduced where a bus is used rather than a train. This was another idea that the industry was far from keen on, and instead they produced their own plan to minimise possessions. Judging by the number of times buses were replacing trains at Lewes in the autumn and winter of 2014/15, it did not seem to be working very well.

It is easy to knock the industry, and indeed it has been a national pastime going back to the days of British Rail and their allegedly curling-up sandwiches, which were actually not like that and were perfectly acceptable, but an urban legend was born.

The fact is that the industry delivers a safe and broadly reliable and professional service, but, just as hospitals suffer when bed occupancy approaches 100 per cent, so the train service becomes vulnerable when it becomes as intensively used as it is today, and with passenger numbers still growing, which of course they would not be if the railway were not as good as it is.

How do we facilitate further growth in passenger numbers on a finite network and at the same time maintain the performance we expect to see from the railway? This is the major challenge going ahead.

Another train matter that was occupying me in 2012 was the proposal that responsibility for monitoring performance be transferred from the department to the ORR. This was in practice a naked grab for power by the ORR and I was strongly opposed, as indeed were the train companies, who saw a conflict arising between that responsibility and the ORR's other roles.

While Theresa was also against, I understood that such a move might look superficially attractive to the centre, and I had to spend some time persuading Oliver Letwin why the idea should be dropped.

Justine had invited my comments on future spend on the railway and I proposed a budget line for medium-size line reopenings, such as Oxford–Bedford, now happily proceeding. Sadly, Lewes–Uckfield is not yet. It seemed to me that large projects such as HS2 were being handled direct by the department, and small projects like new stations were being picked up by the LSTF. But nowhere was there a fund for medium-size schemes. In theory, the devolution to regions should fill the gap (although the Tories hated the word 'region' as it reminded them of Labour structures), but by 2015 there was precious little evidence so far that it was doing so.

I also pointed out that the 'Passenger Demand Forecasting Handbook ... generally has hopelessly underestimated demand on reopened stations and lines' and needed revising. When the line to Alloa reopened, the train was so crowded it took longer for passengers to pay on arrival and exit the station than it had done to make the journey along the reopened line.

In July 2012, the Dalai Lama was making one of his regular trips to Britain and, as often was the case, he wanted to meet some parliamentarians.

My interest in Tibet is long-standing, pre-dating my election to the House of Commons by some years. My interest had been stirred by some hard-hitting reports in the press during the 1980s, from journalists such as Jonathan Mirsky and Nick Davies.

The more I read, the more appalled I became. Here was a peaceful society with a unique culture that had been brutally treated by the Chinese over decades. What was happening was no less than the eradication of an entire culture – cultural genocide.

In 1959, when the Chinese invaded, there were over 6,000 monasteries in Tibet. Ten years later, there were just thirteen. Hundreds of works of art and sacred religious artefacts were destroyed.

And while western countries were making noises about human rights violations elsewhere, there was barely an official murmur about Tibet.

I discovered that Britain had a special place in Tibet's history, having been the only country apart from China to have witnessed the independent status of Tibet prior to the Chinese invasion after the Second World War. This is important, as China maintains that Tibet had always been part of its territory, but this was patently not the case.

Tibet had its own currency, its own stamps and, more crucially still, its own government and its own foreign and defence policy. China had to pay tax on its goods entering Tibet.

In 1904, Britain and Tibet signed the Lhasa Convention. China objected, and Britain replied: 'Tibet is not one of the eighteen provinces of China.'

The Simla Convention was signed between the two countries in 1914, a treaty to which China was not a signatory.

As late as 1942, the Foreign Office said: 'The Tibetans have every moral right to their independence for which they have fought successfully in the past, and we are committed to support them in maintaining it.'

The tragedy was that Tibet did not apply for membership of the United Nations when it was set up. Had it done so, history may well have taken a more favourable turn.

Because of our interaction with Tibet, Britain for decades and almost alone did not accept Chinese sovereignty over Tibet, but rather the curious concept of suzerainty, which the dictionary defines as a state having some control over another state that is internally autonomous.

If I am driven by anything in politics, it is compassion, and a hatred of injustice. Both were triggered in the case of Tibet, and I returned to the issue again and again in opposition, introducing debates in 1999, 2005 and 2008, as well as tabling many parliamentary questions.

Other MPs asked me why I bothered, and one suggested this reflected my role as the patron saint of lost causes. Maybe it did, but I felt I had to do something, particularly given that Britain was really the only country that could challenge the rewriting of history by the Chinese.

In one of the debates, I held up a small Tibetan flag. You are not supposed to use props during any speech in the House, but I needed to make the point that a Tibetan holding up such a flag in Tibet would almost certainly be arrested, tortured and detained, possibly for years. The control the Chinese exert over locked-down Tibet is phenomenal, and unparalleled anywhere in the world.

In the 2008 debate, which took place in the House's second chamber in Westminster Hall, when I sat down after my fifteen-minute speech the Tibetans in the public gallery all applauded loudly and at some length, which is absolutely not allowed, but the Chair could hardly stop it, and in any case, it would have been a hard man or woman who would have tried to curtail the expression of gratitude that the British Parliament was taking an interest in their country. If you are a Tibetan, you are grateful for any positive development, no matter how minor.

I was incandescent when the Labour government changed the country's decades-old policy on Tibet, so that henceforth we would recognise Chinese sovereignty over Tibet. We knew, more than any other country, that this was to condone annexation, and if in the world of realpolitik we did have to make this move, we should at least have negotiated a serious price for something the Chinese wanted very badly from us. Incredibly, the Labour government got nothing in return. The Chinese simply opened the till, banked the change in policy, and closed the till again. Whoever in the Foreign Office handled this matter should have been made Governor-General of Pitcairn Island. It was incompetence of the highest order.

As chair of the All-Party Tibet Group, I led a delegation to Dharamsala, the home of the Tibetan exiled community in northern India, including the Tibetan government-in-exile.

The Chinese were aware of my role and I was invited to the Chinese embassy in Portland Place to meet the ambassador, which I welcomed. We each went through the formalities, over endless topping up of tea, setting out our positions, before I moved on to the argument that I thought might actually make some headway. This was that it is in the interests of the Chinese themselves to allow Tibet more autonomy. Why not let them speak Tibetan, and control their own health and education systems? That would take away much of the resentment felt by the Tibetans, would mean less need for a heavy-handed and expensive military presence, and would be widely welcomed across the world.

I sensed this was a line of argument that the ambassador was open to, though I discerned that merely from the mildness of the rejection, compared to the flat disagreement with other points I had made earlier. Given that China cannot be compelled to change its policies, appealing to their own self-interest seems to me to be the most pragmatic way forward.

As part of my role, I had the deep honour of hosting the Dalai Lama at an event he held at the Royal Albert Hall, where I interviewed him on stage. Never have I felt so nervous, nor such a great weight of responsibility on my shoulders.

I was asked to become President of the Tibet Society, the longest-running pro-Tibet group in the world. I gladly accepted, though when I became a minister in 2010, this had to become a ceremonial role.

Nevertheless, I was delighted to receive an invitation from the Speaker, John Bercow, to join him, Fabian Hamilton, the principled and affable Labour MP who had replaced me as chair of the All-Party Tibet Group, and a few others for lunch with the Dalai Lama on the occasion of his visit to the House in July 2012.

But then an instruction came from the Prime Minister. No minister was to meet the Dalai Lama. This followed a huge amount of pressure the Chinese government had brought to bear following his previous visit earlier in the year when he had met the PM and DPM. Following that, and the various meetings he had held with political leaders, even though in a spiritual rather than political capacity, the Chinese had frozen dealings with the UK on many levels, including ministerial visits.

I thought this was well out of order. It was a private lunch and I had been invited in my capacity as a long-standing member of the All-Party Tibet Group, not as a minister. And in any case, it was a private lunch without media present.

My anger was shared by Tim Loughton, the Conservative

children's minister, who was also a member of the All-Party Group and had been with me to Dharamsala.

I was in two minds whether to ignore what I regarded as kow-towing by No. 10 but I did not want to start another coalition row, for I figured Cameron would be bound to raise the matter with Nick Clegg. I also realised that Tim was in a more difficult posi-tion than me, without a coalition shield, so in the end we decided not to go but to write to the PM after the lunch.

The Lib Dems at No. 10 subsequently told me that they had been surprised I had not simply gone to the lunch, and that had I done so, they would happily have defended me to the hilt as they shared my view on the matter. Pity I hadn't known that beforehand.

Tim and I therefore sent a strong letter to the PM, writing:

> We ... are of course aware of the wider agenda and the sensi-tivities which exist. We do not believe, however, that justifies in any way a blanket prohibition on a minister meeting a reli-gious leader in private in a non-ministerial capacity, and we think this crossed a line. Our absence from this small private lunch is deeply embarrassing for us in terms of our long-stand-ing Tibetan connections, and will have been registered by the Speaker, to whom we were obliged to offer late apologies, and doubtless will not have passed unnoticed by others. The note [we had been sent] is tantamount to saying that Brit-ish foreign policy on Tibet is whatever China wants it to be.
>
> There was tremendous pressure put upon each of us at the eleventh hour not to attend, including a phone call from a Foreign Office minister, in a way that seems to us to be out of all proportion to the issue at hand ... While the policy on Tibet ... is clearly a matter for the Foreign Office and not for us, we are bound to record that our close observation of this

matter over many years has led us to conclude that, where Tibet is concerned, the Chinese government does not respond positively to any conciliatory gesture by the British government, but instead interprets this as a sign of weakness and so makes further demands for concessions.

The whole affair in our view has been very poorly handled...

The Prime Minister did not even give us the courtesy of a reply, which I thought was pretty shabby, though I did notice that at the next reshuffle two months later, Tim Loughton, who was widely regarded across the House as having done a good job as children's minister, was sacked.

After we had pushed unsuccessfully for a reply from No. 10, Tim and I were eventually offered a meeting with the Foreign Secretary, William Hague.

When we met in the commanding surroundings of his office, I set out our concerns in calm and moderate terms, and then Tim added his piece, in far from moderate terms, in fact in terms that would have pushed the conversation past the 9 p.m. watershed, had it been broadcast.

William Hague received all this with good humour, and set out his thinking on dealings with China, in his usual impressive manner. He was at his least impressive in defending the decision to bar us from that private lunch. It may be fanciful on my part, but I came away having concluded that the decision had been taken at No. 10, not in the Foreign Office, and he did not really agree with it, but that may have just been effective smoothing of feathers on his part.

Ironically, after all that, I was the first minister back into China, in January 2013, as part of the slow thaw, which I thought odd, given my well-known views on Tibet. Perhaps it was because the previous year I had received the Chinese Transport Minister and it would have been difficult to unpick the return invitation.

We duly arrived in Beijing, under strict instructions from the Foreign Office not to take any phones, iPads or other electronic equipment into the country. We stayed at the residence of the British ambassador, the building a wonderful relic of the bygone influence of Britain, as so many of our embassies and residences are. I was told that the residence would be bugged so to be careful what I said.

A ministerial visit to China is a highly formal process that replicates what has been agreed beforehand in private. It was made plain to us that if we deviated very far from what had been agreed, the meeting would be terminated.

The minister and I sat in comfortable chairs at one end of a room, both facing down the room, with a table between us on which sat some flowers. Down each side of the room were representatives from each country, facing each other, so at right angles to us. I presumed they were in some sort of pecking order, with the most important closest to the minister. Nobody apart from me and the Chinese minister spoke during the meeting, which lasted about half an hour.

It struck me that this was all rather more redolent of Imperial China than of a communist regime but I thought it prudent not to say so.

The minister began, contrary to the script, by apologising for the air pollution. It was indeed really bad, with a visible chemical haze all over the city, obscuring views, and you did not have to be out long before you felt an unpleasant rasping in your throat. Nevertheless, given the Chinese tendency not to want to lose face, I had not expected this.

According to the US embassy, which monitored the air pollution and published the results, much to the annoyance of the Chinese administration, levels were about twenty-five times the maximum safe level while we were there.

The visit generally was interesting, if limited. The thaw had not permeated the desired schedule, and I was kept away from any areas that might have a Tibetan connection.

On the return trip from Beijing, we travelled via Hong Kong, which was much fresher, tidier and generally cleaner than mainland China. While there, I launched some new buses from the UK, which I was delighted to learn had destination screens made in Lewes.

Buses are apparently of great interest to small boys in Hong Kong, and I was besieged by about fifty of them, all terribly excited by the bus I was on.

While in Hong Kong, we had breakfast in some old colonial setting with British businesses. The breakfast menu looked like it had been frozen in aspic, even if the food was not, in about 1954. It was very British.

I asked the businesses present for their take on matters, and what message they wanted me to take back to the government in London. I could not have anticipated that their main concern was that the government should stop raising the prospect that we might leave the EU. That seemed a long way from Hong Kong. I duly took back that message, though with zero impact.

Chapter 20

I was determined to use my ministerial position to make a positive difference for the environment. That, after all, had been the driving force that had got me into politics in the first place.

In opposition I had shadowed the environment brief but concluded that this was not the best approach. Firstly, environment is not seen as a mainstream issue but a niche one, and indeed one only to be given attention during the good times. Second, too much of it seemed too abstract and divorced from everyday life. Climate change, the ozone layer, deforestation, polar bears: these are all important but you will not find them on the front of the papers or being discussed down the pub or in the supermarket.

Sometimes the issues we discussed were just too esoteric. On one occasion while in opposition, I was invited on to *Newsnight* for a live discussion on the hydrogen economy. Having had a manic day, I was not able to prepare for this and decided I could probably busk it. I do not know what excuse the Labour minister had, nor Jeremy Paxman, who was interviewing us, but it quickly became apparent to me that none of the three of us knew what we were talking about. My wife, watching at home, thought the whole thing was hilarious.

I decided that, to make a real difference, I needed to look to a mainstream department, where a change of direction could make a real beneficial change for the environment. I decided they were the Treasury and transport, and as I was unlikely to be trusted with the first, either shadowing or in government, I would aim for the second.

So, in opposition I made a pitch for transport and was made shadow Secretary of State by Nick Clegg, translating into Transport Minister in 2010.

In that role, there were obvious connections in my portfolio, which covered cycling and walking, buses, trams and trains. But there were other parts of my portfolio rather more hidden that were also significant.

One rather opaque area covered fuel quality. This was to blow up due to the issue of tar sands, or oil sands, as officials preferred to call them. These unconventional fuels were predominantly being exploited in Canada and were hated by the green groups because of the carbon footprint generated both by the extraction methods required and by their eventual use. And of course, by opening up another source of fossil fuel, they could help to keep prices down, so making cleaner forms of energy less attractive.

The relevant Commissioner in the EU, the Danish Connie Hedegaard, was determined to do all she could to discourage their use. This ran counter to the Foreign Office's preferred priority, which was to keep Canada happy. Crucially, the Foreign Office was of course the department that co-ordinated policy in respect of EU policy, which in this case was something of a challenge.

I did not like either position. While I sympathised with those concerned about the environmental impact of tar sands, the way the EU Commissioner was handling it, singling out tar sands alone for special treatment, seemed to me to be unwise and counter-productive. Equally, those in the Foreign Office who wanted to keep Canada sweet seemed uninterested in the genuine environmental issues that tar sands raised.

Their positions were matched by the various interest groups, as I discovered when I met, separately, green groups and industry. I was also conscious that I did not want to damage my green credentials and those of the Lib Dems by being left at the end holding the baby, a tar baby. Worryingly, there seemed little interest in, or knowledge of, the environmental aspect anywhere else in government.

The problem was exacerbated by the fact that fuel quality was regulated in the EU by two overlapping and to some degree contradictory directives – the Fuel Quality Directive and the Renewable Energy Directive – and, to make matters worse, under the auspices of different commissioners. The division was mirrored in the UK, where the DfT led on the first, and the Department for Energy and Climate Change (DECC) on the second.

I sent Justine a long note on 3 February 2012 to alert her to how the problem was shaping up and to let her know I was off to meet Connie Hedegaard to try to move matters forward. It was a somewhat depressing meeting, in that the Commissioner was determined to press ahead with her approach, rather than consider more palatable alternatives that might well get her to the same point.

I sent Justine another note on 20 February. 'This could be a big issue,' I wrote. I then referred to an EU vote due on 23 February to 'allocate a specific (and high) value to tar sands and a general all-encompassing default value to conventional crudes (which make up about 99 per cent of the EU's supply)'. If enacted, that would severely limit the likely use of tar sands in the EU.

The green lobby was very much in favour of the EU proposal, I told Justine – there had recently been a Greenpeace 'siege' of the department – and the week before, Desmond Tutu and seven other Nobel laureates had called on the UK government to change position.

I added: 'The level of activity is such that even the Labour Party has noticed and Maria Eagle wrote to me last Monday asking me to make an oral statement ahead of the 23rd.'

As a government, we had agreed to abstain on the 23rd; it had taken a lot of lobbying on my part to stop us voting against, as the Foreign Office had wanted. We also agreed not to make this public ahead of the 23rd, so as not to weaken our negotiating position.

My note went on:

> I am assuming the Commission's proposal will not secure the necessary two-thirds majority. Under normal circumstances, the promoting Commissioner would recast the proposal but having met Connie Hedegaard a few days ago, I think it highly likely she will take the nuclear option and push it up to the Council of Ministers, where, as I understand it, it only needs 51 per cent ... The agreed UK position only holds for the committee so there will have to be another write-round ... My own preference, for both environmental and political reasons, if push comes to shove ... would be to support the Commission's proposals, but I suspect that may not be the prevailing view across government, particularly at the FCO.

I had been helped by John Ashton, the Foreign Secretary's special representative on climate change, whom I had called up in January. He was very switched-on, bright, and both understood and was sympathetic to the environment. He helped hold Foreign Office officials in check. I gathered that they and, to an extent, junior ministers were the problem rather than the Foreign Secretary himself.

The key vote in the EU had been indecisive, with 89 supporting votes for the Commissioner's proposal, known as Option 1, to single out tar sands for adverse treatment, 128 against, and 128 abstentions including the UK, Germany and France.

On 14 June, I wrote to William Hague to get agreement on our negotiating position. I framed the letter as carefully as I could, given that I had to keep indifferent or even hostile departments on board, not to mention ensuring this did not turn into a coalition issue, which would not have helped.

I suggested our ultimate aim should be 'the objective treatment of all crude sources … via a methodology that sets specific default values for each crude source'.

I genuinely thought that was right. I did not want to give tar sands a free ride, but nor did I want to pick on them exclusively, as the EU Commissioner did, not least because there were other conventional fuel sources that were just as damaging, if flaring on site was taken into account. I was surprised and disappointed that the green groups seemed uninterested in conventional fuels, which made up 99 per cent of supply. They seemed to me to want some sort of totemic victory rather than to address the whole issue.

I suggested to the Foreign Secretary that our objectives, in priority order, should be:

1. Equitable treatment of all crudes;
2. Minimising the burden on industry and consumers;
3. Maintaining our environmental credentials;
4. Implementing measures to ensure a competitive market;
5. Addressing Canada's concerns where they align with ours.

That last point was a sop to the Foreign Office and was couched to really mean nothing very much.

I added, for good measure: 'There are strong environmental and political reasons which steer the UK towards supporting the Commission's proposal and which I believe would make it hard for the UK to vote against.'

My approach won support, or at least failed to engender fatal opposition, and that became the UK government's position for the time being.

In the meantime, I continued to engage with Connie Hedegaard in the hope that she would be prepared to be more flexible, given the indecisive vote that had occurred. I suggested that she should prepare an impact assessment, which she agreed to do. The next key vote on her side was put off until 2013.

Meanwhile, the lobbying continued. On the green side, I was subject to a highly personalised and vicious campaign funded by the retail chain Lush, which delivered leaflets attacking me in my constituency. The fact that I had done more than anyone else to move the government in their direction cut no ice.

It was, I am sorry to say, typical of the attitude of many green groups throughout the parliament. They attacked the Lib Dems, who they thought had not gone far enough, failing to recognise the huge effort we were putting into environmental matters and the real progress we were making, but they left the Tories alone. They were kicking their only friends inside the tent. It was deeply unfair, but more than that, it was crass.

Incredibly, the same approach was even taken by some Lib Dems. I picked up my local paper, the *Sussex Express*, one day to find I was being slagged off over tar sands by our own MEP Chris Davies, who had not even taken the trouble to discuss the matter properly with me, thereby demonstrating an absence of both common courtesy and political sense. With friends like that, who needed the Tories?

On the other side, big oil was issuing dire warnings to the Treasury and others that the price of fuel would rocket unless their preferred solution, known as Option 0, was adopted. This was one default value for all fuel sources, whether conventional or unconventional, whether high in carbon or not, so putting tar sands on a level with every other crude source.

In May 2013, I met the Canadian minister Joe Oliver at his request. I was not desperately keen to do so but I thought it would be a discourtesy not to, and a refusal would not be well received at the Foreign Office. I was trying to exude an air of reasonableness. I was in no doubt, however, that if the fact that we had met became public, the green groups would accuse me of selling out or betraying the environment.

In July 2013, the EU assessment I had asked for became available. It showed that pump prices under any option would only increase by a maximum 0.3 euro cents per litre. This was good news.

Opinion elsewhere in government, including in Vince Cable's business department, was hardening in favour of Option 0, which I regarded as the worst option environmentally.

To head this off and break the logjam, I came up with a new option, which I called Option 0+. This set a single default level but allowed lower values to be ascribed to an individual feedstock where evidence was produced to justify this. I had called it Option 0+ as I thought psychologically it sounded closer to 0 than to 1 and therefore might just get past those elsewhere in government who had to agree to our negotiating position.

I also suggested that we did not need to say anything publicly on Option 1 'until the smoke has cleared'. Privately, I did not want to rule this out in case it came down to a binary choice between 0 and 1, in which case I would argue for 1.

The tactic worked and the government in September agreed to push Option 0+, despite scepticism from Sajid Javid, then at the Treasury. The option was timely, as the Commission was at last beginning to look for a compromise, and interest in Option 0+ began to pick up as our diplomats in Europe, armed with a clear line, started to sell it.

The other environmental matter I had to deal with in parallel with tar sands related to another ongoing EU discussion: maximum emission limits for vehicles. Again, I was to take the greenest position in government, and again I would be personally targeted by the green groups in my own constituency for not delivering 100 per cent of what they wanted.

The matter had first come up early in the parliament when Philip Hammond and I had to agree a position on maximum van emissions. As usual, industry was maintaining that a significant tightening could not be achieved, something they always said. We had settled on 147g CO_2/km.

Since then, good progress had been made and I thought a maximum of 135 could be delivered by industry, a point I put to William Hague in a letter on 11 December 2012. I also wanted to keep the door open not just on finalising a 2020 target, but on setting a 2025 one as well.

The industry was broadly opposed to the latter, yet they were always telling me, with some justification, that they needed certainty over long-term policy, given the long delay between investment and results, and I thought setting a 2025 target did just that.

I was able to secure agreement across government on most of what I had argued for, except that I was blocked on my move to change the van limit from 147 to 135.

Meanwhile, I was subject to another highly personalised attack in my constituency, this time from Greenpeace. Following this, I wrote to Doug Parr, their chief scientist, whom I had known and worked with over many years.

The letter read: 'I was disappointed by the event you staged in my constituency on Monday 13 May, regarding the negotiations in Europe on new car CO_2 levels, which I felt was both unwarranted and unfair.'

I reminded him that I operated an open-door policy, was always happy to see Greenpeace, and 'all you have to do is pick up the phone'.

I went on:

> We have worked well together over the years and you must know of my genuine commitment to environmental issues. Frankly there are many others around far more in need of a reminder of the importance of the environment and the dangers of climate change. As a supporter of Greenpeace I would like to see you spend more time on them rather than attacking those who are trying to do the right thing in difficult circumstances. I particularly resent the suggestion that I am trying to 'water down' measures to protect the environment. Why would I do that when I have spent my entire political life campaigning for the opposite?
>
> In addition I am not happy that you chose to target my constituency where I serve as the local MP rather than the Department for Transport where I work as a minister. I do not know your motivations for this – as I am sure you appreciate this distinction – but I do not feel it is at all appropriate. You have deliberately sought to damage my reputation locally, and to do so based on an erroneous and misguided assumption as to my motives.

I also told him that a member of staff had complained to me of being intimidated by Greenpeace activists.

Finally, I picked up on recent criticisms he had made of me in respect of tar sands.

> Your statement refers to *my* decision. If only it were that

simple! These matters must of course be agreed cross-depart-
mentally and across the coalition. I would be happy to explain
to you the mechanisms of decision-making within government
if that would be helpful to you. They are, I fear, rather more
multi-dimensional than you appear to realise.

I met Doug Parr shortly afterwards to elaborate. I told him I did not
mind working against the grain. Indeed, I was used to it. I was prepared to challenge those opposed to what he and I wanted to achieve,
whether in government or elsewhere, to spend a lot of time on issues
which frankly had little political payback, and to live with the criticisms in the media that flowed from challenging vested interests.

What I found debilitating, however, was for green groups to treat
me, and the Lib Dems more generally, as the major villain of the
piece and seek to damage my support in my own constituency, the
only consequence of which, of course, would be a Tory MP.

Greenpeace and others in the green movement should be helping the Lib Dems, not attacking them, I told him. Almost without
exception all the major advances on the environment had come
from us – the green investment bank, the big increase in use of
renewables, the massive investment in sustainable transport – and
we had achieved this not with the help of Greenpeace and others
but in spite of them.

In short, they needed us in government, but by their actions they
were undermining our chances of staying there. They relied on us,
and almost never met the Conservatives, but decided to bully and
shame us, rather than working with us, as a way of making progress.

I told Doug that, personally, I had had enough of these tactics,
and was asking Nick Clegg for a move at the next reshuffle away
from an environmental role.

Accordingly, Nick and I had a conversation in early July, when I asked for a move and we discussed the Home Office as a possible destination. Shortly after that, my wife and I went to see *Relatively Speaking* at Wyndham's Theatre in Charing Cross Road. By an amusing coincidence, we were allocated seats MI5 and MI6.

I had not lost my interest in green issues – far from it. In fact, in May 2013, I sent Nick a long note, setting out what I thought we as a party needed to do between then and the general election. This included a recognition that the Tories had given up on the environment, and we needed to work better across departments to compensate for this. Nick agreed, and asked David Laws to take on this task.

Before all that, the discussions and negotiations on the emissions issue were unfolding favourably, with not a little help from some really good (and undervalued) DfT officials. We had a reasonable environmental outcome, and we had also managed to protect our niche manufacturers.

But then No. 10 interfered. This was almost never a good thing. The people at the centre did not normally have the detailed knowledge of a subject to appreciate the nuances and to be able to finesse it well. They combined that lack of knowledge with an arrogant air of superiority that they knew best, they worked in the heart of government, they were more important than those toiling away in departmental outposts.

On this occasion, Angela Merkel had rung the Prime Minister to ask for help in delaying the vote on emissions. In return, Cameron asked for something inconsequential, which she readily offered.

He was advised by Ivan Rogers, then head of the secretariat covering European and global issues in the Prime Minister's office. He doubtless thought he was being clever in recommending this deal. He was actually being shafted, as was the British car industry at the expense of German manufacturers.

Nor did the Lib Dem channel work. The information had been passed on to Julian Astle, working for David Laws in his capacity as Cabinet Office minister. Julian did not think to check with me, with Vince Cable, with Ed Davey, or with anyone who might actually understand the issue.

When I found out what had happened, I erupted, even warning Julian Astle that I would cause him physical damage if he was within range.

Nor was I alone. Ed and Vince were far from happy, and the motor industry was furious.

I wrote in uncompromising terms to William Hague on 28 June, pointing out that the decision taken was at odds with the position we had agreed across government, and that our car manufacturers had concluded that the PM had decided to help the German car industry at their expense.

I wrote:

> Throughout the negotiation, Germany has been pushing for weakening of the 95g CO_2/km target that applies from 2020 by promoting 'super-credits'. Their position is not concerned with CO_2 reduction, rather it is one taken to boost the long-term competitiveness of premium German brands such as BMW, Daimler and Audi over their rivals in the global marketplace, including Jaguar, Land Rover, Aston Martin and McLaren. These much smaller UK manufacturers cannot benefit from 'super-credits' and rely on important provisions within the regulation that protect their competitiveness and support the diversity of vehicle manufacturing here in the UK. Ensuring niche and small-volume derogations are maintained is a UK priority for this negotiation...
>
> The agreement due to come before Coreper [the final tier

of official-level negotiations under the Council of Ministers] was the result of months of painstaking negotiation and met all the UK's requirements for a deal. The decision to delay Coreper discussion could have far wider consequences than it may have first appeared. It now makes it easier for the Germans to build a coalition of opposition under a new presidency and with the ascension of Croatia. In particular it makes it more likely that they will attack the niche derogation.

I would like to register my significant disquiet at the recent decisions taken to support the German bid for delay and make clear that we should not support the German proposals to weaken this regulation for the benefit of their automotive sector over ours. It is crucial that any decision to change our negotiating position be agreed by proper process and European Affairs Committee write-round.

I copied this to the PM, DPM, Ivan Rogers and Sir Jeremy Heywood.

At the same time, Vince Cable and Ed Davey both independently wrote in similar terms about this spectacular own-goal.

Ivan Rogers was rewarded for his diplomatic efforts by being promoted to the position of our permanent representative in Brussels, effectively our ambassador to the EU.

As for the green lobby, I noted that by July 2015 they were bemoaning the fact that the new Tory government had within weeks acted to sweep away the 'green crap'. Subsidies for wind and solar power had ended, taxes on renewable energy had been increased, plans for zero-carbon homes had been axed and the flagship energy efficiency scheme had been closed. They were writing to the government to express their concerns. They might as well have gone to watch the cricket. By their actions, they had helped to create the position where after 2015 there was a

Tory-only government, anathema to their interests, and one they had failed to cultivate. Meanwhile they had lost their friends and lost the plot.

Chapter 21

The first reshuffle, discounting small moves to replace individual ministers who had had to resign for personal reasons, did not take place until 4 September 2012, nearly halfway through the parliament.

That, to my mind, was welcome. Prime Ministers all too often reshuffle ministers for no good reason: to give the appearance of control or activity, to distract from other issues, or just because they can.

The reshuffle had in fact been expected in July but was delayed until early September. The way the coalition worked was that, right at the start, David Cameron and Nick Clegg agreed on the division of places, so how many Cabinet places each, how many ministers of state, how many under-secretaries. But it was left to each party leader to choose who filled those places. The PM could not veto Nick Clegg's choices and vice versa.

The appearance of serenity and organisation could be misleading. When the coalition was formed, Norman Lamb, whom Nick Clegg had intended to put into the Department for International Development, was left without a ministerial post because Nick miscalculated how many places he had to fill. He was hurriedly made a deputy whip as a consolation prize and had to wait for the 2012 reshuffle to have the oversight corrected.

Similarly, as mentioned, I do not think Justine Greening's Heathrow views were factored in when she was made Transport Secretary.

The public sometimes assume that ministers are promoted on merit, and sacked only when they are not up to the job. The 2012 reshuffle certainly gave the lie to that idea.

So we saw Charles Hendry sacked from his position as Minister of State at the Department for Energy and Climate Change not because he had performed badly, but because he understood the brief too well, and was therefore too independent-minded for the Chancellor in particular and, sin of sins, was much too close to the Lib Dem Secretary of State in outlook.

The reshuffle also saw the removal of Tim Loughton from the education department. Tim was well regarded but he had stood up to Michael Gove, and had annoyed the Prime Minister over Tibet, so had to go.

The Tory reshuffle moved their party noticeably to the right, which was widely picked up at the time. What was less noticed was that George Osborne's fingerprints were all over it rather than the Prime Minister's. The Chancellor has been placing his protégés all over government.

Just consider some of the people who have been junior Treasury ministers (or the Chancellor's PPS in the case of Amber Rudd) between 2010 and 2015 and then gone on to Cabinet posts:

Justine Greening (Transport Secretary then International
  Development Secretary)
Nicky Morgan (Education Secretary)
Greg Clark (Communities Secretary)
Sajid Javid (Culture Secretary then Business Secretary)
Amber Rudd (Energy Secretary)

Others widely regarded as being in the Osborne camp have also prospered, including Matthew Hancock and Greg Hands.

The 2012 reshuffle saw a complete clear-out at the Department for Transport save for me. Everyone whom the Prime Minister and the Chancellor could remove was removed. There was a view in the Tory centre that the department was somewhat off-message, that it had become too Lib Dem and not Tory enough.

Justine Greening was absolutely devastated. She had been in post for less than a year and most certainly did not want to move. But within the hour she was on her way. She walked down the corridor, past my office towards the lift, her face strained and taut, staring ahead, I think trying not to cry.

I went out to try in some sort of inadequate way to sympathise and comfort her, but when I spoke it was as if I was not there. I tried again but she simply pressed the lift button and waited. And then she was gone. I felt rather sorry for her. She had brought a freshness to the department and handled her brief reasonably well.

Mike Penning had got himself promoted, as he had told me he would a couple of weeks earlier. He was off to become Minister of State for Disabled People at the Department for Work and Pensions.

Theresa Villiers, who had twice been passed over for Transport Secretary, finally made the Cabinet as Northern Ireland Secretary. I was pleased for her if a little surprised. Apart from anything else, Northern Ireland was not an obvious posting.

I viewed the situation with some trepidation. The Department for Transport had been a happy ship with good relations across the coalition, but I was conscious that there had been mutterings in the centre about the need to reset the department in a more Tory direction. I feared the worst. Frankly, I had been lucky to have been able to work with collegiate Tory colleagues – even Philip in early coalition days was someone you could do business with – but I knew very well that there were plenty who were not.

To my surprise and relief, the new Transport Secretary was Patrick McLoughlin. Patrick was well liked by everyone, as far as I could tell, despite having been the Tory Chief Whip. Certainly, Alistair Carmichael, then Patrick's deputy, told me he was good news.

Patrick was that relative rarity, a working-class Tory who had made it to the Cabinet. He was proud of his roots as an ex-miner and hung on his wall an election poster from when he had stood for the Tories, in a coalfield area in the 1980s, proudly wearing his miner's helmet.

I did not like what the Conservatives had done to the mining industry in that decade, but I reckoned it must have taken some guts for a miner to stand for election then as a Tory in the heart of mining country.

Patrick had actually been a minister in the department before, in the previous Tory government, between 1989 and 1992, when he had covered 'roads and motoring'. Twenty years must be one of the longest gaps between departmental appearances.

Some of the officials in the department were a bit sniffy at first at the idea of having someone with Patrick's background at the top, but he gradually won respect across the board, and quite right too.

He brought with him two special advisers, who, unlike many of their creed, were human beings first and political appointments second. Julian Glover, the ex-*Guardian* journalist and partner of Matthew Parris, was friendly and helpful to me in a way that went quite a long way beyond what was necessary. When I left for the Home Office, he would send me a text saying, 'Come back.'

The other special adviser was Ben Maskell, whom we called Little Ben, in an affectionate rather than derogatory way.

In opposition, I had been very combative, and I think a lot of Conservatives did not relish working with me for that reason. But I have always taken the view that you play the cards you have been dealt, and that means adjusting to circumstances. I had been told by both the PM and the DPM that they wanted me to make the coalition work, insofar as my input was concerned, and that was what I sought to do.

Nick Clegg had also told me on my appointment that, naturally, he wanted me to put a Lib Dem stamp on the departments I was in, so we could show that we had made a difference and delivered Lib Dem policies.

At the Department for Transport, it proved eminently possible to meet both these objectives so there was really no reason to be combative. Indeed, apart from souring the atmosphere, it would have been counterproductive.

Early on in the life of the government, on 7 December 2010, the Public Administration Committee had summoned Mike Penning and me to give evidence on how the coalition was working. I imagine they thought that there would be fireworks. In fact, it was harmony personified, with a bit of gentle, good-natured ribbing from each of us. Philip Hammond had insisted on seeing us the day before to remind us to present a unified front. He need not have worried.

With Philip, there was an acceptance that both sides had to gain from the coalition, and we were after all in the honeymoon period.

Justine was more Lib Dem-leaning in her outlook anyway, and Patrick displayed both characteristics: a willingness to give the Lib Dem in the department space to achieve things, and a benign attitude towards the objectives I was pursuing, in public transport and electric vehicles.

The three new ministers arrived and they and I assembled in Patrick's room.

'I suppose I ought to welcome you all to the department,' I said, and they laughed.

The new Minister of State was Simon Burns, who I soon gathered was not very well disposed to his coalition partners. There was a connecting door between my office and his, and Theresa and I used to pop in and out when we had an issue to discuss, or just to say hello. Within an hour of Simon's arrival, the door had been locked.

I thought this rather unfriendly but decided there was no point in raising it. Gradually, we built up a reasonable working relationship. Nevertheless, I was in Simon's office much less than I had been in Theresa's.

Simon changed the feel of the office quite markedly. Theresa had barely inserted much of her personality into the room, so when she left, it looked largely unchanged. Simon, on the other hand, did not hide his interest in American politics – oddly, I thought, for the Democrats rather than the Republicans. He had worked on the Hillary Clinton campaign and had a picture of her on his wall to prove it.

The third new Conservative was Stephen Hammond, who, in many people's eyes, should have been there on day one of the coalition. Stephen unsurprisingly wanted to cover rail – everybody always did – but I refused to relinquish the areas I had painstakingly carved out for myself.

I made the point to Patrick, which he accepted, that I was at that point the transport minister with the most up-to-date knowledge, so it would be perverse to reduce my portfolio. In the end, Patrick concluded that the portfolios as they were pre-reshuffle should remain roughly the same.

Patrick and I got on very well, even to the extent that in May 2013 he came down to my constituency to make a helpful intervention on the possibility of reopening the Lewes–Uckfield line. He is the only Tory to have featured positively in some of my political leaflets locally. I say 'positively' because we did use the Chancellor from time to time in a less flattering way.

Patrick and I had relatively few policy disagreements. The main difference related to the issue of roads reform. I was not against the idea of creating a plan for investment, rather than opting for the stop-start approach that had been the norm for decades. Nor was I against Highways England being created.

I did, however, object to the lazy assumption that traffic was going to grow substantially, especially as that was at odds with recent evidence and the view of some academics that we were approaching 'peak car'.

In a memo of 3 October I wrote to him:

> I have a number of serious concerns about the proposals set out in Michael Dnes's submission of 27 September on Roads Reform ... I question the basic premise that there is a need for a substantial road-building programme. Of course some new road capacity is necessary, particularly to deal with bottlenecks, but in my view the network is reasonably comprehensive. In addition, road use, unlike rail use, has been flat-lining.

I then referred to the department's 1994 report, the Strategic Advisory Committee on Trunk Road Assessment, which proved conclusively that providing more capacity simply generates more, new journeys, and diverts traffic away from rail.

I also pointed out that the proposals as framed would disincentivise the take-up of low-carbon vehicles.

This nearly all fell on stony ground, though Patrick did seem to take the point about cheaper, more targeted schemes and came up with the pinch-point fund, something I supported.

It seems I had little impact on officials, either, for a subsequent submission, on 10 June, made the claim that traffic volumes would increase by 46 per cent by 2040. This was despite the fact that levels had stabilised over the previous ten years. Company car mileage had actually dropped 40 per cent between 1995 and 2007. The suggestion that we needed massive road-building to meet anticipated demand was a return to the failed policy of predict-and-provide that I thought had been terminally discredited.

Nor did I have much luck with my Lib Dem colleagues. Neither David Laws nor Danny Alexander, my two key colleagues in the centre, objected to the idea of a big road-building programme, though they did think any announcement should be linked with measures to incentivise greener cars and rail.

The other policy decision Patrick took that I disagreed with was the decision to ensure the franchise for the east coast main line was put out to tender before the election. Because of previous failed franchises, this was being run by the state, and well run, too. It was popular with passengers and returning a healthy profit to government coffers.

I was not philosophically against tendering the route, and accepted that it should return to private hands and that a private sector operator might increase the flow of money to the Treasury. But it made no sense to me to bring this forward for tendering when it was working well and when there was a priority to sort out the west coast franchise, which was then going through some turmoil.

In essence, I thought Patrick was taking the wrong operational decision for overtly political reasons – to ensure the line was once again in private hands before the general election, in case Labour won.

I also thought the reliance on short extensions to franchises, which was then becoming something of a habit, would mean less money for the public purse, a hiatus on longer-term investment from the train companies in those franchise areas, and a potential challenge to the legality of the practice.

I spoke to Danny Alexander about these concerns and formed the impression he agreed with me, but when he finally wrote back to Patrick, it was to sign off Patrick's proposals, even though the letter acknowledged that, under the new programme, all but three operators would receive an extension to their existing contract without a tendering process.

Overall, though, these were rare quibbles and there was, happily, a high degree of common purpose between Patrick and me. He gave me enough space to pursue my portfolio relatively freely, for which I was grateful.

One area where we did not make as much progress as I would have liked was in London. As early as July 2010, when we were discussing the first round of cuts, I drew Philip's attention to the very generous travel concessions that were built into the base budget. I was not against the concessions but thought London ought to pay for them, and our baseline calculations should be amended accordingly.

Later, I wrote to Justine Greening about the way London had been prioritised for cycle safety funding.

> I note that you have approved a £15 million grant to TfL for cycle safety in London. As you know, Theresa and I have reservations about additional funding for TfL, and I would prefer any money available to be much more widely spread. It is also not clear to me how such money would be spent. I also think whatever money is handed out might sensibly be match-funded as a condition.

I also wanted to make progress on the issue of pedicabs. These cycle rickshaws had sprung up in large numbers in the West End, but I was concerned that they were unlicensed, even unregistered, and I worried in particular about the potential exploitation of vulnerable passengers. Where they existed elsewhere in England, and it is true that very few did outside London, they were required to be licensed as taxis.

The law relating to taxis and indeed hire cars, which are legally different, was a mess. For one thing, completely different laws applied in London compared to elsewhere in England. I won agreement that the Law Commission should be asked to look into the whole matter with a view to making recommendations to rationalise and update the law, some of which dated back to the 1840s. By August 2012, they had come up with seventy-three provisional recommendations, including keeping the division between taxis and hire cars, and setting taxi standards nationally rather than locally.

This was all going to take time, so I wanted to make progress with pedicabs ahead of the Law Commission's final report, even though I had asked them to consider this aspect as part of their work.

I raised the matter with Philip Hammond, who asked me to delay any action until after the mayoral elections, which I agreed to do. As soon as they were out of the way, I wrote again to the Secretary of State, by now Justine Greening, but she seemed untroubled by the position and there it rested.

Then there was the issue of London rail decentralisation. Boris Johnson was empire building, seeking to extend his writ far beyond the London boundary. I objected, as did Tory MPs from Kent, on the basis that his plans would have inevitable negative impacts on rail services outside London.

'Rail users who have no vote in the London mayoral elections would be affected by his/her decisions. There is a real risk that services would be inevitably prioritised by the mayor to aid his/her electorate at the expense of the longer-distance journeys,' I wrote in a note to my fellow transport ministers. That particular battle was largely won.

In April 2013, it was another round of cuts, and once again, I thought London was being let off lightly while others took the pain. I was damned if we were going to see support for buses or for local transport schemes outside London cut while London carried on wasting money.

Exasperated by this, I drew up a document entitled 'London Waste' to demonstrate to Patrick how money had been squandered and how cuts could be made without affecting front-line services.

On capital expenditure, I wrote:

> Given the additional 1 per cent savings we will now have to find ... I think we really do have to look at the 38 per cent of budget which will go to the capital. In my view there is significant waste in London which should be dealt with as a way of releasing funds for London ... Why should people in the Derbyshire Dales lose because of bad practice in London? My view is there is a good case for loading a much higher percentage of cuts on London than anywhere else.

Stephen Hammond made a good point in support of me which was that if Boris had a big cut, he would almost certainly appeal to the Chancellor and have money allocated direct from the Treasury, thereby in effect increasing the transport budget in total.

Boris in fact had a habit of engaging directly with the Prime Minister or the Chancellor, and much less with the Transport Secretary of the day. He would never engage with me, despite my portfolio being highly relevant to London in many ways. Indeed, I only officially met him once in three and a half years, and that was at a Tube station event. He did not like Lib Dems and was highly partisan.

My London Waste document covered the following:

- Cable cars: originally supposed to be privately funded, the cable-car crossing at Greenwich ended up having £24 million of public money allocated, yet numbers of passengers using the facility were dropping, and it was costing Transport for London £500,000 a month to run. Meanwhile TfL had spent a further £150,000 on opinion polls about cable cars.
- Cycle hire scheme: what was promised to be cost-free to the taxpayer had ended up as the most expensive in Europe. Usage of the scheme had fallen from its peak.
- New Routemasters: the first eight buses had cost £1.4 million each, compared to around £190,000 for a normal double-decker. Development costs had doubled. The use of conductors was to be met by TfL, meaning either a substantial extra cost or, alternatively, what was increasingly happening: many new buses operating without conductors or open platforms, thereby defeating the entire purpose of the new bus.
- The requirement for special features on London buses that are not required anywhere else and which drive up the cost, for example central doors and roller blinds. And each bus had to have £18,000 spent on removing these features, which nobody else wanted, before it could be sold on.
- Poor timetabling, meaning Oxford Street was seeing 800 buses an hour, causing very slowed-down journeys.
- Outdated working practices on the Tube, costing taxpayers millions.
- The huge waste of money on developing plans for a 'Boris Island' airport that everyone knew was going nowhere.

I cannot help thinking that had this been anywhere else in England, or if London had had a Labour mayor, the government and its right-wing allies in the press would have ripped into this. Nor would the Chancellor have been so unquestionably generous to London as he regularly was.

Boris did not handle transport in London at all well, but he got by with a mixture of his own signature bluster, extensive cover from senior Conservatives and, most of all, excellent support from the talented Peter Hendy, moved in the summer of 2015 to shore up Network Rail as their chairman.

There were a couple of issues in transport where, as I prepared for a move from the department, I recognised I was not going to win. They were in themselves not large issues, but I had nagged away at them, that being an approach that often did bear fruit.

The first of these related to what were drily known as Sections 165 and 167 of the Equality Act. In layman's terms, this was about requiring taxi drivers to help people with disabilities. You might think this was uncontroversial. Not a bit of it.

It did begin that way and, by way of preparation, we enacted Section 166 in October 2010. This exempted taxi drivers with a medical condition from the requirements under 165 and 167.

After a while, people began to wonder, not unreasonably, why 166 was in place but not 165 and 167. The question was raised with me by Dai Powell, who chaired the Disabled Passengers Transport Advisory Committee. (Incidentally, the Tories, as part of their cull of quangos, wanted to abolish this committee, but I was in the end able to save it.)

The fact was that this had run into trouble with Mark Prisk, then Minister for Business and Enterprise, and the relatively new government policy not to impose burdens on small businesses.

It seemed to make no difference that the burden in this case was officially classified as zero. It was still a theoretical burden, so had to be opposed.

I asked Miles Gibson, a civil servant at No. 10, to help. Miles was the Prime Minister's adviser on planning and transport.

As this was unfolding, the department's officials had managed to persuade Mark Prisk to withdraw his small-business-related objection, but alas, Miles Gibson had briefly raised the matter with the Prime Minister at the end of a long meeting. The PM had replied off the cuff by saying that taxi drivers should not be compelled to help disabled people, and so put the kibosh on the whole thing.

I was surprised and had expected the PM, of all people, to be more sympathetic to the needs of the disabled.

I asked Justine if she would help, but this drew a blank. I went to see Oliver Letwin, who was always prepared to listen. He was sympathetic but warned that it would be difficult to make progress if the PM had already made up his mind. Together we worked up a scheme to ensure the power was not misused by councils. I offered to produce a guidance note for the councils. He thought this a satisfactory way forward and did raise it with the PM, but to no avail.

Lastly, I asked Nick Clegg to raise it at one of his regular bilaterals. He was not against doing so in principle but pointed out that there were always more pressing matters he had to raise in the limited time the two of them could spend together. I do not think he ever did so.

And there the matter rested.

The other long drawn-out and ultimately futile issue related to Moving Traffic Offences.

Part 6 of the Traffic Management Act 2004 extended to the rest of England those powers already in force in London for councils to enforce moving traffic offences such as cars driving the wrong way down one-way streets. It had never been taken forward, however, and it was a regular ask of local government that it should.

In December 2011, I had asked officials to undertake a short consultation and was told that there was not much enthusiasm for this. Local councillors to whom I passed this on did not believe this, so I looked at the individual responses myself and found they were more rather more supportive than I had been led to believe. I was not best pleased.

I was aware of the potential sensitivity of the issue, given the Tories' 'war on the motorist' rhetoric, so I sounded out Miles Gibson at No. 10, who said he thought what I wanted was fine and I could proceed to a write-round.

I proposed making available to councils all the powers London had with the exception of those relating to box junctions. I was concerned that motorists in London were sometimes being unfairly penalised when they entered a box with their exit clear, only for another vehicle to pull out in front of them, generating an offence. I wanted enforcement of box junctions to remain with the police.

Justine gave me the green light, agreeing with me that box junctions should be excluded.

By late April, however, she was getting cold feet, worried that the move might provoke the allegation that this was a new 'war on the motorist'. I pointed out that it would only affect motorists who broke the law, and also that this power was included in a deal reached between the government and Sheffield as part of a devolution agreement for the city.

She was still nervous, so as a compromise, I suggested three pilot areas, which could neatly sweep up the city deal asks. She agreed to this, but officials then advised that this would require changes to regulations and would take the department eighteen months to deliver.

Given the skewed report I had received about local councils' views, I did not necessarily believe this, but let it go on the basis that, if true, changes would in any case be forced by the city deals.

When Patrick took over, I took the opportunity to raise the matter afresh with him in October 2012. I set out the history, to which I added the new fact that the Welsh Assembly was taking the matter forward now.

I argued that it would remove burdens from the police, as civil enforcement of parking had, and was only about enforcement so was not a burden on the law-abiding motorist. I again proposed to exclude box junctions.

I asked for his agreement to move forward, and he undertook to speak to Eric Pickles, who by that point was the main obstacle, and a large one. Unfortunately, Pickles's position had hardened and indeed he was moving in the opposite direction, wanting councils to discontinue CCTV enforcement entirely.

By 19 March, Pickles was arguing that enactment would mean 560,000 fines being issued each year. His was a preposterous figure and can only have included the box junctions I had already excluded. However, if he was arguing that there were 560,000 incidents of the law being broken that were going unpunished, that seemed to me an argument for action rather than inaction.

He trotted out the old chestnut that this was a 'war on the motorist', 'especially if implemented alongside the separate DfT write-round seeking to increase the level of parking fines … by a third'. They had not risen since 2003 and were well behind London's, which had steadily increased. Of course, he was blocking that matter as well.

And so the reshuffle came and I was, as I had expected, moved to the Home Office in a promotion to Minister of State. I left the department with fond memories.

The industry, and indeed the department, which had viewed me with a mixture of suspicion and concern when I was first appointed, came to be warm towards me in a way that I found rather touching.

In 2012, I was given a special award at the annual UK Bus Awards, officially for longevity – I was the first ever buses minister to make the event three years in a row – but I think more out of affection. The fact that I invariably managed to time my appearance to coincide with some financial handout for buses of course helped.

On my third appearance, the after-dinner speaker was John Prescott and I used some of my contribution earlier in the evening to gently, and I think almost endearingly, wind him up in a way that everyone in the ballroom at the Hilton in Park Lane found amusing except him. When it came to his turn, he made some rather rude remarks about me, without the benefit of humour, before launching into a tirade about the shortcomings of the bus industry and how Labour would sort them out. It was the most ill-judged speech I think I have ever witnessed and was not appreciated by the audience.

Very shortly after I was moved to the Home Office, I received a special one-off award at the National Transport Awards for Outstanding Contribution to National Transport. I am told that this had been planned before I was reshuffled.

The award was presented by Patrick McLoughlin, who was typically generous in his comments. I cannot think of many other Tory secretaries of state who would have been prepared to give an award to a Lib Dem junior minister in their department.

In March 2015, just before the election, I came across an article in the trade magazine *Passenger Transport*, the regular column 'Great Minster Grumbles' – written, we are led to believe, by an insider at DfT headquarters, Great Minster House. The article reviewed all the ministers who had served in the department over the parliament and nominated me for first prize as the best minister, by a whisker over Patrick McLoughlin.

'Our Whitehall Insider' wrote:

> The real surprise was Norman Baker, who I think we all came to like and respect … We all thought he was going to be a nightmare to deal with … but unlike many ministers, he listened, thought about the issues and changed his mind – and admitting publicly that he had.

That was nice. I will always look back on my days at the DfT with fondness.

Chapter 22

In many ways, I was very sorry to leave the Department for Transport. I had enjoyed my brief and felt I had achieved a lot. My relations with my Conservative colleagues, ministers and special advisers, had ranged from business-like to very good. The civil servants had been supportive and, after I encouraged them, good at coming up with creative ideas.

I was especially lucky with my private office, where, under Jo Guthrie and Alex Philpott, I had had so many super people helping me, like Katy Budge, Joe O'Leary and Adam McIntee. Everyone was friendly. People talked to you in the lift. Jean, the lovely tea lady, made sure I was kept topped up. It was fun.

The Home Office was literally across the road, but it might as well have been on another planet.

I waited in the reception area to be collected. Up on the wall were photographs of the Home Secretary and the Permanent Secretary, Mark Sedwill. Every other department I had been to had photographs of the ministerial team in the entrance area, but not the Home Office.

I was met by the Lib Dem special adviser who covered the Home Office and the Ministry of Justice, Alex Dziedzan, who took me upstairs. I like to think I can feel the atmosphere of a building. This one felt dry and oppressive.

The building was separated into three sections named after three seminal historical figures, Mary Seacole, Robert Peel and Elizabeth Fry. Accordingly, you would see signs stating 'Peel and Fry', which I always thought mildly surreal, but nobody else seemed to. The Home Office does not do surrealism, at least not deliberately.

The building was much newer than the one I had come from, and was in fact built on the site of the old Department of Environment and Transport at 2 Marsham Street, where, many years before, my mother had worked as a civil servant. Sadly, she did not live long enough to see me as a minister.

My room was perfectly adequate though small compared to the unnecessarily cavernous space I had had across the road. There was limited natural light, for security reasons, and there was no art to brighten the place up, so I had some pictures brought across from my old office in the DfT.

These had come from the government art collection, itself housed in an anonymous building off Tottenham Court Road which I had visited in May 2011. Clearly, by that point, and with Buggins's turn firmly operating, what was left of the collection looked rather unappealing. I did, however, find amongst other works an interesting black and white photo of a traditionally dressed civil servant holding a bowler hat in front of his face, and a photo of Old Aberdeen, not far from where I was born.

My transfer to the Home Office took place as part of a Lib Dem reshuffle with no Tory counterpart, that having taken place in July, and my move was widely regarded as the most eye-catching one.

Opinion was sharply divided between those who were delighted, especially Lib Dems and those on the left, and those who were horrified, notably those firmly on the right and what remained of the Blairites.

I met the Home Secretary briefly on the day of my appointment for a short five- or ten-minute introductory chat in her office. Thereafter we would always meet in her office. Unlike the various transport secretaries I had worked to, she never came into my office, and I would never see her in those of the other Tory ministers either.

Her room was quite barren and looked like it could be evacuated of all traces of its occupant within a matter of minutes. I was led into her room by her private secretary and sat down at a long table. She had a pile of files on her own desk which she was working through, requests for authorisation for communications interceptions, it appeared. She got up from her desk and came to sit opposite me. She bore the icy smile of a snow queen.

I learnt the next morning that my transfer had generated a welcome present from the Home Secretary's special advisers in the form of a hatchet job in the press. Two friendly journalists had rung me up to tell me what was going on. The spads had been furious that I had been moved to the Home Office and had briefed against me. I had moved from the sunny beach to the snake pit.

As would so often be the case, the *Daily Mail* was their chosen vehicle, and they majored on David Kelly. The *Mail*, of course, had serialised my book when it came out and had run editorials supporting my investigations, but that was then and this was now.

Publicly, I denied there was antagonism.

'I had a very friendly chat with Theresa last night,' I told Radio 4. 'If she was angry, I didn't notice it.'

That was almost true.

My first proper meeting with the Home Secretary came that day and was a tense one. I told her that I did not expect to be briefed against by her special advisers. I had proved myself to be a collegiate minister at the DfT, working in harmony with my Conservative colleagues. I expected the coalition to work on a proper basis, here as much as anywhere else.

I did not want to have this confrontation in our first substantive meeting, but I sensed that if I did not put down a firm marker in response to this head-on challenge then I would be sunk.

She said she did not think her spads were behind the press stories. I told her bluntly that I had been told they were by two different sources. She said she would investigate.

During my time in the Home Office, I concluded that while Theresa May did not initiate such behaviour herself, she gave her spads considerable latitude coupled with a general steer, and did not look too closely at exactly what they were doing, which as a consequence gave her deniability.

Her spads were very different from the friendly pair I had been used to at the DfT. They were ruthless in pursuit of their party goals and took no prisoners. Coalition for them was an unwelcome necessity to be tolerated, and any party advantage that could be gained at the expense of the Lib Dems was fair game. In that attitude, they reflected the views of the Home Secretary, only magnified.

And just as I would never see Theresa in my room, only exceptionally would I have a visit from one of her three advisers: Nick Timothy, Fiona Cunningham and Stephen Parkinson. I would, however, occasionally pop into their room to say hello, which I think rather disorientated them.

Of the three, I had been told Stephen Parkinson was the most Lib Dem-friendly, and he seemed to have been allocated as the contact point. I came to suspect that this was because he was the most junior of the three, rather than because of any empathy for the Lib Dems. He was in any case not particularly friendly.

Fiona Cunningham was the spad whom officials seemed to dislike most, but I concluded that she was the one most likely to see the need for a sensible working relationship. I did not myself dislike her. I just thought she was doing her job.

Not long after my arrival, Fiona and I arranged to go for a drink, which apparently generated a good deal of interest from officials.

'I would love to have been a fly on the wall,' one of them told me the next day, pumping me unsuccessfully for a report of the meeting. It had in fact been perfectly civilised, friendly even, if robust. We would do it again another couple of times.

I was, however, troubled by her relationship with Charles Farr, a very senior official working as Director of the Office for Security and Counter-Terrorism. It was not the relationship per se that concerned me – that was none of my business – but the fact that I needed to speak to officials frankly and with complete confidence that what we discussed would not be communicated to Conservative special advisers.

Charles Farr was a colourful character who had served in Afghanistan with MI6, supplying money to Afghan warlords in return for them discontinuing their production of opium. He had been passed over for the top job at MI6, and indeed for the job of Permanent Secretary at the Home Office. According to *The Guardian*, several officials threatened to resign if he were appointed to this post.

I told Charles Farr of my concerns and he assured me that he would approach our dealings professionally, and indeed insofar as I could tell, he did so. I did also make my concerns known to the Permanent Secretary, Mark Sedwill, who told me with a straight bat that the arrangement had been cleared by his predecessor. I concluded that he did not approve either.

After the row over the hostile welcome I had received, there then followed an extended dispute with the Home Secretary over portfolio allocations. I had inherited Jeremy Browne's policy areas, and now the Home Secretary said she wanted to rebalance these, by which she meant removing serious crime from my portfolio and transferring in two minor areas, animal experiments and firearms.

This was an open attempt to exercise power to the disadvantage of the Lib Dems, and to minimise what I would be able to do in the department.

I told her that she could move her Tory ministers around as much as she liked, but the portfolio allocation to the Lib Dem in the department was a coalition matter and I would have to agree it or it would not happen.

I was not in fact totally certain of my ground, but the Home Secretary did not challenge the statement. I told her if she wanted to transfer serious crime from me to James Brokenshire, the security minister, she would have to put together a package that was equivalent. Actually, I could see that the change she wanted was a logical one in terms of a portfolio fit for him, so I did not oppose it in itself.

Over the next fortnight, Theresa became more irritated about my failure to agree, and kept pressing me, but I stood my ground. In the end, I said I would accept a change if child exploitation was moved into my sphere, along with the other bits she had already identified, one by one adding sweets to the scales. She did not like this idea, and I was by now also getting irritated, so I indicated that in that case, we would just have to carry on with the portfolio split that had applied in Jeremy's time. Shortly after, she agreed to the deal I had suggested.

I did not like operating in this way, but if she was going to be as hard as nails then I had to be too. It was tiresome but necessary. Sink or swim.

To my dismay, I discovered that the coalition rules and conventions that had applied from day one at the Department for Transport were largely absent. While the former had been run as a coalition department, the Home Office had clearly been operating as a Conservative department with a Lib Dem in a corner. I had to re-create basic procedures, such as access to papers, that had applied from day one at the DfT.

There, I had had access to the Secretary of State's work diary so I could identify meetings that it might be helpful to discuss beforehand or sometimes attend. So I would sit in occasionally on, say, discussions about aviation strategy. Each of the transport secretaries recognised that it was sensible to understand the Lib Dem perspective at an early stage to prevent problems occurring later.

I would see submissions sent to other ministers for decisions and occasionally write them a note or just pop my head round the corner. They would do the same in reverse. Sometimes, the Secretary of State or another minister would flag up an issue I had missed and ask for the Lib Dem view. For my part, I was sensitive to the touchstone issues for the Tories and would alert them to anything I was doing that I thought they would be interested in.

This was not the Home Office way, where there was no acceptance that I had any business to get involved in issues outside my portfolio. The Home Secretary never really accepted that the Lib Dem minister in the department had a wider duty to the coalition to keep an eye on matters beyond his or her portfolio.

It might be thought that she would have seen the value of that approach after the 'go home' vans fiasco, where Jeremy Browne had been kept out of the loop, but it seems not.

The Home Secretary even objected to my wish to be regularly given top-level briefings by directors covering areas outside my portfolio, but I went ahead anyway. Apart from anything else, I would be expected to be up to speed with other matters in the department for Commons debates and questions, and for TV and radio appearances as a Home Office minister, so it was stupid to try to keep me in the dark.

At the DfT, we had regularly helped each other out across portfolios. For example, when I announced the successful schemes from the Local Sustainable Transport Fund, all of us would head out to different towns and cities to ensure we maximised the good coverage that could be had.

For my part, I had for example become involved in HS2, representing the department at a meeting in Scotland and appearing on *Newsnight*. One year I even gave the key address in International Shipping Week, a subject about I which knew close to zero, reminding me of the appointment of a shipping minister in the 1920s who maintained the only justification for his appointment was that he was completely at sea.

On my first day in post, I learnt there was to be a meeting of Chief Constables with the Home Secretary and Damian Green, the policing minister, but I was not invited, even though I was now Minister for Crime Prevention. I raised this with the Home Secretary's office and was told she strongly advised against my going. No good reason was given, so I went along anyway, to the visible annoyance of Theresa. Tiresome but necessary.

It was trench warfare, with every inch of ground having to be fought for. There was no generosity of spirit, and if there had ever been a coalition honeymoon effect in the Home Office, it had certainly worn off after three and a half years.

In one sense, I could understand the resistance I was encountering from Theresa and her special advisers, given that I was seeking to change things three and a half years into the coalition. But the fact was that all I was seeking to put in place were basic arrangements that should have applied from day one – and did elsewhere in government.

Theresa never wanted to give ground, which occasionally led to direct action on my part, as with the meeting with the Chief Constables, but more usually to a complaint to the Permanent Secretary, Mark Sedwill.

Mark was in my view a very good civil servant who, like the best civil servants, understood politics to a high degree and was therefore able to be safely and completely apolitical. I learnt to trust his judgement and his fairness.

When I raised procedural matters with him, he would usually rule in my favour, no doubt to the annoyance of the Home Secretary and her political team. This was because I did not normally bother him unless I was reasonably sure of my ground. Nevertheless, a lesser man might have taken the line of least resistance and bent to the will of the Home Secretary or her special advisers, rather than judging the matter on its merits.

Many civil servants did bend and were genuinely frightened of her spads, who were not above shouting at them. One of my visits to Mark Sedwill was to complain of them doing just that to the officials in my private office, which I was not going to tolerate. I told him that that must never happen again, and it did not.

What was in place, at least as far as senior officials were concerned, was close to a thinly veiled reign of terror. The tramlines were laid down by Theresa's spads, and woe betide any civil servant who went outside them. Officials who did not please found themselves shunted out to cul-de-sac postings elsewhere.

What a contrast to the DfT, where Justine Greening had invited her officials to come up with good ideas. No small acts of love at the Home Office.

I thought this was not just nasty but an approach that smothered ingenuity and innovation in a rather central Soviet way.

The officials most under the cosh were those in the department's press section. Lines came down from the spads office and this exact language had to be used. The answer was to be substantially the same no matter how much the question changed.

Shortly after I arrived, a draft quote on drugs came up for me from the press office, drugs falling within my portfolio. The line I was offered was so tired it was pushing up zeds, and made me sound like an identikit Tory. I changed it, but then it was changed back by Fiona Cunningham. In the Home Office, it was normal practice for the Tory spads to have the final say on all press lines, even from the Lib Dem minister.

I stormed down to the spads office, much to the amusement of Rebecca Whitfield, one of the team in my private office, who followed me down, not wanting to miss anything. I opened the door and the Principal Private Secretary almost jumped out of his chair with shock. Apparently Jeremy had never done this.

An argument followed. I said I was not having words made up for me and moreover I was not going to have quotes that made me sound like a Tory. We came to a messy compromise.

Again and again the issue of press lines would arise, and I ended up discussing it with the Home Secretary on a number of occasions. She said I had to remain within agreed government policy, which I naturally accepted. That was not the issue, I suggested, and challenged her to find one line I had put out that was outside agreed policy. She did not cite one, instead shifting the argument to say that lines from all ministers should sound consistent. That was why it was important that the same phrases were used again and again.

I countered that staying within agreed policy did not mean I had to sound like a Tory and there were different ways of expressing the government line.

On a practical basis, I pointed out that the lines suggested for me (and other ministers) were so repetitive they were being largely ignored, and we were missing opportunities to get our message across.

She was rock solid, however, with not a chink of light glinting through, and in the end I took it to Mark Sedwill, who ruled that her spads could not change my press quotes against my wishes.

'Unless factually inaccurate,' he wrote, 'the line cleared by the minister responsible should be taken as the final version.'

If the spads objected to what I wanted to say, and we could not agree, then they would have to refer the matter to the Home Secretary, who could overrule me.

The Home Secretary had not wanted this, saying of the spads: 'They are my voice.'

It was a revealing statement, but one with which the Permanent Secretary disagreed. Her voice could overrule me. Theirs could not.

This ruling reduced the number of incidents, and for my part I exercised a degree of self-restraint. But matters then began to deteriorate again, particularly over drugs issues, which were one of the big flashpoints across the coalition.

The spads objected to some terminology I wanted to use and I refused to change it. I was then told the Home Secretary had decided in their favour.

My understanding of Mark Sedwill's ruling was that where there was a deadlock, Theresa and I would discuss it, not that it would be referred to her by the spads and I would be told the decision. I refused to put the quote out and it was issued in the name of a 'Home Office spokesman' instead.

After this had happened a couple of times, it seemed to me that we were in effect reverting by other means to the previous arrangements I had succeeded in changing.

I made it known that if this continued, I would bypass the system and phone up the journalist in question direct, issue the quote

I wanted, and then inform the press office so they had a record of what I had said. I did in fact call their bluff and do this once.

This new tactic proved more effective and I did not have to use it again.

The civil service, except those working in immigration who were of the True Faith, seemed secretly rather pleased I was taking on the spads, who were widely disliked. Unlike officials, I could not be moved sideways or shouted at.

Officials all across the department started being quite helpful, even if it was largely under the radar. I encouraged them to discuss policy options with me and tell me what they really thought the best solutions to any particular problem were. This was a novel approach for some, apparently.

My own private office had no choice, of course, but to be above the radar, and, as my DfT office had been, were helpful and supportive. It must have been more difficult for the Home Office lot, however, and I was grateful to the team.

Everything, but everything, was a battle. My request for a bike was met with silence, followed over the days with responses intended to make me give up. They did not yet know me very well.

When I kept pushing it, I was told that it would be an unnecessary expense. I pointed out that a bike costs next to nothing, unlike the car and chauffeur they had allocated to me. Ah, but they have been paid for, I was told. The bike would be extra. Well, get rid of them, I replied. Alas, cannot be done, was the rejoinder.

After a couple of weeks dancing round the issue, I went to the *Mail on Sunday* with the story, and how they were trying to force me to have a car and chauffeur. It did the trick.

A couple of days later I was told they had solved the problem. It turned out this meant borrowing my old Brompton from the DfT. It was a neat civil service solution. I had my bike but they had stuck to their point of principle that money should not be spent on this. And the car and the chauffeur could continue to wait downstairs, unused by me.

And yet still it was not sorted. They wanted me to keep the bike in some downstairs car park area that was so remote and difficult to access that the chances of making it to the Commons within the eight minutes allowed for a vote were zero. Finally, I got them to agree to keep it near the entrance, which is what should have been offered in the first place.

If cycling was difficult, so was recycling. There seemed to be no provision for this, so I asked my new private secretary, Stephen Knight, to try to make some progress. This turned out not to be at all simple, as there was no provision in the relevant contract. The answer from the cleaners had been to separate out the recyclables from the general waste and leave them on Stephen's desk. What he was supposed to do with them was not clear.

My efforts to avoid using a ministerial car were successful, in that I simply refused to use one. The civil service could not make me get into a car but they could make the alternatives as difficult as possible.

Aside from the travails over the bike, they were resistant to giving me an Oyster card, even though travelling by Tube was the most obvious way to travel round London. I finally got one in February, several months after I arrived at the department.

The most ludicrous episode occurred when I was visiting UK Border Force at Kew. I had, as usual, refused to be taken by car from central London, not least because it was clearly going to be slower and less certain in its time of arrival than a train. When we got to Kew, it was raining heavily and I did not fancy the walk of half a mile or so to the location, so decided we ought to take a taxi for the last stretch.

The civil service never wanted me to travel by taxi for the same reason they did not want me to use a bike: there was a ministerial car available. On this occasion, the official who was with me, aware of the strictures, rang the office to check that we could use a taxi. Absolutely not, we were told, but if we could wait there, they could probably get the ministerial car there by three. It was then half past one. We took a taxi.

Incidentally, while at the DfT, I had been horrified to learn that the departmental spend on taxis was a whopping £38,292 for the six months from August 2011 to January 2012. One journey cost £720. I sent the Permanent Secretary a note on this in late August 2012 but uncharacteristically forgot to follow this through. Some MP should ask a written question, and also of the Home Office.

Meanwhile, in my role as co-chair of the Greening Government Committee, I discovered that over the past year, the Home Office had been responsible for 3,412 domestic flights, of which 1,493 were between London and Manchester. There was clearly a long way to go to get the Home Office to behave rationally, let alone environmentally, in its travel arrangements.

There was some light relief when we all – the ministerial team, the Permanent Secretary and the spads – were invited by Theresa to Christmas lunch, even if this did not finally happen until early January.

We duly assembled one lunchtime in the basement of Osteria Dell'Angolo, the restaurant immediately opposite the Home Office in Marsham Street. I arrived a few minutes late and took in the room and its atmosphere of slightly forced jollity.

A terribly polite discussion about the wine ensued, with everyone settling for red except James Brokenshire and me, who went for the Gewürztraminer.

To lighten the atmosphere, I started telling anecdotes, and recall for some reason referring to the jazzman Eubie Blake, who, on reaching 100, had said if he had known he was going to live that long, he would have taken more care of himself.

The others laughed, very slightly hysterically I thought.

A few days later, each of the ministers received a bill from Theresa for £58.74.

Chapter 23

The Home Secretary and I were always supportive of each other in public while I was a minister. Apart from anything else, that was just good manners. This included when she gave evidence to the Home Affairs select committee – which, with Keith Vaz as chairman, was always keen on mischief-making – for which I thanked her. I reciprocated by stoutly defending her from an unfair attack on *The World at One* that questioned her commitment to violence against women issues, where she had actually been very sound.

After that appearance, I bumped into Jeremy Browne, who clearly thought I had gone native, with the implication that if so, there had not been much point in replacing him. I should record that Jeremy and I always got along fine, and I sought his advice on matters occasionally, especially on drugs.

By his own admission, however, Jeremy had not enjoyed the Home Office, much preferring his previous posting in the grand surroundings of the Foreign Office. They used to run India from his magnificent room there. The qualities he required there were not the same as required at the Home Office. And Theresa May was not William Hague.

Some people assumed everything had settled down after the initial furore between myself and the Home Secretary. Others who were more in the know assumed that there was a deep antagonism being played out beneath the surface.

Actually, both groups were wrong. I never felt any animosity towards Theresa May. Indeed, I respected and even admired her. She was clearly competent and it is no mean feat to survive so many years as Home Secretary. She was brave, for example in taking on the Police Federation, and also principled in her beliefs, even if I did not always agree with her principles. You do not have to agree with someone, or even like them, to acknowledge their strengths.

The problem was that I did not like the way she ran the department. She would argue that without this vice-like grip at the centre, she would not have lasted so many years in post, and perhaps that is true. But the price of that was a climate of fear in officials, a gloomy air of drudgery around the department, and the stifling of ideas and innovation. We could all see the stick, but where was the carrot?

From my point of view, this approach was compounded by her insistence on running the Home Office as a Tory department rather than a coalition one. The fact that this tendency was so pronounced was a primary reason I had been sent in by Nick Clegg, to reassert the Lib Dem part of the coalition.

In another department, where there were fewer differences between the parties, this might not have mattered so much, but it did in the Home Office.

It did not help either that she was generally reluctant to delegate very far to her ministers, Tory or Lib Dem, and would intervene in really quite small matters. I regularly sought to raise this general issue with her, but somehow there was never time in our bilaterals to get round to it, even after I had discussed it with Mark Sedwill.

In the end, her helpful private secretary produced her a note to aid a discussion, but that did not happen either, and I was forced to write to her formally on the matter. Her secretary meantime just disappeared one day. The rumour was that he had been sent to the civil service equivalent of Siberia for not being sufficiently on-message.

There were areas in my portfolio where we did agree, such as on alcohol, domestic violence and child sexual exploitation, and we worked well together. We did not do so on drugs. Overall, the only latitude she would give me was the latitude to agree with her.

Outside my portfolio, the flashpoints across the coalition were immigration, Europe and what we termed the 'snoopers' charter'.

I found her reluctance to embrace the coalition frustrating and it limited the opportunity to build bridges.

It may be that a particular issue in government divided the parties neatly and cleanly on different sides, but it was actually much more common for the division to be between the Tories and Lib Dems in one department and the Tories and Lib Dems in another, or between one department and No. 10 or No. 11.

I would regularly make this point to Theresa, but to no avail. One such trigger generated a note from me to her on 27 October 2014:

> I also learnt from the weekend papers of your challenges with the European Arrest Warrant. As you know, I share your view on this matter, so it is a pity you have not asked me to use my influence with my Lib Dem colleagues at No. 10 and elsewhere.
>
> In the end, the extent to which you involve me is I suppose a matter for you to decide. I would however reiterate that by seeking to exclude me, you are missing the opportunity to pull all the levers available…

Occasionally there were issues where my party was uninterested and where I would find myself working with a like-minded Tory to get what I thought was the right result, such as on animal testing, where I worked with Oliver Letwin. Equally, I would sometimes be asked by a Tory colleague to help influence one of his or her Tory colleagues on an issue.

So, across government the Tories and Lib Dems did work in this integrated fashion, while of course retaining individual party loyalty. It is this mature approach that meant the coalition worked well and lasted the full five years.

The Home Secretary was different. For her, acknowledgement of the coalition was predominantly through the regular bilaterals with Nick Clegg that were established before I arrived in the department. No other Tory Cabinet minister had such bilaterals, instead largely sorting matters out with their Lib Dem minister at departmental level.

So there were issues where the Home Secretary and I were in agreement, but the blockage to progress was at No. 10. I thought we should have worked together more closely in these situations, as I would have done at the DfT with my Secretary of State, to try a pincer movement on No. 10, through both Tory and Lib Dem channels.

This was in fact more necessary at the Home Office than it might have been elsewhere. For one thing, No. 10 was always wary of the Home Secretary, who it was assumed was interested in the top job. For another, her spads were not well liked at No. 10 and so did not have the influence they might have had.

But the Home Secretary was not keen on the pincer idea. Perhaps she did not trust me.

One such area was alcohol. By Home Office figures, alcohol abuse cost society around £21 billion a year, an enormous figure. This broke down into £11 billion in antisocial behaviour, £4 billion to the NHS and the rest in lost productivity. The total figure dwarfed income to the Treasury from alcohol duty.

The total damage to society each year from illegal drugs was estimated to be about £10 billion, so roughly half the cost of alcohol damage. Alcohol was of course far more pervasive in society, but even so the gap was stark.

The government had been backtracking on the one measure I thought was likely to be effective at minimising harm, namely minimum unit pricing. Alcohol harm was disproportionately associated with cheap, super-strength lager and cider and cheap vodka, obtained via off sales. These would be caught by minimum unit pricing.

The other benefit I saw was that such a policy would reduce the price differential between pubs on the one hand and supermarkets and corner shops on the other. I was keen to support pubs, both because they are part of the fabric of our communities and because they provide a controlled drinking environment.

But before my time at the Home Office, this had been watered down to a proposed ban on sales below cost, which accounted for a microscopic proportion of alcohol consumed. I had to take the introduction of this through the Commons and relied heavily on the excuse, in fact not unreasonable, that we had to wait for the outcome of legal action that had been taken in Scotland against minimum unit pricing before deciding whether to proceed.

Had this been the only issue, I could have lived with that, but it was not.

In February 2014, Theresa and I had been lobbied by the drinks industry, who wanted a blanket national extension to opening hours for pubs on evenings when England were playing in the World Cup. We both thought that this was not justified, but of course individual pubs and clubs could apply for extensions as normal, if they wanted to.

This was wrongly presented as a ban on extensions, leading to a headline in one Sunday paper: 'They drink it's all over, it is now'.

The next day, the Prime Minister announced at an 11 a.m. press briefing that there would be a 'consultation' on a national extension, but in the side-briefings to journalists it was made plain that this was a formality and that the decision to go ahead had already been taken.

Neither Theresa nor I had been consulted, or even warned about this. She was understandably livid for a whole range of reasons.

First, they did not seem to understand the issue, as they were talking about 'a national solution with local options'. This was in effect what we were proposing.

Second, as Theresa rightly remarked to me, this would likely lead to increase in antisocial behaviour and domestic violence – there had been a small increase in the latter associated with the 2006 World Cup.

Third, it undermined generally the alcohol strategy we had been pursuing.

Fourth, it was just plain discourteous.

As so often, No. 10 was acting in a way it did not really understand, though arrogantly believed it did. In this case it was being driven by the power of the drinks industry, which had no hesitation in going to No. 10 when it did not like the line it was getting from the Home Office.

The Home Secretary then had a wheeze to consult on either national or local exemptions, the latter of course being the unvarnished status quo. Six of the nine formal consultees, such as the police, opted for the latter, with only beer and football interests preferring the former.

That notwithstanding, No. 10 told Theresa that we were having a national derogation and that was that. She was not best pleased and told me she had stripped the Written Ministerial Statement that was required down to the bare minimum and given it an obscure title (Alcohol Licensing).

I suggested we would need to have a meeting, including her spads, to talk about where this left our alcohol policy.

I was continuing to put pressure on the industry to deal with specific problem areas. One of these was inappropriate marketing. I called industry representatives in and laid out in front of them photographs one of my officials had taken – alcohol displayed next to children's clothing, for example. They clearly did not want to act, so to ginger them up, I released the photos to the *Daily Mail*, who did a nice piece, which woke them up.

With unilateral action by us having been shut down by No. 10, we were working towards an alcohol summit by cajoling the industry to come up with firm proposals on a voluntary basis.

I had asked officials to make it plain to them that the Home Secretary and I were deadly serious in our intent and would follow through with new rules and regulations if the package they produced was inadequate.

This was largely a bluff, but they could not be sure. The language from officials and my own piece in the *Mail* were clear signs that we were indeed serious.

In early July, with the summit just two or three weeks away, the industry had produced a package of sorts, but I felt they had not gone far enough.

A draft invite letter came up to me for approval. I felt it was too soft, and amended it to stress that we expected results and concrete proposals from the summit, not vague promises of things to come. I sensed that the industry would be quite happy to play for time, with the election less than a year away.

The Home Secretary had been sent a draft at the same time and had independently decided that the wording needed to be strengthened.

But then came the bombshell. No. 10 said it did not want a summit to take place at all, or for us to say anything about the industry pledges.

This was mad. We had, against the odds, negotiated a worthwhile package of measures, which was a good-news story for the government. And now No. 10 wanted to smother the whole thing.

What could be the motivation? Had they been got at by the drinks industry? Was it a case of 'barnacles on the boat' – the idea that government should concentrate only on big-picture issues? Was it putting the Home Secretary firmly in her place? Was it just pique that we had got so far despite their opposition?

Nick Timothy came to see me in my office, the first time he had done so since I was appointed. He gave the impression of being as incandescent as I was. We agreed to try a pincer movement on No. 10, and I briefed Alex Dziedzan accordingly.

This was partially successful, with No. 10 agreeing that the summit could be held. But they insisted that there should be no pre-publicity, and only an obscure, web-based story afterwards, in which we were not to be critical of the industry.

A submission came up from officials which summarised this, and I dropped the Home Secretary a note saying that this was ludicrous. Her deadpan reply was to tell me that this was the deal with No. 10 and was I 'content'? I was not content, of course, but I recognise *force majeure* when I see it.

It was clear nothing could be done before the summit, but afterwards was a different matter. I briefed Nick Watt of *The Guardian* about the story over a rather fine lunch at the Cinnamon Club so that he would spot the web story when it was published.

Nick duly published a piece but, to my consternation, it appeared a day early, and only online. If the Home Secretary noticed the piece, she did not mention it to me. I was pleased that Nick had used my line that the government was 'burying good news'.

I had not told the Home Secretary I was doing this, largely in fact to protect her. As a matter of course, I had since 2010 been fixing lunches with journalists through my constituency office rather than via my departmental office. I discovered early on that after one leak to a paper (not from me), No. 10 had gone through all ministers' diaries to see who had had lunch with that particular journalist, so I had taken precautions from that point on.

Whether because of effective lobbying from the industry or just petulance on the part of the Prime Minister I do not know, but an extraordinary instruction was issued that nothing should be issued ahead of the election to attack alcohol interests. So extreme was this direction that I wondered at that point whether the question of election donations to the Conservative Party might be relevant.

The direction was relevant because there was a further alcohol-related issue I was pursuing, namely the establishment of pubs on motorway service stations.

Under the 2003 Licensing Act, this had been explicitly banned but, presumably due to a defect in the law, Section 176 allowed sales from privately owned service stations, which in fact as a result of privatisation in the 1990s now made up nearly half of all service stations. With a green light from Theresa, I had been working up proposals to close this loophole.

The spur had been the decision by J. D. Wetherspoon's to open a pub, the Hope and Champion, at the Junction 2 service station on the M40. This had been given permission by the local district council, South Bucks, in January 2014. It was rumoured that this was under threat of an expensive appeal, though I never checked this out.

Either way, it struck me as a really bad precedent and I was keen to prevent further pubs from opening. Did we really want drivers stopping for a pint before they got back in their cars and drove off?

We were already being lobbied hard by the police on the need to reduce alcohol availability at motorway service areas. This was about to make it a whole lot worse.

In March, I asked officials to work up the necessary secondary legislation as soon as possible and was given a timeline showing it could be accomplished by October.

We started going through all the laborious processes involved, such as notifying the Reducing Regulation Committee, writing to the devolved administration in Cardiff, and then to the government's own Home Affairs Committee, the clearing house for domestic legislation. Discussions on the package, which also included an easing on selling alcohol at overnight lodges, had taken place informally with other departments likely to have an interest, such as Transport, Business and Culture, the latter for tourism reasons, and all had been positive.

However, the Prime Minister was adamant. No matter that colleagues across government in both parties wanted to close the loophole, no matter that the police were strongly in favour, as was the public, judging by the reaction to the original M40 story. We were to take no action to stop pubs opening on motorways. And that was that.

Another issue where the Prime Minister intervened personally and unhelpfully related to gun licences. The fees for these had not increased since 2001 and I could not understand why. I popped round the corner to see Damian Green, who had had responsibility for this area before I arrived, to ask him for his advice. He told me he had himself tried to correct this but had been 'shat upon from a great height' by No. 10. He wished me well.

I did some digging. It turned out Damian's efforts had been

blocked by a combination of the Prime Minister himself and Owen Paterson, who had said that an increase would 'affect our people'.

Yet the police were estimated to be around £18 million out of pocket, that being the shortfall between the cost of processing applications and the fees they received. This was scandalous at any time, but especially when police budgets were having to be cut.

The answer from No. 10 was for the police to become more efficient at processing the applications, and it is true that there was work to do here, but they did it. By the time I took over the portfolio, the overall estimated cost to the police of processing an application had been reduced from just shy of £200 to around £90, but this was still way above the £50 fee charged.

Even the shooting lobby found all this rather embarrassing. It was also conscious that an incoming Labour government might do rather more than cover costs, notwithstanding that they had uselessly failed to do anything between 2001 and 2010.

This particular point had occurred to Geoffrey Clifton-Brown, a leading Tory MP in shooting circles, who collared me to ask why there was a delay in increasing the licence fee. He suggested that both our interests would be served by an increase to the level where the police break even, introduced before the election. I told him I agreed, as did the Home Secretary, but advised him bluntly that he needed to speak to the Prime Minister, who was blocking any increase, despite all sides now being in agreement on the way forward.

For my part, I briefed out the story to the *Sunday Times*. The next day, the Home Secretary gently told me off, but not so you would really notice.

The article was useful, however, in alerting the wider public to the issue. For instance, Martyn Underhill, the Dorset Police and Crime Commissioner, went so far as to issue a press release on 21

August, saying he had written to the Prime Minister 'to express his disbelief' at what had been done.

'David Cameron needs to justify this stand-alone decision and reassure the cynics amongst us that this isn't about his personal hobby, the party faithful and extreme lobbying,' he wrote. He added that he estimated the issuing of gun licences in Dorset was being subsidised to the tune of £250,000 a year.

Finally, in March 2015, just before the election, my successor Lynne Featherstone announced an increase in fees from £50 to £88.

Chapter 24

In February 2014, I arrived at the department one day to find Mark Harper had resigned as immigration minister as an issue had arisen over the immigration status of his cleaner.

I was sorry to learn this and did not think that a resignation was really justified. However, I knew the media well enough to recognise that if he had not resigned, he would doubtless have been hounded until he did. Indeed, the *Daily Telegraph* was already starting down that road, digging out earlier material about his expenses.

As it was, resigning quickly was an astute move, and he was then able to come back into government after a short period out, and indeed be promoted to Chief Whip after the 2015 election.

Mark could not be anything other than a Conservative given his beliefs, but he was quite popular with the Lib Dems because he played coalition straight. He had had the difficult task, before he came to the Home Office, of being No. 2 to Nick Clegg, and had succeeded in being loyal to Nick without tarnishing his Tory credentials. It was an impressive performance.

Mark's approach meant he and I were able to have sensible discussions about the Immigration Bill in a way that minimised coalition tensions. In return for agreeing to some of the changes the Tories wanted, we secured the end of child detention, and managed to remove some of the more extreme proposals, such as making teachers responsible for checking the immigration status of children. Having reached an agreement, Mark honoured it.

Apart from being sorry at losing Mark, I was unenthusiastic that he was replaced by James Brokenshire, promoted within the department. I had nothing against James on a personal basis, but he was widely regarded as a sort of teacher's pet. He also lacked the political skill of Mark Harper and made something of a hash of his first big immigration speech.

Of course, it was not easy to present a good front to a policy that lacked intellectual coherence.

While the Home Office gave the impression of wanting to pull up the drawbridge against anyone it could, other parts of government were making the case for a more relaxed line, particularly for those who wanted to enter the country from China.

The Tories were tied in to the absurd and completely arbitrary target for annual net migration of no more than 100,000. This was a Tory target rather than a coalition one – we were not going to touch it with a bargepole. Apart from anything else, because it is not possible under EU law to prevent access to the country by EU citizens, it was like setting a target for the maximum number of days each year it should rain. By 2015, the immigration figure was 198,000. It was astonishing that the Tories were still hanging on to this target – or aspiration, as it now seemed to be.

The consequence, however, was that because the numbers of Poles, Romanians and others from Eastern Europe could not be controlled, the Tories sought to clamp down on those who could, even though this often made little sense: business people who wanted to invest, tourists with money and students who wanted to study, including high-value postgraduates.

In March 2014, a group of Tory backbenchers led by the MP for the Cities of London and Westminster, Mark Field, called on the

Prime Minister to tone down the rhetoric on immigration, which they said was damaging as it was discouraging foreign students who would be good for the economy.

It was therefore no surprise that the Immigration Bill ran into trouble in the Lords on the subject of student migration. I wrote a long note to the Home Secretary in March to suggest how defeat in the Lords could be avoided. I saw no value in running straight into a brick wall.

The government also suffered a defeat in the Lords, entirely predictably, on the proposal to deprive UK nationals of their citizenship under certain circumstances. It was a nasty proposal, to leave a UK national stateless, and reinforced the view that the Tories cannot be trusted with our basic rights. In a contest between political expediency and rights, the Tories will ultimately always opt for the first over the second. Those pushing for the UK to exit the European Convention on Human Rights and who somehow believe a British Bill of Rights is an adequate substitute may well find they are exchanging cast iron for cheap plastic.

Generally, the Home Secretary and the Prime Minister could not resist tinkering around endlessly with the immigration rules and regulations, like continually picking at a spot. And immigration officials, picking up the mood music, would continually offer tweaks here and there. While there were undoubtedly abuses to be ended and loopholes to be closed, it did not make sense for the orderly process we had established between the parties for the Immigration Bill to be picked at in this way.

There was also quite unnecessary conflict over one particular cross-government process: the 'Review of the Balance of Competences between the UK and the EU'. This was a dry, analytic process, as far as the Foreign Office was concerned, just to set down how things stood. That was also the view of nearly everybody else, but the

Home Office's Tory spads could not resist the temptation to try to make the review that related to asylum and immigration into a tool that justified what they had done to date and – even more so – what they wanted to do in the future.

The original draft from officials had been broadly fine, but then it was sexed up. Another battle ensued, tiresome but necessary. I wrote a six-page note to the Home Secretary on 18 November 2013 about the neutral paper, now politicised.

> Its tone does seem to me to be tendentious in places and to appear to rely on opinion and perception as much as evidence. Where evidence is used, it appears to be partial and biased. I am advised that it has not drawn on relevant and authoritative studies which have been widely quoted in the press and academic literature and that there are a number of errors.

Amongst the changes were the removal of evidence that demonstrated the value to the UK arising from the free movement of people, and the creation of a misleading picture on benefit eligibility.

No other department had tried to twist this exercise as had the Home Office.

Other portfolio duties were no less important, but less contentious – even harmonious – between Theresa and me.

One big area was violence against women and girls, where I chaired the national group of key interested parties. Theresa was very sound in this area and I arrived at the department in time to see through new measures she had created: the Domestic Violence Disclosure Scheme, which enabled a person to ask the police whether their partner had a record of violence, and the Domestic Violence Protection Order, which enabled a woman subject to violence in the home to stay put while the perpetrator had to leave for a period, a reversal of what normally happened. They are excellent creations.

During my time, I visited a couple of refuges, one with Theresa and one alone, in my own constituency. I felt very conscious that I was a man and tried to be very careful in what I did and said.

I was encouraged that both refuges had a positive atmosphere and clearly were safe havens, doing a good job. Unfortunately, we were seeing refuges across the country shut, due to cuts in local government support. Even where they stayed open, councils were sometimes imposing conditions that generated extra cost for no gain, or, worse, undermined the refuge itself. Some had begun specifying that women who arrived had to be from that council area, failing, it seems, to see that the last thing a woman who is vulnerable to violence wants to do is to stay in the same area.

The Home Office did what it could, but Eric Pickles at CLG did not seem interested, and certainly showed no appetite for intervention. In the end, it took a sharp letter from No. 10 in September 2014 to galvanise CLG into action.

'The Prime Minister was very concerned to hear of the closure and scaling back by a number of local authorities of domestic refuge services…' it began.

'In the next fortnight, we would like you to develop policy options that can be implemented quickly to ***stop any more refuges from closing***.'

These paragraphs, with the original stresses, give a fair flavour of the letter. I was delighted. It was the best letter I saw come out of No. 10 during my time as a minister.

Theresa and I did not completely agree, however, on the subject of brothels. I was concerned by the fact that two sex workers who choose to occupy a house together for safety reasons can be prosecuted for running a brothel, thus forcing women out on to the streets, where it is less safe.

Furthermore, the law still includes in its definition of a brothel any premises 'which are resorted to for the purposes of lewd homosexual practices', whether or not for gain. This seemed to me to be a throwback to a different era and I thought it should be changed.

Police operational responses to prostitution varied significantly across the country, but incidents of violence were declining in Merseyside, where the police had taken a more relaxed view of the use of houses for prostitution in preference to streets.

I formed the impression that Theresa might be persuadable on the merits of reform, but I came to this conclusion late in my time in the Home Office, so was not able to test this very far.

I was pleased to make some real progress on the issue of female genital mutilation (FGM). I had been vaguely aware of this before I was promoted, but was horrified to learn the gruesome details. How could a parent have this inflicted on their daughter?

My interest coincided with coverage in a couple of papers, most notably the *London Evening Standard*, as well as active and effective campaigning from some brave women who had had the misfortune to have undergone FGM themselves, such as Leyla Hussein.

Theresa was also sound on this issue, but the Home Office's commitment was not matched all across government, where it was not really on the radar, and certainly not in Michael Gove's education department, which was actively hostile to intervention at school level.

My way around this was to create a ministerial declaration, pull together a group of ministers and get different departments signed up. The declaration itself was relatively anodyne, so as to get maximum endorsement, but still useful, not least in the precedent it set.

Many departments signed up. This helped isolate Michael Gove, who was eventually pulled into line.

I was also making good progress on getting all faith groups to condemn the practice. Contrary to popular belief, no religion requires FGM to be carried out. The response from the different groups, from Muslim to Catholic, was universally positive.

Another major part of my portfolio related to child sexual exploitation. It was becoming apparent during my tenure that the practice had been, and probably still was, far more extensive than anyone had thought. The lead police officer, Simon Bailey, the Chief Constable for Norfolk, told me that if police forces investigated all the leads they had, they would literally be able to do nothing else. One force was increasing the number of officers allocated to the task from two to eighty. They all, of course, had to be taken off other duties, and at a time when police numbers were falling.

It became clear, through an excellent if depressing report by the Deputy Children's Commissioner Sue Berelowitz, that there was a major problem with the sexual exploitation of girls in gangs, where the advances in women's rights over the previous fifty years appeared to have left no trace. This was also an area where we looked for help to Michael Gove's department, but looked in vain.

I wondered whether the overall level of child abuse that was now being identified had always occurred, but in the past it had just been accepted, or whether the incidence was increasing. Either way it was horrible.

The Home Secretary was brave and principled in facing up to the huge issue of historic child abuse, though regrettably, despite this being my portfolio, she would not involve me in the choice of chair for the inquiry, or even acknowledge either my suggestions or my concerns about individuals I understood to be in the frame.

Had she done so, I might have saved her from the embarrassing sequence of events that followed.

Another area I covered related to animal experiments. This again was something I had taken a close interest in, going back to 1997. I did not like the use of animals in procedures that were sometimes painful or distressing for the animal.

More fundamentally, I thought back to the discussions I had had almost twenty-five years earlier with Simon Hughes in the early hours of the morning when finishing off 'What Price Our Planet?' I was uncomfortable with the Christian ethos of humans having dominion over all other living things. The key word for me was respect.

In practical terms, I recognised that the use of animals in experiments could not simply be stopped overnight, but I felt much more should be done to identify other means of assessing the safety of products and ingredients so that in due course, probably many years from now, alternatives to the use of animals would be so well developed that we could close the door on animal experiments.

I was therefore pleased to launch with David Willetts the first ever government document setting out a route map to reduce the use of animals, and moreover it was a plan that the industry accepted, even if nervously.

I also secured an increase in funding to develop alternatives. Ones already in use were providing reliable data and doing so more cheaply.

At the same time I took a hard line with those in the industry who failed to look after animals in their care properly. There was a serious incident that arose at Imperial College, where I required the person responsible to depart.

So I was pursuing a nuanced line, albeit one more reforming than previous ministers had taken. My line, and my aspiration for an eventual end to the use of animals, was reported accurately by the BBC but then hyped up inaccurately by a sub-editor, suggesting I wanted a ban forthwith. I complained to the BBC, who accepted that the story was inaccurate and changed the heading.

In the meantime, the inaccurate story led to an angry letter to the Home Secretary from the Association of the British Pharmaceutical Industry.

Now, I had taken the BBC story with equanimity. These things happen. But I thought the ABPI should have contacted me first, rather than writing to Theresa direct. However, I could live with this.

What angered me, however, was that before I had even seen the ABPI letter, Theresa had written back to them, essentially taking their version of events at face value. I only discovered she had written when I received a copy of the letter she had sent.

I thought what she had done was disloyal and unhelpful, and wrote to tell her so. My position was not what the ABPI had alleged, the BBC had withdrawn the story, and yet she had felt able to reply without taking even two minutes to check with me first.

I concluded my letter:

> It is clear to me, both from this and earlier issues, that it would help the smooth running of the department if we talked more and you did not rely on the prism of your spads to relay what I am doing. From my perception, it appears to be often inaccurate and hyped up.

In between the portfolio issues came the run-of-the-mill Home Office business, including attending cross-departmental Cabinet committees.

At one inter-ministerial meeting on infrastructure in June chaired by Danny Alexander, I was delighted to see Patrick McLoughlin was there to answer questions on what the DfT was doing. Of course, I knew where the bodies were buried and playfully asked him a number of awkward and penetrating questions, to which he responded good-humouredly if not entirely comprehensively.

There was also a long discussion about bricks: why were we importing so many? I chipped in, knowing a bit about the subject, as I had a major brick manufacturer, Ibstock, in my constituency. It is in fact the oldest such establishment in the country that hand-fires its bricks. They presented me with one when I visited them, with my name dug into it. This is a great present for an MP: a unique souvenir, but one which is theoretically worth nothing, so does not have to be declared.

The most memorable quote on bricks, however, came from Vince Cable, concerned about imports of other products we should be making ourselves: 'Bricks are the tip of the iceberg.'

Away from Cabinet committees, there was also the need to respond to Commons adjournment debates, so called because rather bizarrely, the government whip stands up at the beginning and says, 'I beg to move that this House do now adjourn,' even if it is the first item on the day's agenda.

There were fewer adjournment debates for the Home Office than there had been for the DfT, but still a goodly number.

In April, I responded to one from Robert Syms, the Poole MP. He briefed me in advance on what he wanted to say, which I always encouraged so I could give the MP whose debate it was, irrespective of party, the best answer I could.

His issue was rented houses being used for hen and stag parties, and he regaled me with tales of blow-up dolls and nude waiters. I told him that referring to those would certainly ensure some coverage for the issue, if not for the waiters. 'I do hope they are wearing bow ties,' I added. 'There is such a thing as decorum.'

The debate itself almost resulted in an embarrassing shambles. At 10.45, one of my private office team, the affable Pat Duncan, had come into my office 'for my eleven o'clock appointment'. I looked at the clock and told him I was rather busy finishing something off.

'It's only 10.45,' I said. 'If the appointment's at eleven, come back then.'

At 10.55, he came in again, and stood there quietly, in his gentle West Country way. It is only then that I discover that my appointment is the debate in Westminster Hall in the Commons, and I have five minutes to get there.

'Jesus, Pat!' I exclaim and run for the lift. There are six of them, all pitifully slow. The only good thing that can be said about them is that they are better than the ones in the DfT.

Outside, with Pat in tow, I hail a taxi, which then gets stuck interminably at workmen's traffic lights, barely ten yards from where I had boarded it. I beseech the driver to do a U-turn and take a different route. If either the MP whose debate it is or the minister is not there for the start, it is likely the debate will be lost, and I did not fancy explaining this away to Robert Syms, or indeed to the Home Secretary.

At the lights at Parliament Square, I tumble out and hare across the path in front of the cathedral, scattering tourists in all directions, dodge the cars to cross the road, barge past the police at the main entrance to the House, and run down to Westminster Hall. I make it there at 11.01.

Fortunately, there is a government whip on the bench and my Lib Dem colleague Adrian Sanders in the chair. Between them, they have held the debate for just long enough for me to get there.

Robert Syms begins his speech while I get my breath back and drink some water. Luckily, I had had the presence of mind to grab my speech on the way out of the office.

In debates, the minister is supported by at least a couple of civil servants to whom notes can be passed by the minister to help get answers to points raised, thus informing the ministerial reply.

The Poole MP makes an interesting point and I turn round to pass a note to officials only to find they are not there. At 11.15, just as he is sitting down, seven of them come in. Why on earth are there seven of them, and why were they not there for the start of the debate?

It turned out that there were two from the Home Office, two from DEFRA and two from CLG, plus Pat, and they had missed everything that the MP had said. Apparently, although six of them had been on time, they had waited for Pat, whom I had left in the taxi while I hared across the road, before coming in! The civil service at its worst.

Both at the DfT and the Home Office, I was staggered by how little civil servants understood how Parliament works. I would regularly have to explain procedures and conventions to them. They would confidently tell me the time of a vote, which I would then check and correct them. They would tell me I had to be in the House to vote on a Ten-Minute Rule Bill, and I would remind them that ministers do not vote on such occasions. In the end, I arranged for my private office to spend an hour or two in the Lib Dem Whips' Office to have a crash course.

The same week as the debate occurred, on the Wednesday, I was in Lewes. I had a long-standing social engagement in the afternoon that had been in the departmental diary for quite some time, and I took the opportunity to visit the town's prison in the morning. I had been to see it many times in my local capacity, but here was an opportunity to discuss departmental issues, and in particular the prevalence of drugs in the prison. They were everywhere, I was told, especially the new so-called legal highs.

At ten past ten, a call came through from my private secretary, Stephen Knight, to tell me I had to return to cover a thirty-minute debate on rural crime at 2 p.m.

This was the first I had heard of this debate. It had not come up on Monday at our regular ministers' meeting when we discuss the week's business.

It turned out that the debate had originally been allocated to DEFRA, that being the department that covered rural issues – the clue being in the departmental name – but at the last minute they had backed off and were maintaining that the Home Office should cover it, which had been interpreted as meaning me, as the Minister for Crime Prevention.

I told my office point blank that I was not doing it, that I had had this afternoon slipped for weeks, and that I was slipped for all votes for the rest of the day. It was unacceptable to bounce this on me in this way. DEFRA had been allocated it. DEFRA should cover it.

I carried on with my visit, being shown various sections of the prison, but when the governor and I returned to his office, there was a message waiting for me, this time from the Home Secretary's office. It was from her private secretary, telling me I had to be on the 12.20 train.

I rang him up and repeated my earlier reply: I was not coming back. I suggested that DEFRA should be leant on to find a minister. If we had to cover it, I knew for a fact that Damian Green was around, so why could he not take the debate?

It was rare for me to book any time off and I was not going to rush back to handle a mess not of my making.

In the end, Damian did cover the debate, and it turned out most of the issues raised, such as police numbers, fell into his portfolio anyway. That did not stop him subsequently giving the Permanent Secretary both barrels for the inadequacy of the briefing.

The next day, I received an email from James Kirkup at the *Daily Telegraph*, asking why I had not taken the debate. This had the fingerprints of the Tory spads all over it. I explained the situation to him factually and he agreed that what I had done was perfectly reasonable. No story appeared.

In May and June, there was a huge coalition row over knife crime. The Tories had been pushing for a 'two possessions and you're in' policy. I thought this unattractively populist and simplistic, and felt that it fettered the discretion of judges. I had, however, let it go through the Home Office on the basis that you can only fight so many battles at one time.

Other Lib Dem colleagues, however, had taken a different approach, and I learnt that the write-round letter to other departments for clearance had been blocked by both Danny Alexander and David Laws.

Nick Clegg was then ambushed at the Home Affairs Committee, the clearing committee he chaired on domestic policy, by a combination of Theresa May, Michael Gove and Philip Hammond, but he refused to give way.

Full details of the spat then appeared in the next day's *Daily Mail*, written up predictably in a manner hostile to the Lib Dems. It also linked the story to the tragic stabbing a couple of days earlier of the 61-year-old teacher Ann Maguire, knifed by a fifteen-year-old pupil. Any suggestion that the law the Tories wanted enacted would have prevented the stabbing had it been in place at the time was both offensive and absurd.

Tim Colbourne from Nick's office asked me if I could work up any alternative proposals and I offered him the option of expanding the effective work the Home Office was doing on gangs. It was a Bank Holiday Sunday, but within a couple of hours, officials had come up with a detailed package, exactly what I had asked for, indicating how we could spend relatively small sums of money and have a noticeable impact. I was very impressed and congratulated them.

Both Nick and Tim were enthusiastic about the ideas, but not about what the Tories had done. Tim emailed me:

> Just got off a conference call with Nick. We agreed to work up an alternative proposal based on the stuff you sent ... The mood is very angry indeed – not just Nick, but also Danny and David who had their letters leaked. So no prospect at all of accepting the mandatory minimum proposal and a collective view that we need to respond in the strongest possible terms to Gove.

Michael Gove was believed to be behind the *Daily Mail* story.

The Tories decided to push ahead anyway, confident no doubt that Labour, so authoritarian on Home Office issues, would support them. They briefed the lobby for 12 June that the two parties would be voting differently across the coalition, with Tory ministers abstaining. The fact that knife crime was down 46 per cent from 2008 seemed to get lost in the mix.

June saw possibly the worst week in government for the Home Secretary, certainly her worst week during my time at the department.

Relations were strained not only between Michael Gove and the Lib Dems, but between Michael Gove and Theresa May as well. The DfE seemed to be increasingly out of line with other departments and was unhelpful on a whole range of issues in my portfolio where both the Home Secretary and I wanted help, from compulsory personal and social education (PSE) in schools, to the provision of information about drugs, to FGM. On the latter, the Education Secretary had finally been forced to do something after some damaging front-page headlines and a private letter from me urging him to act. I suspect the first of these was more significant than the second.

But on other areas he would not give way, and this clearly irritated the Home Secretary, who openly challenged him at a Cabinet committee she was chairing where I and other Lib Dems were present.

Then, in June, the niggling burst into the open big time. Michael Gove had openly criticised the Home Secretary and Charles Farr to *The Times* over their handling of extremism in schools and the alleged Trojan horse plot to infiltrate schools in Birmingham.

In this case, the Trojan horse contained more than Michael Gove bargained for. He was forced to apologise for his part in the briefing war that ensued.

It was not just the Home Secretary who was annoyed. Fiona Cunningham, as often, reflected her boss's mood magnified. She was also upset with Gove, who had referred publicly to her relationship with Charles Farr.

Fiona took the extraordinary – and fatal – step, in the early hours of the morning, of posting on the Home Office website a brusque letter from the Home Secretary to Michael Gove, criticising his record. In it, May accused Gove of failing to take action when the extremism threat was first brought to his attention in 2010. It also commented unfavourably on his call for Muslim girls not to wear headscarves in school.

With some goodwill, she might have got away with it, but there was precious little goodwill between Downing Street and Theresa's spads. Here also was a chance for No. 10 to clip Theresa's wings.

Fiona needed a lifebelt but Craig Oliver at No. 10 threw her a block of concrete instead. Cameron wanted her head and she had to resign.

Shortly before she did so, Fiona was spotted wandering down

Great Smith Street and past the DfE, not too subtly, to gauge the media interest. She was briefly filmed by the BBC. A few minutes later, the reporter got a call from Andy Tighe, the civil servant in charge of the Home Office's press department, to raise the issue of her being filmed.

'She's over twenty-one and on the public highway,' came the reply.

'Do you intend to use it?'

'What do you think?'

It is interesting to note that following the 2015 election, Michael Gove was made Secretary of State for Justice, which looked very much like a move by Cameron to create problems for Theresa May, though in any contest my money would be on the Home Secretary.

I was actually rather sorry about what had happened. For a start, in any policy showdown between Theresa May and Michael Gove, I was firmly on her side. Secondly, Fiona and I had actually got to a stage where we had a sensible working relationship. I had even come to quite like her. I certainly much preferred dealing with her than with either Nick Timothy or Stephen Parkinson.

Fiona was to be replaced by Liz Sanderson, a features editor at the *Mail on Sunday*, but the spads' office was also augmented by the addition of Will Tanner as the Home Secretary's 'policy adviser'.

Will Tanner was a civil servant, but was to be based with the spads. He was allocated areas of responsibility, as the other spads were, and was to answer to Nick Timothy. I thought the concept of a civil servant answering to a spad had gone out when Gordon Brown took over from Tony Blair, after the reign of Alastair Campbell.

The number of spads is set by the coalition, and this looked like an arrangement to add an extra one by the back door. There was also a question as to whether he was actually knowledgeable in the policy areas he had been allocated.

I was handed an internal email which had come from Alice Jewels, the Home Secretary's assistant private secretary, on drugs. It referred to 'special advisers (Will/Stephen/Nick and Alex)', which seemed to make my point for me.

I raised the matter with the long-suffering Mark Sedwill, who said Will would not be providing political advice, but agreed to remind colleagues that Will must remain, and appear to remain, politically neutral.

I also had to complain to Mark that a press line had gone out, generated by the Tory spads, criticising something Nick Clegg had said on drugs which clearly related to manifesto policy. I pointed out that this was a party matter as it related to the next parliament, so any response should have come from Tory central office, not the civil service. Furthermore, because the issue related to my portfolio, the line should have come to me for clearance, which it had not. Mark by and large agreed with me on the first point, and strongly on the second.

I did not take any enjoyment from having to continually challenge matters, but I was only too aware that if I did not, the abuses would get worse.

Nick Timothy was minded to get elected to Parliament, and was seen less around the ministerial floor than his colleagues. He became very shirty when I was in the spads' office and mentioned this one day. I think he misunderstood me. From my point of view, the more he was out of the building, the better.

As it turned out, No. 10 was to get its revenge on him, and Stephen Parkinson too, allegedly for not canvassing in the Rochester by-election. He was removed from the candidates' approved list as a punishment.

It was hard, as a rule, to feel much sympathy for Nick Timothy, but I did think he had been hard done by on this occasion, not least because the special advisers' employment terms precluded such involvement. The code of conduct says special advisers who want to take part in election campaigns must first resign.

In the same bad week for the Home Secretary came water cannon. Boris Johnson had announced he wanted to deploy the machines and had even taken some steps to secure some. This was a crude attempt to bounce the Home Secretary, whose decision it was as to whether they could be deployed on the UK mainland.

Theresa was taking her time over the matter, months, in fact. She had genuine doubts about whether this was a good idea, and was also conscious that, because police officers might have to move areas to use them in the event of a major incident, the training costs would be substantial.

In addition, I had made it clear that this was not something I supported, for that reason and others, including the damage it might do to the concept of policing by consent, and the fact that an individual in Stuttgart had been left blinded by their use. But this was not strictly a coalition matter, rather an operational decision for the Home Secretary.

Nevertheless, I asked for a briefing, to which she objected on the basis that it was not in my portfolio. She was not still not accepting what other Cabinet ministers accepted, namely that the coalition minister in a department had a right, even a duty, to be across the live issues in the department.

Once again I had to get Mark Sedwill to intervene on my behalf. Mark, who was normally very even-tempered, did on one occasion tell me that he had not secured the position he had in order to engage in shuttle diplomacy up and down the corridor. I sympathised, but suggested that point would be better made to the Home Secretary.

On 12 June, a No. 10 spokesman reported that the Prime Minister had given his support in principle to water cannon, though the final decision lay with the Home Secretary. It did not take long to work out that Boris was up to his old tricks: going straight to No. 10 and bypassing whatever Cabinet minister or junior minister was getting in his way. I felt angry on Theresa's behalf. This was an operational matter and nothing to do with the Prime Minister, who cannot possibly have had access to the detailed analysis that had been prepared in the Home Office.

I was pleased to see that Theresa finally decided in July 2015 to refuse the use of water cannon, leaving Boris rather high and dry.

In that same difficult week, there was a lot of noise in the media about the operation of the Passport Office. As far as I could tell, while there had been a problem, it was now largely sorted, with close to 100 per cent of passports being delivered within the approved timescale. However, the alleged problems had been blown up, quite effectively for a change, by Labour, which succeeded in painting a picture of a Home Office slightly out of control.

James Brokenshire was summoned to No. 10 to explain to the Prime Minister what was going on. He was kept waiting for ages before being sent away again, told that the PM no longer wanted to see him.

There were further ministerial changes in July, when the second Tory reshuffle took place. On this occasion, there was no matching Lib Dem event. At the Home Office, Damian Green lost his position, one of a number of moderate Conservatives to lose out, along with Ken Clarke and Greg Barker. Overall, the reshuffle built on the one the previous year and signalled a further shift to the right, though we did see the end of Owen Paterson at DEFRA, which we in the Lib Dems shed no tears over.

Damian's replacement was Mike Penning, whom I had worked with at the DfT. Mike was to the right of Damian politically, but he was a friendly face and I was glad to see him.

At my old department, there was yet more upheaval. Stephen Hammond was unaccountably sacked and was understandably angry. He had, so far as I could tell, done a good job.

'The Prime Minister needs to remember that loyalty is a two-way street,' he said to me darkly when I commiserated with him in the voting lobby. On his way out but still able to conjure up a transport metaphor.

In his place, the department gained John Hayes and Claire Perry. I presume the extra ministerial post was to help in the Commons, where transport ministers were kept busy, and where the pressure had increased following the appointment of my Lib Dem replacement, Susan Kramer, who was based in the Lords.

John Hayes was regarded as something of a buffoon, and I was told that Patrick McLoughlin had tried unsuccessfully to prevent his transfer to the DfT.

Of course, we as Lib Dems were merely observers of the Tory reshuffle, just as they were of ours. From a personal point of view, I was most disappointed to see William Hague resign. I thought he had been a really good Foreign Secretary, and had shown a welcome if unexpected interest in issues close to my heart, such as the need to tackle FGM and to protect endangered species. His line on Europe, too, was much more balanced than it had been when he had been Tory leader.

The new Foreign Secretary was Philip Hammond, who looked very chuffed as he walked along Downing Street. While I did not doubt Philip's competence, having worked with him, I did not think this was a very good appointment. Sorting out the overspends at the MoD was one thing, handling delicate diplomatic matters was quite another. And of course he was more two-dimensionally Eurosceptic than his predecessor.

The Tory reshuffle followed the European elections, which had produced catastrophically bad results for the Lib Dems. We lost all bar one of our seats, only Catherine Bearder in the south-east hanging on. There were mutterings that we should change leader and change strategy, even leave the coalition, but the general view was that any Plan B looked even worse than Plan A and the only realistic option was to sail on and hope the wind would change.

Unusually, I asked to see Nick to discuss where we were. I did not normally bother him, knowing how busy he always was. I told him that while I thought he was doing a good job (which I did), and while the papers were being deeply unfair to him (which they were), we needed some changes.

In particular, I said that we needed to get more and different Lib Dem faces out there, not just his and Vince's. We needed to look broader and more female. Why was Jenny Willott, our Cardiff MP, not being used more, for example?

I also complained that his spads were giving him advice without checking first with the relevant Lib Dem minister, or ignoring ministerial advice, sometimes even undermining it. This, I pointed out, weakened our leverage in our departments, if officials and indeed Tories concluded that we had limited traction at the centre.

I gave him the example of a speech he had made on FGM that I had known nothing of until after delivery although I was the lead minister on this. It did not even mention the Home Office and I thought sounded amateurish and unbriefed as a consequence.

The answer, I suggested, was a box on all submissions to him headed 'Lib Dem Minister's Views' which should be completed before a sub is sent to him.

Nick held a Lib Dem event one Saturday at Chevening, the country residence in Kent he shared with the Foreign Secretary. It was making the most of the sunshine before the storm clouds moving ominously closer would finally burst.

I brought the family in my fun summer car, a red 1971 Triumph Herald convertible. Danny Alexander was suitably impressed and insisted on taking a photo of me next to the car with its hood down. He remarked that he had thought I was anti-car.

'Not this one,' I replied.

One of our girls went swimming with Nick in the big lake close to the fabulous house while I began a tour of the building. The old kitchens and washing rooms have been preserved untouched from a bygone era and were particularly interesting. I mused that they must have needed a staff of well over a hundred to run this place in the past.

At the end of what had been a very pleasant afternoon, Nick thanked me for our chat a few days earlier, and said he would indeed ensure we widen the Lib Dem arrowhead. He also thanked me, excessively effusively I thought, for my help with the Data Retention and Investigatory Powers Bill, known unattractively as the DRIP Bill.

This Bill was a piece of emergency legislation to ensure that the capability of the state in relation to communications data was not dangerously eroded. It would not, I think, be sensible to explain the full background, but suffice it to say that I was clear the Bill was necessary to maintain existing capability.

That was no reason, however, not to seek to achieve some useful policy gains on the back of it. Accordingly, I sat down with our Lib Dem policy advisers and our knowledgeable Cambridge MP Julian Huppert to draw up a list of asks that we would put to the Conservatives as the price for supporting the Bill.

This included a sunset clause for 2016, which would enable a full and proper post-Snowden debate to occur. We also asked for, amongst other provisions, a new independent privacy and civil liberties watchdog, a restriction on the length of time data could be held and a reduction in the number of public bodies able to access the data.

To my astonishment, the Prime Minister agreed to the whole list when it was put to him by Nick, bar a slight slipping for the date when the sunset clause would expire. I wondered if we should not have asked for even more.

The Home Secretary was livid about the concessions, though whether she was consulted by the PM then overruled, or not consulted at all, I was not clear.

The Bill was unveiled on 14 July and received royal assent just three days later. The Labour Party had decided to support the Bill, though that was hardly a surprise. With ID cards, ninety days' detention without trial and the rest, they had proved themselves to be more authoritarian than the Tories on such matters. Their whole tactical approach to home affairs appeared to be to put themselves to the right of the Tories on most matters. I sometimes wondered what the university professors, media types and smart Hampstead set who supported Labour thought of all this. I can only assume they did not know.

Of course, that did not stop Labour trying to claim credit for the package of safeguards to the Bill that we as Lib Dems had negotiated, and they briefed *The Guardian* accordingly, but they did not get much traction.

Notwithstanding the safeguards, two MPs, the Tory David Davis and Labour's Tom Watson, initiated court action to challenge the Act.

The Home Secretary in fact took a hard line on any matter that related to interception or data retention. She was very concerned to provide the security services and the police with whatever technical solution was available, and seemed to see the civil liberty consequences that arose as something of a nuisance, rather than a genuine issue to be addressed in tandem. She was quite technocratic in outlook.

She was especially wedded to what was popularly, or unpopularly, known as the 'snooper's charter', something Nick was strongly against. She seemed oblivious to the concerns raised by the revelations of Edward Snowden about the scale of surveillance undertaken by the United States and its allies – but then, frankly, so were the public, *Guardian* editorial writers and Lib Dems aside. Whether it is the result of the internet or something else I do not know, but the public, especially young people, seem much more relaxed about personal information about them being available to the state, indeed to anyone, than previous generations would have been.

I resolved upon arrival in the department to see whether any progress might be made in this area. It was right that damaging gaps in capability should be addressed, but also right that basic liberties were not damaged in the process. Rights are hard won and easily lost.

In November 2013, I met with Charles Farr and officials from the Office for Security and Counter-Terrorism to discuss communications data, and subsequently received a submission detailing proposals they believed should be taken forward. I also arranged to speak to the professionals on the front line, and undertook visits to the relevant section of the Metropolitan Police, to MI5, MI6 and to Cheltenham to visit GCHQ, as well as the relevant people in the Home Office itself.

I concluded that there were indeed gaps in the system that should be closed, particularly in relation to internet protocol address resolution. Whereas a fixed-line connection will generally have a dedicated IP address, this is not the case with mobiles, where providers have only a limited number to allocate so share them between customers, before reallocating the same address to another group a split second later. The Met took me through a case where they had been stymied in trying to identify the location of a vulnerable child who had made a call using a mobile.

The sheer scale of the growth of the internet is mind-blowing. By 2015, it would take a person five years to view all video crossing IP networks in just one second. The number of networked devices is now twice the global population.

The 2013 Queen's Speech had contained a commitment to act on IP addresses, and the Lib Dems had accepted that action was necessary, but the Home Secretary wanted to hold out for a bigger package of measures containing in addition rather more controversial ideas, including legislating to ensure retention of weblogs data.

Based on what I had learnt from visits and briefings, and also the public domain information from those concerned about the consequences for civil liberties, I wrote a detailed note setting out how I thought agreement could be reached across the coalition. Given its very sensitive nature, I only sent it to two people: Nick Clegg and Theresa May. Nick told me it went too far, and Theresa said it did not go far enough, which suggested to me that what I had proposed was indeed the basis for a coalition compromise.

A new front was opened up by Duncan Hames, the MP for Chippenham and then PPS to Nick Clegg. It followed a provocative speech made by the Home Secretary at the 2014 Tory Party conference in which, returning to her favourite theme of the Communications Data Bill, she accused the Lib Dems of being 'outrageously irresponsible' for blocking the legislation. She said this had led to the National Crime Agency having to drop twenty cases as a result, including thirteen threat-to-life cases involving children.

Even allowing for conference drum-beating, this was a bit thick.

Nick certainly thought so and wrote a strong letter to the Home Secretary in which he refuted the claims she had made.

> The reality is that these cases have nothing to do with my decision to block the Communications Data Bill. The cases were dropped because it proved impossible to match IP addresses to suspects' mobile devices. As you well know, I supported and continue to support measures to solve this 'IP matching problem' ... Those children have not been put at risk by my party. Rather, they have been put at risk by the woeful inaction of your department.

Following that, one of Theresa's spads, with or without her knowledge, briefed the *Daily Mail* (where else?) with the line that the Deputy Prime Minister was a 'wanker'. We had hit a new low, and once again the Home Secretary's spads were pushing the envelope.

As a result of this briefing, Duncan Hames initiated a formal complaint to Mark Sedwill, pointing out that this was a clear breach of the special advisers' code of conduct, which says such individuals should avoid personal attacks. Some hope!

One of the more bizarre duties I undertook as Home Office minister was to conduct a ceremony in March 2014 to award an OBE on behalf of the Queen.

The deserving recipient, Professor Marianne Hester, had lived in the UK for decades but had retained her Danish nationality, and Denmark, it transpired, does not allow dual nationality.

There are therefore a small number of overseas citizens each year who receive an honour, and it seems these are bestowed by the relevant minister. I had in fact made some mileage out of some of these honours in opposition days, when some seemed to go to rather dubious characters.

There was nothing in the least dubious about Professor Hester, who was quite rightly being rewarded for her sterling work on tackling domestic violence, and who came across as a friendly and genuine person.

That made it rather a pity that the room that had been allocated in the Home Office for the ceremony was a rather soulless one, but then they all were. The atmosphere was not helped by the addition of some rather sad-looking sandwiches, but Professor Hester seemed happy enough.

There is a form of words for me to read out before I formally hand over to her the box with the OBE in it. It is the first time I have seen one close up. I also have to hand her a brown envelope, which apparently provides details of her rights to access St Paul's Cathedral, as well as letting her know what to do if the OBE goes missing. I asked officials what happens if a loss does occur, but nobody seemed to know. Perhaps it is a matter where the royal exemption to the Freedom of Information Act applies.

Chapter 25

The whole question of Britain's relationship with Europe had simmered away potently throughout the parliament. It was obvious on day one that the chasm in the Tory Party that had been there for decades had not closed.

It was not as though David Cameron had not registered the problem. In his first speech as Tory leader back in 2006, he observed that the Conservatives had alienated voters by 'banging on' about Europe.

Not banging on about Europe was part of his long march to detoxify the Tories, to take what Theresa May had referred to as the 'nasty party' to the doors of respectability in time for the 2010 election, moving the Tories to the centre, hugging hoodies – or was it huskies?

So you would have thought that David Cameron, in his preparations for No. 10, would have had a clear strategy to neutralise the issue in his own ranks.

Not a bit of it. He had, it seemed, learnt nothing from the Thatcher years, even less from the Major years, when the mild-mannered Prime Minister with a wafer-thin majority was repeatedly held to ransom by 'bastards' on his own backbenches.

David Cameron was naive if he believed that merely exhorting his own troops not to bang on about Europe would have any effect.

So instead, apparently caught off guard, he retreated, red line by red line, in a futile attempt to buy peace, more Neville Chamberlain than Margaret Thatcher.

By December 2011, the man who professed that Britain needs to be at the heart of Europe ending up losing 26–1 in a key EU treaty vote, then vetoing the will of the other EU members. How to win friends and influence people.

By 2013, he was warning that exit from the EU was a possibility, but still maintained that 'I do not want this to happen'.

In 2014, the PM put himself in the embarrassing and self-defeating position of trying to stop Jean-Claude Juncker from becoming president of the European Commission.

He tweeted: 'I've told EU leaders they could live to regret the new process for choosing the commission president. I'll always stand up for Britain.'

He asked EU leaders, referring to Juncker: 'Is that the type of person you want for the future?'

The answer to that question was yes. The PM publicly lost the vote he had forced 26–2. In what way was isolating the UK, and insulting the man he would now have to deal with, standing up for Britain?

Then we had the promise of a referendum, which when conceived must have looked like a good wheeze to get him past the election in 2015 but in the cold light of day looked like a prison of his own making, as the Eurosceptics in his own ranks pushed him to define success or failure in any renegotiation.

The red lines kept being rubbed out and moved backwards. After the 2015 election, he made it plain that ministers would be expected to campaign for Britain to remain in the EU following successful treaty renegotiations or resign. Within twenty-four hours under a hail of internal fire, that position too had been smudged over.

Conservatives are unionists, but David Cameron almost lost Scotland in his first term as Prime Minister and was endangering the other union in his second.

It need not have been like this. The man who once called himself the 'heir to Blair' (though it is not a comparison he seems keen to make any more) could have generated his own Clause 4 moment. If, in 2010, he had picked a fight with a couple of his less attractive Eurosceptics, he could have come across as a strong leader. He would of course have won any vote on Europe, with the Lib Dems in coalition, and so what if a couple of Eurofanatics had left the party? They would have found themselves in the wilderness, and be a warning to others of a similar mind.

But instead, he has caved in time after time, in the delusional belief that at some point the anti-EU MPs in the Tory ranks will draw stumps and be satisfied. But throwing meat to tigers only makes them stronger. A great many of them will be satisfied with nothing less than EU exit.

So why did he not act to lance the Europe boil in 2010? Nick Clegg thinks that the one thing the Prime Minister was desperate to avoid was being seen as a weak leader. Perhaps that is the John Major inheritance for him.

Nick thinks we all underestimate how vulnerable the PM felt within his own party after the 2010 election, which his troops think he should have won with an outright majority. Actually, most independent analysts think he did very well in 2010, gaining 108 seats, going from 198 to 306. His detoxification strategy had worked.

But that was not the view of his backbenchers, so he dared not take them on. The irony, of course, is that this laid him open to the very charge he was keen to avoid: that of being seen as a weak leader. He seems to have thought that keeping his party together, at almost any price, would keep the lid on the fractures that exist and which would betray his lack of control over a large element of the parliamentary Conservative Party.

It also betrays a running theme of the Tory approach to the 2010–2015 parliament. Nine times out of ten they would put politics above policy, even if this just brought short-term relief. The Lib Dem mistake in government was to put the long term ahead of the short term, to put policy ahead of politics.

All too often, a Lib Dem minister would come up with a good idea, present it neutrally as a government policy, sometimes not even mentioning in radio or TV interviews that this was a Lib Dem idea. Who now knows that the seminal pension reforms of the coalition came from Steve Webb, that these were Lib Dem creations?

Our own private polling told us the depressing picture. Our policies were popular, but with one or two exceptions, such as the raising of the tax threshold, the public thought they had originated with the Tories.

To some extent, this was probably inevitable given the greater firepower of the Tories, including the vast resources available to them, compared to the small change we had to play with. And of course the Tories had ready access to a number of national papers open to presenting a Tory point of view sympathetically. We did not have the equivalent.

Partly it was down to our own failure to link policy with party, and while we successfully communicated some of the Tory policies we had stopped, like the right of employers to fire at will, we were much less good at saying what the Tories had stopped us doing, which would have given a clearer idea of what we were trying to achieve in government.

The Tories played their part in fostering the image of the Lib Dems as the party of blockers. Whenever the Prime Minister or Chancellor had to reach a compromise disliked by their backbenchers, they would be told it was a result of Nick Clegg's insistence, even where the Prime Minister had been in agreement with the Lib Dem leader.

The public perception of us was also hurt by the tendency of the Tories to adopt, magpie-like, policies that we had originated and which were gaining public traction, even where they had opposed them earlier. They were shameless in their ruthlessness and opportunism.

Take the Regional Growth Fund, which Nick Clegg had begun pushing in 2010. The Chancellor's view then was that devolution of this kind was 'a load of crap', that Whitehall knew best. But then it started becoming popular, and he also began to realise, with his political antennae tuned, the opportunity for the Tories to create a distinct and potentially popular message in what were predominantly Labour-voting areas.

So now we have the Northern Powerhouse and really quite radical devolution to cities like Manchester, all championed by the Chancellor, even if it does not seem to have been considered in any depth. For example one of the carrots dangled in front of local areas if they agree to an elected mayor is the ability to adopt London-style control over bus services, something the Tories strongly opposed while I was at the DfT.

This particular offer seems to have been made by the Chancellor without thinking through the consequences, and indeed by bouncing it on the DfT, which has been left to pick up the pieces.

Or there was childcare, another lonely furrow the Lib Dems ploughed before the Tories adopted it as their own. They would demand concessions for Lib Dem childcare proposals in the government's forward financial plans, yet now trumpet their enthusiasm. Much of this is still short-term, not thought through. The increase to thirty hours' entitlement for three-year-olds was made by the Tories simply to 'shoot Labour's fox', they having offered twenty-five hours.

But what did they – do they – actually believe in? Their magpie tendencies may have been very effective politically, but they also imply a party, at the top at least, that will pick up anything shiny in an indiscriminate manner, a party bereft of vision, intellectually hollowed out.

David Cameron, asked before 2010 why he wanted to become Prime Minister, replied 'because I'd be good at it'. Good, perhaps, at being chairman of the board, squaring people, offering reassurances. Steady as she goes, don't rock the boat. But where is the boat heading?

Chapter 26

When I arrived at the Home Office, I inherited the drugs portfolio from Jeremy Browne. Drugs was a coalition fault line, with the Lib Dems believing the 'war on drugs' was not working and a different approach should be tried. The Tories saw this, wrongly, as a remnant from our beards and sandals days.

Nick Clegg had wanted a root-and-branch review of drugs policy through a royal commission, which the Tories were stoutly against. The compromise had been the creation of an International Comparators Study, which was about three-quarters complete by the time I arrived.

Jeremy was generally regarded as about the most right-wing of the Lib Dem MPs, but that was a crude simplification that missed key aspects of his belief system. He was mainstream liberal on drugs, and indeed much else besides.

One of the first issues that arose was khat. This is a flowering plant found in Africa and the Arabian peninsula that has been chewed by local communities for thousands of years. It produces a mild amphetamine-like effect, and is regarded as less harmful than tobacco or alcohol by the World Health Organization.

The Home Secretary had decided to ban this in the UK, ostensibly because she was worried about the UK becoming a trading hub for the substance. Jeremy had taken the view that she was wrong and my examination of the facts had led me to reach the same conclusion.

I told the Home Secretary that I could not in all conscience take the ban through the House and we agreed it would be handled instead by James Brokenshire. I was regularly challenged on this in the House, and gave the reply that as this had all been decided before I arrived, as it had, it was only sensible for an existing minister to handle this. We just about got away with that, though the defence vanished when Karen Bradley took on the task after the reshuffle that followed Mark Harper's departure, she having arrived after me.

I undertook a series of visits as part of my drugs work. One of these was to a clinic in Chelsea, where I expected to see predominantly heroin users. There were certainly a number, but the largest group consisted of alcoholics. The staff there told me it was more difficult to rehabilitate an alcoholic than a heroin user, which is not at all what I would have expected.

They explained to me that heroin was like food, in that it created a craving that had to be met, but if it was, then a normal life could be followed. In many cases, of course, the need to secure money to buy the stuff led to crime and a chaotic lifestyle, but that need not be the case.

Other visits were overseas, to complete the research for the International Comparators Study. The one that made the most impression on me was to Copenhagen, where we visited a social centre for heroin users run by a startlingly and radiantly fit 63-year-old who had been injecting heroin for just shy of forty years.

As well as the games rooms, art areas and the like, there was a display cabinet of curiosities he had collected over the years. These were mostly from the nineteenth and early twentieth centuries and featured products that had been openly available at the time, promising health cures and pick-me-ups.

It seems just about every banned drug has been commercially available at some time, corralled into service by the potion producers of the day. Cannabis, cocaine, opium, they were all there, opium in products designed to help children get to sleep.

We also visited a state-approved heroin consumption room, or, more colloquially, a shooting gallery. There I saw individuals enter, say good morning, be handed a clean needle by a trained nurse, inject themselves, then leave. I saw one man calmly lie down on the ground, remove his trousers, and shoot up into his groin. I wondered what they did when they ran out of veins.

Some were clearly on their way to work and stopped to shoot up just as you or I might stop to buy a paper. It was a calm and clean environment, and one fully supported by the residents of what was a middle-class area. Since it had opened, the numbers of people injecting on the street and leaving needles lying around had shrunk dramatically.

We also went to see the area known as Christiania, having been advised to dress down and lose our suits for the occasion. This is an extraordinary place, a self-run rough-and-tumble expanse of some eighty-four acres in the middle of the city that used to be used for military purposes but which now houses a tolerated alternative lifestyle, hidden behind glamorous streets of expensive shops.

There are no proper roads and only haphazard lighting. There are, however, plenty of stalls selling various strains of cannabis resin, cafés galore, a yoga centre, even a bath house. It resembled a 1970s hippy festival without the music.

Christiania polices itself and bans hard drugs, as well as photography. Gawping tourists are not welcome. There are around 900 regular inhabitants.

The place is unique and a fascinating social experiment. As I wandered around with my officials, I tried to imagine what the Home Secretary would have made of it. It was, I imagined, rather different from her constituency of Maidenhead.

In my work, it became very apparent early on that one really big problem was that of so-called legal highs. These are substances created in chemistry labs in China and elsewhere, often based on old research papers from the 1970s and 1980s that can be found on the internet. They are designed to mimic the effects of 'traditional' drugs like cannabis, cocaine or acid. They also tend to be professionally packaged to look like approved products, and are to be found in high street shops, garages, even ice cream vans, rather than via some shady dealer.

The world is not used to large numbers of new drugs coming onto the market, and the systems employed by governments take some time to find, identify, consider and then ban them, whereupon a small tweak is made to the chemical composition and the whole cycle begins afresh.

The worry from my point of view was that these new products were not safe for human consumption. Indeed, the very fact that they were developed from research that had been abandoned was testament to that. I firmly believe that the synthetic cannabinoids are more dangerous by some distance than the grass and resin that had held sway previously.

I decided to set up an expert panel to examine the problem and come up with recommendations, and asked my officials to find a range of people with differing perspectives, from the police, the local authority world, the health profession and the like. I gave them free rein and asked them to tell me what they thought, and not to second guess what ministers might want to hear.

At the time there were a number of different approaches being tried. In this country, we had introduced a way of banning substances quickly, and much more quickly than most other places, but it still left us chasing the chemist. We were always behind the curve.

In New Zealand, they were taking a radical approach, looking to license some lesser substances and control access and quality that way. The theory was that this method would move people on to less harmful substances.

In Ireland, they had decided on a blanket ban of psychoactive substances, including some of a very low impact such as poppers.

I was genuinely keen to see what the panel would say and to give them space, wanting to rule nothing in or out. As far as I was concerned, I was open to whatever solution would minimise the harm to society, and to young people in particular, from these substances. I just wanted to know what would work.

Unfortunately the Home Secretary interpreted this suspiciously, thinking I was hankering after a sort of faded 1960s policy, which I genuinely was not. She did not believe I was motivated by a desire to reduce harm. In her eyes, if I were, I would axiomatically support more repressive policies. She did not seem to ever question whether such policies would actually work, or might even be counterproductive.

Matters were not helped by a report on the front page of *The Times* in early March. This followed a press briefing I had given with representatives from the expert panel. Over-interpreting my open-minded stance, the splash sensationally suggested that I wanted to allow dangerous drugs to be sold on the street. This was rubbish, and the reporter, Richard Ford, rang up to apologise, blaming the sensationalism on the sub-editors.

Meanwhile the Home Secretary and her spads had gone into overdrive. They implied I was trying to bounce them into accepting the New Zealand approach. For my part, I thought that they were exploiting the incident to try to gain some ground. I was presented with the same tired old press lines to clear, which as usual I rejected.

There was more of the same a week later after I had appeared on a Channel 5 programme on legal highs. There I had set out, very fairly I thought, the problem and the various approaches being taken around the world, without expressing any sort of preference.

I also made the point, as I frequently did, that the term 'legal highs' was unhelpful, as it implied some sort of official approval, a sanctioned alternative to illegal drugs. Theresa agreed with me that the term was unhelpful but was not prepared to try to gain currency for an alternative. I suggested 'chemical highs', which I thought sounded suitably unattractive, or 'untested highs', even more so.

Unknown to me, following the programme, the Tory spads had caused a press line to be issued saying a licensing regime, as in New Zealand, was definitely ruled out. It seems they were not prepared to wait for the expert panel to report. Presumably, if the panel then came up with an endorsement for a New Zealand-style regime, all their expertise would be discounted.

I thought this was discourteous to them, discourteous to me and hostile in coalition terms. It was also par for the course.

The Home Secretary and I had yet another argument along well-worn lines, lessened only by the fact that at that stage I did not know about the line that had been issued. As always, we met in her office, sitting facing each other on hard chairs across a bare table. We never used the sofa in the corner. As always, she was smartly dressed, and that day wearing an attractive shade of green, a colour that suited her but increased the impression of coldness.

I told her she was entitled to hold me to coalition policy but reiterated that I had the right to express that in my own words.

I was not a Tory minister. I also told her, referring to the robotic press lines her spads had created, that I was not a speak-your-weight machine.

And if she was going to criticise me for presenting coalition policy, just because it was in a manner she did not like, what was she going to do about James Brokenshire, who had just made an idiotic speech about the 'metropolitan elite' and their cleaners, which was either a sideswipe at Mark Harper or crass beyond belief?

Later I got a text from Theresa:

> Norman, I gather you are on *Newsnight* to talk about legal highs. Please remember our conversation about this. I note that the review is about maximising the impact of the Misuse of Drugs Act and the enforcement response to the new drugs market. In other words the government's position is that we are looking at tougher action not that we are looking at licensing head shops. Theresa.

I replied:

> As always I will present agreed government policy which is to minimise the dangers from legal highs and for the review panel to be evidence based in considering all options to achieve that. As always I will express no preference. Your spads in seeking to rule out one option are not following agreed terms of reference. Norman.

I felt obliged to follow this up with a note to the Permanent Secretary. I was reluctant to drag him into this but he had been our ambassador in Afghanistan so I was sure he would cope with a little spat like this.

The spat turned out to be a mere skirmish for the main event, the finalisation of the International Comparators Study.

The study visits had been concluded and so I began discussing the way forward with officials. They, of course, were horribly nervous, only too aware of the coalition fault line. So they produced a draft worded ever so carefully, in that splendid civil service way. It was largely written by a friendly and professional official called Dan Greaves.

The report looked factually at the countries that had been studied and reported what they were doing. There was then a section headed 'reflections' that sought to draw out some lessons useful for us in the UK, and finally some recommendations.

Needless to say, the whole process had been closely stalked by the Tory spads Nick Timothy and Stephen Parkinson, who wanted to kill the whole thing, or at least mutilate it so it was unrecognisable. They had been unable to do much to date, both because the study was a coalition agreement and also because it was being led by me, not as a Home Office minister but as chair of the Inter-Ministerial Group on Drugs. I had been careful to keep the IMG abreast of progress as we went along.

Once again Mark Sedwill was called in to umpire. The ruling he made, with which I agreed, was that the paper belonged to me as chair of the IMG until it was presented to the department, as it would have to be, at which point the normal departmental and cross-government procedures would kick in.

I took the view, and gently encouraged officials to do likewise, that it might be prudent to make the report as strong as they were comfortable with so that when the inevitable horse-trading began and cuts were made, the end product was still a document worth having.

Anticipating problems after the IMG meeting at which the paper was to be presented, I also wrote a foreword setting out my own views in what I thought were rather modest terms. The Home Secretary did not agree that I should do this and instructed officials not to circulate the foreword. I did not think this was in line with Mark Sedwill's ruling, as it was destined for the IMG, so I simply bypassed this instruction, photocopied the foreword myself, and tabled it at the meeting as a supplementary paper.

Meanwhile Nick Clegg, who had maintained an interest in the drugs issue throughout, raised the matter at one of his bilaterals with the Home Secretary, and pressed for early publication of the study, and she seemed to take this to heart.

I was of the view, however, that there was a compelling case to release the study at the same time as the report from the expert panel into legal highs, or new psychoactive substances, as they were formally called. Apart from anything else, there was an overlap in matters that had been considered. The comparators study had, for example, looked in detail at what was happening in New Zealand.

Politically, I had concluded that the expert panel's report was likely to be much less controversial across the coalition. They were heading for a recommendation close to the Irish model, which would please the Home Secretary, but targeting the dealers and without an offence of possession for the users, which fitted in with the Lib Dem view. Whether it was intended that way or not, it was a neat coalition compromise.

Unfortunately, the panel's review was unlikely to be ready until close to the summer recess, so perhaps unwisely, if logically, I suggested to the Home Secretary that publication of the study be held back so they could be released together.

On 9 July, I sat down with the Home Secretary to agree a way forward with the study. My suggestion was that the report from officials be sent round to other departments without alteration and without recommendations save those where the two parties were in agreement, which I thought optimistically might be about half of them, and that the two parties would be free to make their own recommendations on the others at our respective party conferences in September.

Theresa agreed this approach, subject to her spads looking over the wording of what the officials had produced. We settled that Stephen Parkinson would discuss any comments he had with Alex Dziedzan, the Lib Dem spad, with a view to agreeing a final document. This was to happen within a week, as officials were pressing for sign-off – but then they always did.

A fortnight passed and nothing happened. With summer recess approaching and Theresa due to go off to the Alps, I sent her a note on 22 July, informing her that Alex had received nothing from her spad, and that the matter was now becoming urgent and officials had told me we needed to have sorted this by the end of that week.

Meanwhile Nick Clegg was becoming impatient and had teamed up with *The Sun* to call for an end to the imprisonment of individuals guilty only of possession of drugs. The tabloid was liberal on drugs issues, rather out of character. I suspected many journalists had themselves indulged at some point, and perhaps still did, and found the law rather rigid.

And it was. The Misuse of Drugs Act 1971 came as a reaction to the '60s, as those in power sought to wind the clock back and replace swinging with swingeing. The Act was draconian in its approach to cannabis, and by ending the legal supply of heroin through medical practitioners, it created a black market that multiplied the problem many times over.

Those who are against drugs should be in favour of reform. The notion that just becoming more and more restrictive, increasing penalties and law enforcement, will force down drug use is just a prejudice, and a dangerous one at that, as the International Comparators Study would demonstrate.

I sometimes wondered whether Theresa completely believed the hardline rhetoric she had signed up to. I did not doubt her spads did, but she was a more thoughtful person and rather more nuanced in private than she appeared in public.

She had, for example, very sensibly started to undo the damage of the 1971 Act by allowing heroin to be made available to a narrow category of person for whom methadone was not working. There were three pilot areas in the country where this was occurring: London, Brighton and Darlington.

This was in sharp contrast to the approach advocated at the Inter-Ministerial Group and elsewhere by Iain Duncan Smith, who was obsessed by the notion that those on methadone should have a cliff edge after six months after which they should jolly well sink or swim. A great deal of time at the group was wasted on disproving the merit of this approach. When the answer came back from the experts in a way he did not like, he would cry foul. In the end, we agreed that he would write the question he wanted answered in exactly the words he wanted. But the conclusion came back the same: his idea would not work and would have myriad downsides.

IDS had wanted drug policy to be allocated to him in 2010, and kept up an active interest even after the Prime Minister had confirmed it would stay with the Home Office. Both Theresa and I found this rather tiresome.

Theresa also agreed to make foil available to heroin users to discourage them from injecting. This was something I strongly supported. Smoking the drug was markedly less harmful than injecting it. It did, however, mean the state was handing out drug paraphernalia, potentially opening us up to criticism from the right-wing press and thereafter from Tory MPs.

Theresa was keen that I should present this if required, which I was happy to. But it did show she was sometimes prepared to take a liberal line on drugs so long as nobody noticed.

Nick's intervention with *The Sun* had been well received by the public and he was keen I should capitalise on this. I thought the logical step was to raise the issue of medicinal cannabis. He was not particularly sold on this direction, but I persisted.

My interest had been stirred by a couple of individuals who had been to see me at my constituency surgery to make the case that cannabis was useful in dealing with particular medical conditions and the law should be relaxed to reflect this. I was then contacted in my ministerial role by a group advocating the same, and arranged for them to come in, and for officials from both the Home Office and the Department of Health to be present.

The individuals who turned up were people who were suffering from a variety of conditions which they maintained only cannabis helped with. Other prescribed drugs either did not work or had ghastly side effects. They were articulate, credible witnesses, and their testimonies were both convincing and moving, particularly one eloquent young man by the name of Clark French.

I sensed that the officials had also been impressed, and that a new perspective had opened up for them, just as it had for me. I decided to try to help Clark and his colleagues.

The issue of medicinal cannabis had hardly featured in the work that had been undertaken for the International Comparators Study, except in the sense that we had identified some US states that, in my view, had been citing it as a back-door way to legalisation. Maybe I had been too quick to judgement.

But that would be exactly the suspicion of the Tories in the Home Office, who probably thought I was doing the same thing myself when I raised the issue.

I confess that this issue demonstrated in a general sense how the laws on drugs were rigid and did not work properly, which was a useful bonus, but my prime motivation by some distance was to right a wrong.

Simply put, I felt strongly that it was cruel and inhumane to deny someone a treatment that would help their debilitating condition, and then to prosecute them when they sourced it themselves.

The principle had in fact already been established, in that a cannabis-based nasal spray, Sativex, was theoretically available on the NHS for a narrow range of conditions. 'Theoretically' because it was very difficult to get it prescribed. Yet cannabis was still classed as a Schedule 1 drug, meaning officially it had no medicinal value. This did not make sense. And the Schedule 1 status acted as a red flag to pharmaceutical companies who might think about investigating further the medical properties of cannabis, which had after all been used for that purpose over the centuries, including by Queen Victoria.

I therefore asked for a section on medicinal cannabis to be inserted into the International Comparators Study.

By mid-August there was still no sign, six weeks on, of any comments from Theresa's spads on the study, and no response from her to my memo of 22 July. I resolved that if she was not going to keep to her side of the agreement then neither would I.

My preferred method of operation in the coalition, indeed more generally in life, is to negotiate in a friendly and sensible manner, reach a deal and then stick to it. However, if a deal is reneged on then there has to be a price, or your negotiating position is weakened thereafter on other issues.

Accordingly, I lined up one of the broadsheets and made my call for cannabis to be available to sufferers on prescription. I also announced that I had written to the Health Secretary, Jeremy Hunt, to ask him to look at the matter. I sent an email direct from my Home Office iPad to his private office, knowing that any attempt to route it through officials would be blocked, and even if it were not, it would be asking too much of my supportive private office to implicate them in this.

Within four hours, the Home Secretary, who had been incapable of responding to my note of some weeks earlier, had written to Jeremy herself to rubbish my call – cannabis is dangerous, and so on. So, presumably, is morphine, but they use it day in, day out in our hospitals.

Wearily, I asked Alex Dziedzan to brief Norman Lamb, our health minister, to ensure he had some sort of handle on the replies. The response, when it came from Jeremy Hunt some weeks later, would actually be quite measured, even helpful.

The reaction from the media to my call was pretty favourable, with not even the *Daily Mail* reacting badly. Support came from some unlikely quarters, including the Tory MP Crispin Blunt, who issued a press release calling on the Home Office to back me.

When I next spoke to Stephen Parkinson, to complain that I had been bypassed by the Home Secretary in the process for selecting a chair for the child abuse inquiry, even though the matter fell into my portfolio, he countered by referring to my letter to Jeremy Hunt. I was ready for this and pointed out that if his side did not keep to deal, then neither would I, and where were his comments on the International Comparators Study?

The study itself, written up by civil servants, had proved to be a very useful exercise, in effect the first authoritative review of drug policy in forty-three years since the 1971 Act. It included the following paragraph:

'We did not in our fact-finding observe any obvious relationship between the toughness of a country's enforcement against drug possession and levels of drug use in that country.'

This was dynamite and pulled the rug from under the whole Tory ethos of tougher sentences axiomatically leading to reduced drug use and reduced crime.

It was particularly interesting to see the conclusions on Portugal, which had removed criminal sanctions for drug possession for personal use back in 2001, and therefore had a long period for us to examine. In their place, the country has introduced dissuasion commissions, a lay panel that evaluates the personal circumstances of the individual and refers them to the appropriate place for help.

The study concluded: 'It is clear that there has not been a lasting and significant increase in drug use in Portugal since 2001', adding, 'One of the clearest changes in Portugal since 2001 has been a considerable improvement in the indicators of health outcomes for drug users.'

This was in contrast to the situation in the Czech Republic, where the introduction of harsher laws had markedly worsened health outcomes.

No wonder the Home Secretary and her spads were not keen to release the report, originally timed for release before Christmas 2013. It contradicted their prejudices.

Nor did they seem over-keen to release the report of the expert panel on new psychoactive substances, whose conclusions were in line with the steer I had been given a few weeks before, and would be more welcome to them, in that they broadly endorsed the Irish approach.

I raised this report in a bilateral with Theresa in early September and said I was surprised not to have had any feedback from her. She said the report had not reached her, yet I knew it had been delivered to her office on 21 July and I had written her a note with my conclusions on 1 August. It had, apparently, been diverted via her spads.

I thought the report, unanimously agreed by the panel, was well written, coherent and persuasive. It was also clear by that point that the paint was coming off the New Zealand model, and that country was now reviewing its approach.

Accordingly, I had written a note to Theresa on 1 August, indicating I was prepared to accept all the recommendations with just one caveat, namely the setting of a threshold for what would qualify as a psychoactive substance. I did not want presently legal substances such as poppers to be caught by accident. I also suggested we should get a move on and begin implementing those recommendations that did not require legislation, which included long-overdue education interventions, the sort Michael Gove had regularly ignored.

I was adamant, however, that the report must come out simultaneously with the International Comparators Study, both because they fitted together logically, and indeed were difficult to separate, and also because I knew that if the legal highs report came out first, the chances of the other appearing were significantly diminished.

That battle was won, although the price to be paid was that the recommendations in the study were removed in their entirety, even where the Tories agreed with them. This led to the odd position that the 'reflections' sections remained but led nowhere. This was picked up by a number of MPs. As a matter of fact, the Tories had wanted the reflections removed as well but we had refused.

The Tory spads were keen, for release day on the Thursday, to talk up the legal highs report in order to smother the other one, but Alex and I spoke to journalists ahead of publication and achieved the reverse, with a huge splash on the international study. Nick Timothy was furious on the Wednesday when he found out what we had been doing and that this was attracting the media's attention.

He ordered the study's immediate publication in an attempt to spike coverage. All that did was to increase interest and coverage.

The response from the media was serious and quietly supportive, as it was from those elements of the police system that responded publicly. *The Independent*, sympathetic to my position at the Home Office, described me as 'the only hippy at an Iron Maiden concert'.

The world, and public opinion, had moved on, and the Tories were stuck in the past, repeating in increasingly strident tones rhetoric that no longer convinced.

A major debate in the Commons followed on 30 October 2014, on a motion introduced under the auspices of the backbench committee, a group of backbench MPs who control the allocation of some time on the floor of the Commons. It was helpfully timed, coming just after the simultaneous publication of both the International Comparators Study and the expert panel's report on legal highs.

As I stood up to reply for the government at 2.17, I knew what nobody else in the chamber knew: this would be my last appearance at the despatch box as a government minister. With the international study now out, the delayed Lib Dem reshuffle could finally proceed and would take place early the following week.

It was a good debate to go out on. The Commons was not packed but not empty either, and just about everybody who spoke welcomed the study, with the exception of the Labour shadow minister, the Labour home affairs front bench as usual tacking to the right.

I finished my speech with the following:

> We can no longer rely on the stonewalling about drugs policy in this country that we have so often heard. There is a genuine debate to be had about the proper way forward and it has started today. The genie is out of the bottle, and it is not going back in.

Chapter 27

I decided to announce my resignation through an exclusive interview with *The Independent* and was interviewed by Nigel Morris, a journalist who had always played it straight with me. The headline – 'I resign – and it's Theresa May's fault' – was a touch misleading, but overall Nigel had reported my position fairly.

The story therefore broke with the first edition, at shortly after 10 p.m., and then the dam burst. I had more than fifty texts within an hour. About half were journalists, the rest all supportive comments, from friends, civil servants, Lib Dem colleagues, even a Tory Cabinet minister and a former Labour one.

My old college friend Andy Davey, a Labour Party member but otherwise very sound, congratulated me, and warned me: 'Now for the shitstorm.' He was not wrong.

My resignation from the Home Office caused even more furore than my appointment had. The same people who had been most apoplectic about my appointment were most apoplectic about my resignation.

These were the people who found me annoying and actively disliked me. Maybe it was because I would not play by the unwritten rules of the game and yet mostly got away with it. They would have relished seeing me sacked, or forced to resign. How dare I resign on my own terms?

One even suggested that any minister who behaves in the way I did does not deserve to be in office. So presumably he should resign then?

The Times devoted an entire leader column to telling their readers I was not important, the acreage of coverage they devoted to the subject somewhat undermining their argument.

They also scraped the bottom of the barrel for anything negative they could find on me, then magnified it with a large dollop of innuendo. It was an epic hatchet job. Some of it, such as suggesting that I believe in UFOs, was gratuitously and laughably baseless, and they did eventually print a correction, if grudgingly.

I have always polarised opinion, generating greater levels of both support and antagonism than most MPs do. This was particularly true on a national level, but even locally, our private constituency polling in 2015 showed the same result. It produced overall a very large and enthusiastic positive rating for me, but about 5 to 10 per cent of voters were very hostile.

Paddy Ashdown had said to me when he had stepped down from being party leader in 1999 that it is better to have people ask why you are going than why you are not going.

One after the other, people kept asking me, 'Why did you resign?' to the extent that I began to feel like Patrick McGoohan in an episode of *The Prisoner*.

The general view was that I had resigned over the drugs issue, but that was not so. I had in fact written to Nick in August indicating I wanted to leave ministerial office, and he had asked me to stay on until I could get the drugs report into the public domain, on the basis that if I left before doing so, it would be buried. That was really the only link with drugs.

Those who did not think I had resigned over drugs assumed I had resigned in order to try to hold my seat. That was also wrong. There can have been no guarantee that resignation would boost my vote locally. It might have alienated soft Tories, or those who liked having a minister as an MP. At best, it was far from certain that resignation would have a beneficial effect on the vote in Lewes the following May.

There was in fact no one single reason for my resignation. One factor was that I felt I had achieved as much as I usefully could in the department, especially with the coalition winding up and the election approaching. And after four and a half years as a minister, I wanted a break.

I was pleased with what I had in fact got through – on drugs, tackling violence against women including FGM, moving forward the efforts to counter child sexual exploitation, introducing new crime prevention measures, and publishing the first ever strategy to reduce the numbers of animal experiments.

Because I knew I would be leaving at some point, I had asked each section for which I was responsible to draw up an action plan for the remaining months of the parliament and went through this plan with each one.

Another reason for leaving was that, frankly, I did not want to continue running up a down escalator every day to the election. I described working at the Home Office as 'walking through mud', which was the phrase everyone picked up on. It was not a phrase I had carefully honed or calculated, but one that just came out in response to a journalist's question.

I also made it clear to Nick in my resignation letter that 'in stark contrast to the Department for Transport, I regret that in the Home Office, the goodwill to work collegiately to take forward rational, evidence-based policy has been in somewhat short supply'.

More generally, coalition relations across the board were breaking down. What had begun as a friendly relationship became transactional about halfway through the parliament, and was now beginning to become fractious, as the parties vied for advantage ahead of the election.

There were other reasons for my resignation too. Overall, it just felt like the right thing to do at that time.

I wrote a friendly personal note to Theresa May, and she responded in kind, with some generous comments in return and thanking me in particular for my work in tackling violence against women and girls.

The Prime Minister and the Chancellor were rather more childishly offensive, in a rather snooty, public school way, but then that came as no surprise.

In the wake of my resignation, there was an interesting general analysis in *The Guardian* from Rafael Behr, a journalist always worth reading. He argued that the effect of the Lib Dems in government had been to shunt the Tories off the liberal terrain that Cameron had once laid claim to. By owning issues like human rights and the environment, he argued, we had pushed the Tories to the right. Judging by what happened post the 2015 general election, he may be right.

The rest of my band, The Reform Club, was pleased by the resignation, not because of the politics, but because it led to a spate of plays of our video of 'Piccadilly Circus' on TV, and extensive radio play too. Only Phil Hornby at my local ITV station, Meridian, was sharp enough to use instead 'Endless, Faithless', another track from our album, about a man and a woman splitting up. No matter that it was the one track on the album where I had not written the lyrics.

My constituency party was also pleased, anticipating an easier time on the doorstep, and one of their number, Harvey Linehan, penned a poem to mark the occasion, with the hook of May and Baker, an old established British chemical company that traded from 1851 through to the 1980s.

This was framed with a cartoon from the *Daily Telegraph* that had appeared the day after my resignation, which, reflecting both the time of year and the traditions of Lewes, had me setting fire to a bonfire with the Home Secretary on top. It was timely and amusing, but ultimately inaccurate. Contrary to some assumptions in the media, I had not been attempting to damage Theresa by my resignation. Indeed, I had made the calculation that leaving as I did would actually help her with her own side, as indeed it would me with mine.

I did in fact then spend a lot more time in my constituency, not primarily to shore up the vote, but really because I did not want to be in London and found my constituency and constituents rather more congenial.

I was delighted to be asked to be a panellist on *University Challenge* for my old college, Royal Holloway. I had missed out in the late 1970s, so here was a chance to make up for that.

Our panel of alumni was captained by Francis Wheen, the *Private Eye* journalist, who was positively competitive and responsible for most of our points, though I did score a few hits, including one on Amy Winehouse and another uneducated guess on a science question. Our other two members were Valerie Vaz, the Labour MP, and the pint-sized adventurer Tori James, who was about thirty and seemed to have physically conquered most of the world.

Someone quipped that our team therefore had a Labour, a Lib Dem and a Tori.

We did not win but we were respectably close.

On 11 February 2015, I was inducted into the Privy Council. Nick Clegg had rung me up in the autumn to ask if I wanted to join. I confess I laughed.

I was in two minds whether to accept or not. On the one hand, I regarded it as something of an affectation and I did not particularly want to have an oath administered to me that I was sceptical about.

On the other hand, it did mean you could write to Cabinet ministers and get a reply from them personally rather than a junior minister or an official, which was a practical advantage. I also knew it would annoy some people who would think I should not qualify. And I was curious to see what the ceremony involved, so in the end I decided to accept, but delayed it until the February as the first date offered had clashed with Bonfire Night in Lewes.

The Privy Council is an odd body, a remnant of an earlier era that has somehow not been abolished. Appointment is for life and those inducted henceforth have their name prefaced by 'the Right Honourable', whereas MPs not inducted are simply 'the Honourable'. The former preface persists after you have left Parliament, whereas the latter does not.

The distinction between the two is not widely known or understood – why should it be? – and there is at least one plaque I unveiled which incorrectly described me as 'Rt Hon.'. I suppose subsequent events have now corrected it.

A member also has the individual right of personal access to the sovereign, though only to tender advice on public affairs. I have not sought to exercise this, though the idea of passing on to the Queen my views on a hot topic does appeal.

The Council, whose meetings are conducted in the presence of the Queen, deals with a hotchpotch of responsibilities that over the years have not been allocated elsewhere. These include the affairs of chartered bodies, the 900 or so institutions, charities and companies that are incorporated by royal charter.

The Council is also the body that approves new coinage, as I witnessed when I attended. This seems to be largely and literally a low-level money-making operation for the Treasury.

Meetings are reported in the Court Circular, including the names of ministers attending, and details of the Orders made are likewise public. The swearing-in ceremony, however, is supposed to be secret, on account of the oath that dates back to Tudor times. It is a curious affair.

I was also, following the Privy Council meeting, supposed to destroy the guidance document I had been given about the ceremony. I have not, though whether that means I can be excommunicated or locked in the Tower I do not know.

It was part of the role of the Deputy Prime Minister, Nick Clegg, to conduct these meetings. In earlier times, the task had fallen to Peter Mandelson. There are normally four ministers present, as was the case when I attended: two Lib Dems and two Tories.

After my induction, George Osborne said to me in an oily voice: 'Welcome to the establishment.'

I could imagine at that moment exactly how oily he might have been at school.

Otherwise I used the early months of 2015 to table a few parliamentary questions, though in a quantity that Matthew Parris would have approved of, asked a couple of questions on the floor of the Commons, and introduced a couple of half-hour debates, the first of which was on fracking, where I thought the government, and my party, was in the wrong.

The second of these was my last contribution in the Commons, and, perhaps prophetically, was on endangered species. This is an issue I have always felt strongly about, and pursued throughout my time in politics.

The figures speak for themselves. Twenty-six per cent of known mammal species are now threatened with extinction. There are now more tigers in American zoos than there are in the wild. The number of wild animals on earth has halved in the past forty years.

It was an issue I had pursued both in opposition and at the Home Office, and where the coalition government had made some really good progress, in no small measure thanks to the efforts of William Hague as Foreign Secretary.

The high point was an international conference in London in February 2014, organised very efficiently by the Foreign Office and which I co-chaired. There was real buy-in on the need to protect endangered species, both for the economic value they bring in tourism terms but also because it is simply the right thing to do. The conference produced the London Declaration, which forty-one countries signed up to.

I had also visited the UK Border Force operation based near Kew and was hugely encouraged and impressed by the knowledge, dedication and sheer professionalism of the team there in intercepting movements of endangered species, whether animals or plants. This must be one of the best operations in the world.

As it happens, the timing of my Commons debate, decided by the Speaker, coincided with World Wildlife Day, and with *Animal Countdown*, a four-track EP I had released, without the band this time, on this very subject. I did not think I ought to mention this in my speech, but was not unhappy when the minister who replied, George Eustice, did do so. He told me he had listened to it and it was 'pretty good'. Who was I to argue?

The debate was the last item of business for that day in the Commons and, as normal at the end of business, those few MPs remaining stayed standing while one of the house officials came up to remove the mace from its position in front of the Speaker, while the Speaker himself left the chamber.

As this time-honoured ritual was being performed, I stood there, at 7.26 p.m. on 3 March 2015, reflecting that that might have been my last ever contribution in Parliament. So it was.

Chapter 28

And so Parliament broke up and we all returned to our constituencies to prepare for ... what? Not government this time.

The omens were not good. Our opinion poll ratings had dropped dramatically shortly after joining the coalition in 2010 and never recovered. We had had a succession of poor council election results, and the European elections in 2014 had been a disaster.

We were now, irony of ironies, pinning our hopes on the first-past-the-post system and the incumbency factor for our sitting MPs, who were almost without exception well-liked and respected in their constituencies. Even if we polled a low national percentage, we still hoped to win a fair number of seats due to our local campaigning.

Our private polling suggested that we would certainly lose some seats, not least in Scotland, where the SNP surge was unmistakable, against Labour in some areas, and perhaps where existing MPs were standing down, but the inside view was we should manage thirty, and there was a pathway to about forty-five.

My seat was always regarded as safe by the party, and that was the message the polls in the seat gave, both our own and the one conducted by Lord Ashcroft. Indeed, I went at his invitation to see Lord Ashcroft at his office in Cowley Street for a coffee and a chat. He is an interesting man. He told me that in the light of the first poll, he would not be doing any more in my seat.

And yet something, my political sixth sense, told me things were not quite right, even in Lewes. From December 2014, I had any new staff I took on placed on fixed-term contracts expiring in May, and in January 2015, I renegotiated the terms of my constituency office lease to ensure that if I had to vacate, the terms were in line with the requirements of IPSA, the body that now handles MPs' expenses. I had not bothered taking these precautions before previous general elections. I even negotiated a contract for this book!

I had also been ambivalent about standing this time round. I had done the inquisitive opposition role, ferreting out facts those in power wanted to keep hidden, and I had undertaken four and a half years on the other side of the fence in ministerial office. I did not really want to do either again.

In 2014, I had constructed a grid for myself, setting out the pros and cons of standing again, political and personal. Unsurprisingly, given the incumbent factor in elections, my party, both locally and nationally, was keen I should stand, for fear we might lose the seat otherwise. So I had agreed, and decided that if I were re-elected, I would of course undertake my constituency role fully as always – not least because, unlike many MPs, I actually enjoyed it – but I would be relatively low-key in the Commons.

So perhaps my ambivalence communicated itself somehow to my electorate. I worked quite hard in the election, but not as hard as in previous campaigns.

My team in Lewes, and indeed nationally, had concluded everything was looking fine about three weeks out. I was not so sure, and told my hugely enthusiastic campaign manager, Daisy Cooper, that I thought I was going to lose.

I remembered 1992, and it felt like that. I could see the SNP fear story coming down the track a long way off, and tried to counter this in our literature. I decided the best use of my time would be in Seaford, the biggest town in the constituency and one that sits on the cusp between Tory and Lib Dem.

I think to a large degree that paid off. The Seaford result in the general election had us just ahead of the Tories, and my personal vote coupled with clear messages that we would not support the SNP as part of the government limited the slippage to them.

Overall, the Tory vote in my constituency barely moved, up by less than a thousand. What lost the election for me, and I think many other Lib Dem MPs as well, was the shift away from us to Labour and Green, in my case in the town of Lewes itself.

In the Lewes constituency, the Labour vote almost doubled from 2,508 to 5,000, 5 per cent to 9.9 per cent. The Green vote went from 729 to 2,784, 1.5 per cent to 5.5 per cent. Around 4,500 votes left me for Labour or Green. I lost by just 1,083.

It was no surprise to me that amongst left-leaning voters, the coalition was not popular. But I suppose I had thought that when push came to shove, the people of Lewes town, which is where most of that vote is, would have given us – have given me – some credit for the good things we as Lib Dems had done in government and the Tory policies we had stopped, as well as rationalising that I was seen as a good local MP and the Tory candidate did not even live in the seat. Ultimately, I assumed that they understood what we had correctly been telling them for decades, namely that the seat returns a Tory or a Lib Dem and even if they did not like every-thing we had done, they would prefer me to a Tory.

It was not as though they had not been warned. Polly Toynbee, herself a Lewes resident, wrote in *The Guardian* on 17 April: 'Labour voters ... must lend their votes to Lib Dems in seats that would otherwise certainly go Tory. For instance, Lewes is a yel-low dot in an East Sussex sea of blue. Labour has no hope of winning here...'

It turned out that some who had voted Labour or Green had assumed my majority was such that they could vote this way and still get me, aided by the Labour candidate who was peddling this suggestion. Others wanted to punish us for daring to deal with the Tories and did not, or would not, get past that point in their thinking.

The really exasperating ones were those who came up to me in the street afterwards, in anguish that I should have lost, and keen to tell me what a great MP I had been. When I asked them how they voted, they would say Labour or Green without a shred of self-awareness, as if their actions were somehow unconnected with the result. They were voting for Ed Miliband or Caroline Lucas, or some other person who was not on the ballot paper. It is astonishing how some highly intelligent people cannot seem to get their heads around what is after all a pretty simple electoral system.

It reminded me of a conversation I had on the doorstep way back in my first council campaign in 1987.

'I'm voting for Mrs Thatcher,' this woman told me.

'But she's not on the ballot paper,' I pointed out.

'I'm still voting for her,' she replied majestically.

Some, including a university professor one of our local councillors subsequently came across, said he had thought Labour was going to win, on the basis, it turned out, of the number of posters in his street. He did not seem to realise that the election was not just in his street, or even just in Lewes, but across a whole swathe of towns and villages north, south, east and west.

As it turned out, the Labour candidate could not even get elected for the town council ward he stood for on the same day, a ward that returned six councillors, and Labour as usual won not a single district council seat. Their last in the constituency was in the 1970s.

Neither Labour nor Green have ever won the Lewes seat or even come close and I predict neither ever will. It is a Tory seat, and was such from 1874 to 1997, but on a good day the Lib Dems can persuade enough of what we call soft Tories to vote Lib Dem to give us victory. Those Tory floaters will never ever vote Labour or Green in anything like sufficient numbers, but they might just vote Lib Dem.

So Labour and Green voters cannot elect their team but, by their actions, they can determine whether Lewes returns a Lib Dem or a Tory. They are kingmakers. By their actions in 1997, they got me elected. By their actions in 2015, they handed the seat to the Tories.

1997 had seen a campaign called GROT, Get Rid of Tories, which led to very effective tactical voting, for both Labour and Lib Dems, across the country. This time, Labour and Green voters, annoyed by the coalition, adopted instead a SCAM strategy: Send Conservatives a Majority.

It is odd, but looking back over the parliament and up to and including the 2015 election, I do not feel any real animosity to the Tories, although I feel as if I should. They went into the coalition as they would some sort of business deal. They needed a product and we were the only suppliers in the market. They concluded terms, and by and large stuck to them, as did we.

There was much that the Tories wanted to do that I disagreed with, sometimes vehemently, and I spent a good deal of time trying, with some success, to thwart them, as well as to push through what I as a Lib Dem wanted to see enacted. But bearing in mind we were, and are, two very different parties, I think the coalition worked remarkably well, and indeed broadly served the country well.

Nor do I blame the Tories for seeking to maximise their seats at the last general election. They were, and always have been, the enemy. What else would they do?

Every party was seeking to maximise its seats. It is just that they were rather better at it, and of course hugely better funded. It was perhaps a little tasteless to target Lib Dem seats as they did, but there is no sentiment in politics. Their campaign in the Lewes constituency certainly benefited from a vast amount of money, but they spent it sensibly and tactically, leaving left-leaning Lewes town very much alone, which can only have helped foster a sense of complacency amongst voters there.

Curiously, I feel rather angrier with those on the left, where I put myself on the political spectrum. Throughout the last parliament, the Labour Party seemed more interested in attacking the Lib Dems than the Tories, even when it was in their interest to make common cause with us.

A sensible Labour strategy, in my view, would have been the opposite: to be nasty to the Tories and nice to the Lib Dems, to try to detach us from the Tories and have an insurance policy for a possible hung parliament in 2015 where Labour and Lib Dem could form a majority. Instead, so vile were they, they pushed us towards the Tories.

To me, it was unbelievable to see the tactics Labour adopted for the AV referendum. It was clearly in their own electoral interest for this to deliver a yes vote from the British people. The history of the last century has predominantly been of Tory governments, a situation that can only worsen if Scotland does eventually win independence, which looks a fair bet. Even if it does not, English votes on English laws might have the same effect.

On top of that, the Tories intend to reinforce their position through the redrawing of constituency boundaries, which we stopped them doing in coalition and which they were wedded to. When David Cameron learnt that the Lib Dems had blocked the changes, he lost his rag and shouted down the phone at Nick Clegg, the only time he did so during the parliament.

Yet Labour, in the face of all this, seemed to decide that short-term damage to the Lib Dems was somehow more important than their own self-interest. Had they weighed in with us and the Greens, the AV referendum vote might have been carried and they would not now be facing a Tory majority or indeed a near wipe-out in Scotland.

Even during the 2015 general election campaign, their hatred of the Lib Dems blinkered them to their own self-interest. While they were pouring huge numbers of troops into Sheffield Hallam in a failed attempt to unseat Nick Clegg, up the road Ed Balls was losing his seat.

And their hostility to the Lib Dems on the ground up and down the country pushed people away from tactical voting, with the result we saw in Lewes replicated elsewhere: Tory gain after Tory gain, aiding the formation of a Tory majority government.

There is a strand in the Labour Party that longs for a return to two-party politics, even if that means that the Tories are in power more often than they are now – so long as Labour gets their turn every now and then.

The Green Party also needs to examine its strategy, as Caroline Lucas was frank enough to admit in *The Observer* following the election results, when she regretted 'the loss of progressive MPs like Norman Baker'.

Somewhat oddly, I had actually interviewed her for *The House* magazine back in October 2008, when she had just been elected as the first ever leader of the Green Party. At that time, she came across as surprisingly tribal. The country was divided between her party and 'the grey parties', an amorphous collection of everybody else. Only the Green Party could provide salvation.

But the Green Party was not going to have more than two MPs in 2010, I put it to her, so actually, if we are to stave off climate change, she needed the 'grey parties' to adopt green policies – but if they did, then where did that leave the Green Party? Did her party actually want the sinners to repent?

I also put it to her that the rhetoric coming from the Green Party at that point was more hostile to the Lib Dems than to any other party, yet by any objective analysis, we were closer to them than either Tory or Labour. This, I suggested, was competing for votes rather than campaigning for change.

When she was elected in 2010, I was pleased, and offered to help her work out the madnesses of the House of Commons. But she soon found her feet and has proved to be a good MP, as I predicted she would. The House of Commons needs people like her articulating many of the arguments she makes. But those arguments are not the exclusive property of the Green Party and her tribe needs to decide whether it wants to stand aloof, criticising the 'grey parties' from on high, or actually work within the system to effect the kind of change many of us want to see.

As for the Lib Dems, we are now back to where we were fifty years ago, having slid down the longest snake on the board. We lost 319 deposits, so in more than half the seats, if you discount Northern Ireland. We polled less than 3 per cent in 160 seats, and there were even three where we polled less than 1 per cent. Overall, we only managed 7.9 per cent of the vote.

There is no point in complaining how unjust it is, save to observe that if we had been the most useless element of government ever, if we had been rocked by scandal after scandal, if we had run a really terrible election campaign, it is difficult to think how we could have ended up with fewer than the eight seats we have.

Some will blame Nick Clegg. I do not. The result belongs not just to one man, but to us all, and certainly including those employed at head office expressly to deliver a better result. And it belongs to forces outside our control as well, amongst them the strategies and finances of the other parties, and the approach of the media.

I have served in Parliament under four Lib Dem leaders and in my honest opinion, Nick was the best of the four and absolutely does not deserve the vilification he has had to put up with since 2010. He was not perfect, but his resilience, his cheerfulness, his sheer hard work were admirable, and I was proud to be one of his team.

This is not one of the troops defending the leader for political reasons. There are no such reasons. He has resigned as leader and I am no longer an MP. I can derive no personal benefit from making that statement other than the satisfaction of telling the truth as I see it. If there is any justice, history will be kinder to him than the present has been.

On election night, 7/8 May, I was as normal rung at home by my agent Ann De Vecchi at about 2 a.m., this time to tell me she thought I had lost. She was unusually emotional. For my part, I was strangely calm and philosophical about it all. Somehow I had almost subconsciously known this would happen.

My sadness was not with my personal situation, but with the overall result for the Lib Dems. My concern, fear even, was to wonder who was going to be the voice of liberalism, to ensure that when illiberal, or callous or environmentally damaging policies are brought forward by an untrammelled Tory government, they will be effectively challenged.

Those who voted Labour or Green, arguing that there was no difference between the coalition we had and a Tory-only government, are now learning the hard way, as indeed are the rest of us, just how wrong they were, as a whole range of nasty policies are brought forward by the most right-wing government for thirty years. The Tories will take advantage of the position that has emerged in the House of Commons: a useless Labour Party, a Lib Dem party reduced to rubble, a bunch of Scot Nats yet to find their feet and unsure to what extent they want to get involved in English issues, and a Green Party stuck on one MP.

I had in my head a while before settled on the skeleton of a speech for the declaration in Lewes in the event that I lost, and realised I had not really done the same for a victory. I suppose that latter eventuality was easier to busk.

I recalled John Major's well-judged remarks after he lost the 1997 election, and how a final speech can leave a lasting impression for good or bad. I was determined to try to be gracious, which I hope I achieved.

At the count, the Tory candidate Maria Caulfield looked rather surprised, even alarmed, to have won. She certainly did not seem particularly elated. She made a competent, if short, speech, in which she generously said that going round the constituency, she had been regaled time and again with positive feedback about my performance as the local MP and that if she ended her time as MP with people saying the same, she would think she had done a good job. It was a nice thing to say.

I congratulated her on her victory, thanked her for her kind comments, and said that if, in 1987, I had been offered a deal whereby I would be a councillor for sixteen years, district leader for six, MP for eighteen, and a minister for four and a half, I would have snatched off the hand of whoever was offering me that deal. I had had a good run over twenty-eight years, and it was to be twenty-eight rather than thirty-three. Was that so terrible?

Later, at home, I reflected on my twenty-eight years. I felt I had nearly always been true to myself. I had worked against the grain, by my choice of party, by the powerful people and interests I had taken on, by the unfashionable issues I had championed, in and out of government, and I had won more often than I could have hoped.

And so, after the curtain falls, there is the clearing up to do. The worst bit was having to confirm to my staff in the constituency office that they were now facing redundancy. There was no longer a job to do, nor any money to pay them. They had all been great, and it seemed very unfair that they should all have to lose their jobs. Fortunately, they all found new homes to go to.

There were the offices to move out of, the one in Westminster within a week, the one in Lewes within two months. There was the rented flat in London to vacate. There were the shelves and filing cabinets full of constituents' files, a room full of them, to be professionally shredded.

As a souvenir, I had taken the precaution of buying a ministerial red box about a fortnight before my resignation from the Home Office, although I ensured I was able to buy my old DfT box rather than the one I used at the Home Office.

Meanwhile I received an email from SHY Aviation, asking me if I wanted to hire a private jet, helicopter or yacht for the Cannes film festival later that month. I did not.

Within a month of the election, it all seemed a very long time ago. On the boat from Newhaven to Dieppe, it is not long after you leave port and look back that the coast is a distant sight, and before long it has vanished entirely. So I reflected as I too sailed off into the wide blue yonder.